BRITISH REALIST THEATRE

When John Osborne's *Look Back in Anger* exploded onto the British
stage in 1956, it was described as 'the best young play of the decade
more recently it was dismissed as a piece of 'undiluted misogyn
Clearly the critical fortunes of both Osborne's play and of the 'N
Wave' of dramatists, actors and directors who followed him c
the stage have varied in the intervening years. Unarguably, thou
the period of 1956–1965 was a defining moment in post-war Brit
theatre history, in which new possibilities arose for a contempor
and engaged drama. Drawing on a range of sources, Stephen La
argues that the new theatre should be seen in relation to ot
developments in post-war culture and politics, including so
science, the novel and cinema.

The new theatre was regarded as a realist theatre, drama
the social experience of a working-class under threat from the
prosperity. However, despite the currency of the term, 'realis
the period is imperfectly understood and often crudely ap
Arguing that realism is both a tradition of representation a
critical prespective, Lacey examines the connection betwee
ticular plays and productions, and the assumptions about
atrical form and oppositional politics that shaped the way th
theatre was valued by its contemporaries.

Stephen Lacey is a Lecturer in Drama at the University of Reading
He has worked extensively in community theatre in Scotland an
England.

BRITISH REALIST THEATRE

The New Wave in its Context 1956–1965

Stephen Lacey

London and New York

First published 1995
by Routledge
11 New Fetter Lane, London EC4P 4EE

Simultaneously published in the USA and Canada
by Routledge
29 West 35th Street, New York, NY 10001

Typeset in Baskerville by
Ponting–Green Publishing Services, Chesham, Bucks
Printed and bound in Great Britain by
Mackays of Chatham PLC, Chatham, Kent

British Library Cataloguing in Publication Data
A catalogue record for this book is available from
the British Library

Library of Congress Cataloguing in Publication Data
A catalogue record for this book has been requested

ISBN 0–415–07782–6
0–415–12311–9 (pbk)

To my father, Fred Lacey

CONTENTS

ACKNOWLEDGEMENTS

I would like to acknowledge the support and encouragement of a great many people, for although a book is meant to be the product of one individual, it is frequently anything but that. The research on which this book is based owes a good deal to the collective discussions conducted at the Centre for Contemporary Cultural Studies at the University of Birmingham during my time as a postgraduate student there; in particular, I would like to thank Michael Green for his patience and advice. I would also like to thank my colleagues and successive generations of students in the Film and Drama Department at Reading University, who have helped me to develop my thinking about this material over a period of time. I am especially grateful to Talia Rodgers, for her patience and enthusiastic support in the face of broken deadlines. And many, many thanks to my family – as ever – who had to endure a great deal as this book was nearing completion.

INTRODUCTION

The 1950s was a curious and idiosyncratic decade, which, from the viewpoint of the 1990s, is a reservoir of distant, yet familiar images, close enough to be relevant, yet far enough away to be the object of nostalgia. It was a period of full employment, of prosperity and social stability, of the birth of the age of television, of the 'New Elizabethan Age' and the Coronation; it was also the decade of the teddy-boys, Elvis Presley and rock 'n' roll, of CND and of the Angry Young Men. In effect, these two sets of images are associated with the two halves of the decade, with 1956 as the watershed, marking off a 'then' from a 'now' in cultural and political history.

Theatre's contribution to this cultural moment was the much-mythicised first performance of *Look Back in Anger*. Criticism of *Look Back in Anger* – and what followed it – has a strong smell of the barricades about it. Taylor described it as a 'revolution' (Taylor 1962: 28) and military metaphors abound in most accounts of this 'proletarian upsurge' of emancipated working-class writers in rebellion. Even writers with a more critical stance towards the plays and the theatrical and political values of the New Wave (as we shall call it) accept that this period was 'crucial and formative for what is now the mainstream of British theatre' (McGrath 1981: 9). David Edgar has written:

> The date, 8 May 1956, was the last great U-turn in the British theatre. . . . Certainly, whether Osborne likes it or not (and he probably doesn't) all the subsequent 'waves' of the new British theatre follow the agenda he set.
>
> (Edgar 1988: 138)

This agenda is actually rather hard to specify, whether one looks for it in Osborne's work or in that of the New Wave generally;

1

indeed, the term 'New Wave' is itself highly problematic. Viewed in terms of the plays alone, the moment of the late fifties and early sixties is a difficult moment to map with any confidence: there are no manifestos, no obvious 'schools' of writing (certainly no school of Osborne), and a diverse, if overlapping, set of concerns. This has not changed over the years; indeed, the sense of a defining contextual 'moment' has lessened as traditional literary criteria have reasserted themselves, and independent authorial studies of key figures have become the dominant pattern.

It is also the case that the New Wave, and especially *Look Back in Anger*, no longer appears as seminal as it once did. It seems, quite simply, a different play that we see today from the one that so shocked and inspired its initial audiences. As one commentator recently wrote, 'stripped of its context it now looks like a feeble period piece, occasionally fuelled by Osborne's own rage [and] what looked like politically subversive polemic now looks like mere rudeness' (French 1991). I first taught the play to undergraduates in the late 1970s, when a generation of more revolutionary play-wrights – including McGrath and Edgar – had altered the agenda significantly, leaving students bemused about the politics of this famously 'revolutionary' play. A few years later, its politics had become an issue once more – only this time it was the play's representation of sexuality and gender, its sexual politics, that surfaced, and what had seemed a leftish scream against the con-straints of mid-fifties conformism, appeared as an unpleasant apology for misogyny (see Chapter 1).

It is possible now to write a very different history – probably several different histories – of this over-mythicised period. One such revisionist account would centre on Beckett and Peter Hall's production of *Waiting for Godot* (1955) as the crucial and defining theatrical event (and, perhaps, revalue the work of John Whiting). Such an account would emphasise aesthetically innovatory prac-tices, both in writing and its theatrical articulation, and would not foreground questions of realism. In retrospect, there would clearly be a logic to this, given Beckett's subsequent reputation (notwithstanding the general bafflement that greeted *Godot* at the time).

Alternatively, both Osborne and Beckett have benefited from the dominance of London over the rest of British theatre – what we shall subsequently refer to as the metropolitanising of culture, a theme explored in Chapter 2 – and another history would need to recognise that this is one instance of the general process by which economic and cultural power has been transferred from the regions (and the other nationalities within the British Isles) to southern England and London in particular in the twentieth century. There was, for example, a post-war working-class realist theatre alive and kicking before Osborne *et al.* appeared on the scene, only it was in Scotland. A number of established Scottish dramatists, such as George Munro, Joe Corrie and Robert McLeish, had all written plays set among the contemporary Scottish working-class, and which were performed in the late forties and through the fifties (see Stevenson 1987). Until 1950, Scotland had, in Glasgow Unity, a company the prime aim of which was to perform working-class drama (examples of this, such as Ena Lamont Stewart's *Men Should Weep* (1947), were revived in the early 1980s by the Scottish 7:84 Theatre Company). Munro's *Gay Landscape* (1958), which was produced at the Citizen's Theatre, Glasgow, was transferred to the Royal Court, where it could be seen alongside a burgeoning English proletarian drama, which it in some ways pre-empted. It would be more honest, in many ways, to talk of the New Wave as an English, rather than a British, theatre – albeit one that had strong connections to non-metropolitan, often Northern, social experience.

Yet, without denying the validity of these possible histories, I would still want to argue for the centrality of a version of the period that has *Look Back in Anger* as the defining theatrical event and which privileges a complex understanding of realism. This is partly because, no matter what the play may have become in the years that followed, for its contemporaries *Look Back in Anger* was clearly an *event*, the theatrical (and emotional) significance of which was registered in the obituaries that marked Osborne's death in late 1994. 'It would be hard to exaggerate the emotional importance of *Look Back in Anger* to anyone growing up and facing the world for the first time in 1956', wrote Michael Ratcliffe in *The Observer.* 'I remember a performance. . . which moved me so much that the tears streamed down my face and half the time I couldn't even see the bloody play' (Ratcliffe: 1995). In discussing the play-as-event we must recognise that we are dealing with more than simply the original production, or the moment of theatrical performance. *Look Back in Anger* was toured, televised and eventually filmed; it was commented on widely in both the specialist literary press and the popular media, with both its central character, Jimmy Porter (as an emerging social type as well as a dramatic character) and John

Osborne himself (who was often conflated with his hero) functioning as a shorthand for certain kinds of distinctively post-war social experience. There were, then, a multiplicity of 'texts', each helping to redefine the others, existing in a range of social and cultural as well as theatrical discourses (see Chapters 1 and 2).

The success of the play was an indication that the social and political expectations of theatre had altered – that the space that theatre occupied in the general culture was now different; what was to Kenneth Tynan in 1955 an upper-middle-class social ritual, a 'glibly codified fairy-tale world, of no more use to the student of life than a doll's-house would be to a student of town-planning' (Tynan 1984: 148) was for Edgar 'for a short time at least . . . a mirror in which the nation could observe, stark and naked, its own image' (Edgar 1981: 38) . This view of the significance of the period is one that connects theatre not so much to aesthetic debates as to social and political ones, and which places the new drama in the centre of a much wider realignment in British society, in which many post-war certainties were challenged and redefined.

This is not to argue that the New Wave was a self-consciously 'political' drama in the sense that, say, the theatre of Brecht and Piscator in Weimar Germany of the late 1920s was political, or, indeed, the socialist theatre that flourished in Britain in the 1970s. It did, however, have an ideological role that was often difficult to capture in the prevailing critical languages. The first chapter of this book attempts to provide a framework for understanding this ideological function by drawing on a notion of hegemony. As defined by the Italian Marxist Antonio Gramsci, hegemony describes the way that ideological power is exercised in a given society via the manufacturing and manipulation of consent. Consent, and consensus, is a major theme in post-war politics and culture, referring not only to the machinery of government, but also, at a more profound level, to the operation of an entire culture. On the one hand, consensus described the general agreement between the major political parties as to the general lineaments of economic and foreign policy and the role of the Welfare State; on the other, there was a concerted attempt to win consent to a conservative view of the centrality of the family (and of traditional gender roles within it) and to support for established institutions, such as the Monarchy and the Church of England. The break that occurred in 1956, and which was registered in otherwise disparate cultural spheres, was a kicking against a consensus that threatened to stifle debate.

Hegemony is never complete, however, and because it can be fought and won in every area of social life, it can be resisted in these same areas as well; and if *Look Back in Anger* and the New Wave were ideologically and culturally important, then it was because theatre became one of the main forums in which hegemonic values could be debated and contested.

To approach theatre in this way is to recognise the importance of social, cultural and political history, and much of the first part of this book will give space to establishing the contexts in which the new drama should be read. However, this is not a book of general cultural history, and I have been necessarily selective (often reluctantly so, as this is a fascinating and important period). My approach has been to lay out the most significant 'themes' that connect with the general argument in Chapter 1, and explore additional contextual material in later chapters where it is relevant to the discussion of particular plays/productions. For example, debates about the nature of changes to the class structure in the wake of affluence are indicated in the early stages of the discussion, and are elaborated upon in Chapter 3 in the course of an analysis of some contextual readings of social realism. Where I thought it would be either interesting or useful, I have indicated sources for further reading.

In considering the anti-hegemonic function of theatre in the period, I have decided, not without reservation, to continue to use the term 'New Wave', particularly in the earlier part of this book. To discuss this theatre in this way is not to minimise the differences between the writers and plays, which are considerable, or to suggest an absolute identity of social and aesthetic concerns. New Wave practitioners seemed united only in their antagonism to a dour, restricted national culture and a political establishment that several of them rapidly joined. And the term New Wave does not only refer to a corpus of texts but also to a theatre sub-culture: it is, therefore, very much a moment of theatrical and cultural history, not just a development in the drama, embracing writers, critics, actors, directors and producers, who shared a (broadly) common relationship to the established theatre and social structures (and often similar, lower-class social origins). In other contexts, these similarities would not have been decisive; to consider the terms in which they were significant is part of the project of the first part of this book.

It may be that since the late fifties, the New Wave has become a new establishment, but it is worth reminding ourselves that the 'revolution' has been, in certain important respects, over-sold, particularly if the institutions of theatre, rather than the plays themselves, are considered (see Chapter 2). The commercial theatre structures, against which the new theatre was pitted, did not disappear, and to talk of a New Wave at all is to debate the activities of a highly visible and articulate minority. Nor should we under-estimate the continuities between the New Wave and the 'old' theatre it was presumed to have replaced: *Look Back in Anger* was, after all, a rather old-fashioned play, formally speaking (indeed, its use of many of the familiar conventions of the dominant realist/naturalist tradition was central to its success).

The development of an anti-hegemonic theatre in the decades since 1956 has not been even. The wave metaphor, first coined by John Russell Taylor (Taylor 1962), has a sense of comforting inevitability about it, but this conceals the fact that each 'wave' has been not only superseded but, in important respects, defeated. One reason for taking 1965 as the rough concluding point of this book (given that all periodisations are to a degree arbitrary and restrict-ive) is that it was the point at which George Devine resigned the artistic directorship of the English Stage Company (although it was not a gesture of defeat); but two years earlier Joan Littlewood, the artistic director of Theatre Workshop, had left the company for the second time, disillusioned by the compromises she had been forced to make by an ailing theatre system, and Arnold Wesker's Centre 42, an organisation formed to run arts festivals in conjunction with the labour movement (and which represented an important strand in the cultural politics of the new theatre) began to falter.

The prime focus of this book is not theoretical (although I hope that its theoretical assumptions and critical procedures are appar-ent), and I have tried to find a balance between the contexts of reception and questions of dramatic and theatrical form/tradition: a variety of contemporary sources will be drawn on in order to pursue each of these emphases, particularly reviews. As well as providing a record of a production, rather than a play text, reviews suggest something of the dominant assumptions about what passes as a play in a given period, about what is considered good/bad/serious/original. Reviewing practice may also be openly partisan; the reviews of Kenneth Tynan, for example, were unashamedly supportive of the new drama, and Tynan played a considerable role in its development.

Critical judgements may be particular to the critic, or the journal for which he/she is writing, but are frequently more widely held – are indicative of an *interpretative framework* that is comprised of the main assumptions that a critic brings to bear on the material, and which is rarely his/hers alone. The concept of interpretative frameworks is an important one in this book, for they can be both aesthetic in nature (and refer to dominant models of theatrical form and traditions of representation), and socio-political: sometimes they are both simultaneously, and there is, especially in the initial responses to the New Wave, a constant slippage between formal and ideological responses. Interpretative frameworks are also important to a sense of what constitutes a critical 'moment'. The term is an elusive one, and in the present context refers mainly to a period in cultural history where a variety of developments, which are simultaneously artistic, political and cultural in a wider, more sociological sense, intersect in a way that is registered at the public level – is made *conscious* in a new critical language, a new imagery, that is fashioned for the purpose. Within the New Wave, there are in fact two critical moments. The first is that of Anger, which, properly speaking, belongs to the early or middle years of the decade; in this sense, *Look Back in Anger* is the only truly 'angry' play. The second, which will have a more substantial presence in this book, is that of Working-Class Realism.

A discussion of realism provides us with an additional context that was central to the cultural role that the New Wave was required to play after 1956. This is partly because the languages of realism – diverse and contradictory as they sometimes are – relate questions of form to political and social purposes, and this is a principal reason why debates about the nature of realism are central to this study.

Realism has been used, as Raymond Williams has usefully reminded us, in a number of contexts (see Williams 1977 and 1981), to refer to a set of specific intentions, that are often political and moral in focus, and to describe a particular tradition of representation. It is also a term that is ever-present in the critical discussion of the New Wave itself and of other cultural forms in the period. There are realist novels and realist cinema, too, and all three genres were discussed within the same broadly similar critical frameworks; indeed, the moment of Working-Class Realism, which has a considerable presence in British culture in the period, embraces them all (see Chapters 3 and 4). Realism was also the ground on which certain new developments in the theatre were established, particularly those associated with dramatists such as Edward Bond and John Arden, which entailed the rejection of existing theatre practices (see Chapter 5) and a negotiation with other traditions, for example British popular theatre and Brecht, which were compatible with certain definitions of realism. Indeed, this book follows Brecht in defining realism in terms of ideology and politics rather than dramatic method.

New Wave theatre bears comparison with realist cinema. Cinema, too, had its New Wave, which was largely comprised of figures who already had a presence in the theatre – Lindsay Anderson and Tony Richardson, for example. And the new realist films were invariably based on proven successes in other media; Osborne's *Look Back in Anger* and *The Entertainer*, Delaney's *A Taste of Honey*, Wesker's *The Kitchen* and Behan's *The Quare Fellow* were all made into films. New Wave cinema also helped to redefine the terms in which the originals were read, both signifying a move beyond 'Anger' into 'social realism', and emphasising the degree to which the New Wave in general was a realist theatre. For these reasons, the relationship between theatre and film will be considered in some detail here.

Some concluding remarks: I have assumed that most readers of this book will have at least read the plays under discussion, and I have not included plot summaries, except where they are required for the analysis. Also, I have focused largely on the better-known texts from the period, and most of the plays discussed are those that were thought to be of interest at the time they first appeared; indeed, it is *because* these plays were thought to be of immediate value and were widely debated that they are important to the kind of contextual analysis that follows below. There are some inevitable omissions, as well. In addressing issues around realism, I have reluctantly continued the practice of marginalising certain texts and practices that do not easily fall within its ambit, yet are of interest; the work of women writers in the period – Ann Jellicoe's *The Sport of My Mad Mother*, for example – deserves more attention than it normally receives.

Finally, I am indebted to the kind of criticism that has surfaced in recent general accounts of post-war cultural history, where the questions posed are similar to those asked here. Stuart Laing's *Representations of Working-Class Life: 1957–64*, Robert Hewison's *In Anger* and John Hill's *Sex, Class and Realism: British Cinema 1956–63* have been of particular value.

1

REPRESENTING CONTEMPORARY BRITAIN
Anger, affluence and hegemony

AFFLUENCE AND CONSENSUS

The 1950s and early 1960s was an age that was riven with paradox and contradiction, although this was not always apparent at the time. Given a unity at the national political level by three successive Conservative administrations (from 1951 to 1964), it seemed to be a time of unprecedented social stability and prosperity – especially when compared with the vicissitudes of the 1930s and 1940s, or when viewed with hindsight as 'the last period of quiet before the storm' (Bogdanor and Skidelsky 1970: 7) of the 1960s and 1970s. It is characteristic of the era that many of the major indices of this stability were associated with conservative, even hierarchical, symbols and traditions; the Coronation of Queen Elizabeth II in 1953, Harold Macmillan's effortless 'Edwardian' amateurism, the last vestiges of Reithian formality at the BBC. However, one of the central contradictions of the age is that this conservatism was most apparent when it appeared in response to another dominant theme in the decade, the sense of 'newness', of change, that was felt in all areas of social experience and which helped to mark off the pre- from the post-war worlds. Conservatism in this context is not simply to do with the Tory Party's electoral success (the battle between the major parties in the period was always much closer than the election results suggest) but is much wider, moving beyond the narrowly political into many areas of social and cultural life in the early 1950s, and providing the immediate context for the emergence of new, more progressive, forces in 1956 and after.

As is so often the case, the most profound changes were – at least initially – economic, and were associated with a perceived general increase in prosperity made possible by a boom in consumer goods brought about by the collapse in world commodity prices; the key term is 'affluence', which resonates throughout the decade, permeating the discourses of the popular media, national politics and academic sociology, both cataloguing and symbolising social and economic change.

The social and economic meaning of affluence can be registered in different ways. The statistics are certainly impressive: between 1951 and 1964 total production increased by 40 per cent; the number of cars increased from just over 2 million to 8 million and the number of TV sets from 1 million to 13 million. Average earnings in the period increased by 110 per cent and the average standard of living rose, in real terms, by 30 per cent. Consumer expenditure as a whole doubled in that time and share prices trebled in the 1950s alone. Expressing this in another way, Eric Hobsbawm wrote that by the early 1960s '91 per cent of British households had acquired electric irons, 82 per cent television sets, 72 per cent vacuum cleaners, 45 per cent washing-machines and 30 per cent refrigerators' (Hobsbawm 1969: 263). In addition, full-employment was maintained (unemployment averaged 1.7 per cent throughout the country as a whole – although there were marked regional variations). These changes were not simply conjured out of thin air, nor were they solely due to the economic policies of successive Conservative governments or even the peculiar circumstances of the British economy. The Tories certainly promoted the consumer boom, and reversed Labour's emphasis on controlled expansion of the home market in favour of exports, but these developments had their roots in the technological advances of the inter-war period, and were common to all the major industrialised nations.

In retrospect, the idea of a remorseless and universal affluence, carrying all before it, was disingenuous. Although it was certainly true that the general standard of living rose for the population as a whole in the decade, prosperity was most conspicuous where it could be most easily noticed, in the South of the country, and most selective where it could be ignored, in the North. In any case, Britain's economic performance was outstripped by many of its competitors, particularly on the export front. Significant though prosperity was, it did not herald the demise of systemic poverty. Indeed, poverty of a familiar and structural kind was 'rediscovered' on a large scale in the 1960s – a process in which the arts and media often assisted, Loach and Garnett's television play *Cathy Come Home* (1965) being a frequently cited example.

In this way, affluence was always partly an ideological term, registering not only the statistics of material advance but also certain kinds of explanations for its effects on social and political processes – explanations that consistently supported the idea of Britain as a nation moving inexorably towards a post-scarcity and conflict-free society. Such ideologies may be thought of as 'myths'. Myth, in the sense in which it was used by Roland Barthes, suppresses 'the historical nature and antagonistic content of what it signifies, the temporary conditions of its existence, the possibilities of its historical transcendence' (Hall *et al.* 1978: 232), transforming what is argumentative, contradictory and ideological about post-war changes into self-evident, incontrovertible 'truth'. The experience of affluence, sustained full-employment and the Welfare State gave rise to a new mythology, a new symbolic landscape, which found expression at a number of levels. The cumulative effect of these myths was to present Britain as a unified society, which had successfully solved the major problems that were facing it, and that was essentially at one with itself, held within a self-image that supported, and was supported by, dominant traditional interests. This view of post-war Britain was most clearly articulated at the time of the Coronation of the new Queen Elizabeth in 1953, when the consumer boom had just begun to take off. The *Observer* caught the tone of the prevailing mood, proclaiming that 'this country is today a more united and stabler society than it has been since the "Industrial Revolution" began' (quoted in Laing 1973: 370). The new prosperity and the Welfare State helped to create the conditions that made such explanations of social change possible, by appearing to remove some of the traditional means by which social conflicts have been generated, especially poverty. It was the contrast between before and after the Second World War, between a 'then' characterised by inequality, scarcity, unemployment and social division, and a 'now' presented in terms of full-employment, conspicuous consumption, social insurance and universal welfare (accepted as much by the post-war Conservative Party as by Labour) that allowed Macmillan to proclaim by the end of the decade that 'The class-war is over and we have won.' This was both triumphalist Conservative rhetoric and a statement of what was apparently obvious: that British society in the 1950s was essentially a *consensual* one, pluralist in the way that both wealth and power were distributed.

That Britain in the 1950s could be represented as a society unified by a profound consensus coloured in traditionalist terms

11

was partly because, at the level of national politics, there was a consensus between the dominant political players about the broad outline of national and international policy – a consensus that was embodied in the programme of the 1945–51 Labour governments (see Addison 1975 and Kavanagh and Morris 1994). The main elements of this consensus were: the necessity for full employment; the desirability of a 'mixed' economy, with the State assuming a major role (this included nationalisation as a tool of government policy, and the major power utilities and the railways were national- ised at this time); the desirability of social welfare, universal educa- tion and a health service – the machinery of the Welfare State; and a commitment to the Western Alliance, dominated by the USA and NATO, as the contours of the Cold War began to harden. Nor did this consensus evaporate when the Conservatives were returned to power in 1951. It has become a truism to observe that there seemed to be a remarkable continuity between the policies of the Labour and Tory governments of the period (much to the surprise and chagrin of some of their supporters). The Conservatives adopted much of the social programme put in place by Labour, making a commitment to increase the number of council houses by 300,000 in the early fifties. There was also a general agreement within the Party leadership that the Empire should be gradually dismantled – although this was fiercely contested by the Tory right. The con- tinuity between the two parties in government was particularly evident in the sphere of economic policy; *The Economist* coined the term 'Butskellism', conflating the names of two chancellors from opposing political parties, to denote the similarity between them.

We should, of course, be wary of over-stating the importance of this convergence around the middle-ground; the dissident voices of the Tory right and of Labour left were not silenced, and continued to influence the political agenda, particularly when issues such as immigration (for the right) and public ownership and the Welfare State (for the left) were concerned. However, there is little doubt that the idea of consensus is one that is central to an understanding of both the dominant mythology of the period, and the theatre's role in contesting it.

CONSENSUS AND HEGEMONY

The way that consensus operates to unify a society around certain dominant ideologies has been analysed by the Italian Marxist and cultural theoretician Antonio Gramsci, and the key term that he used to describe these processes was hegemony. Hegemony is often used as if it were synonymous with the exercise of any form of dominating influence over a given sphere of action. However, in the sense in which Gramsci used it, hegemony applies to a particular way in which power (and especially class power) is exercised *ideologically* in a particular historical period and is only possible under certain historical conditions. If we term it ideological, then we must recognise that it is so in a complex sense; it is not reducible to a set of ideas or polemics (although it may also be that), nor to physical and political coercion, but is rather a 'concrete phantasy, which acts on a dispersed and shattered people to arouse and organise its collective will' (Gramsci 1971: 126). Hegemony is, as Raymond Williams has argued, 'a whole body of practices and expectations: our assignments of energy . . . a set of meanings and values which as they are experienced as practices appear as reciprocally confirming' (Williams 1975: 26).

Ideologies may be described as hegemonic to the degree to which they all appear to move along the same path, constituting a form of ideological 'common sense' within a society, a sense of reality, beyond which it is often difficult to move. Seen in terms of the distribution of power in a society, hegemony is the way in which subordinate groups come to understand their relationship to, and position within, that society through the definitions of dominant groups. This applies to the way that all ideologies, particularly the central ideologies of an age, are organised, but what gives hegemony its distinctive character is the way that it is structured around the *managing of consent*, and this is why the term is so relevant to the discussion of Britain in the 1950s (see Hall and Jefferson 1976).

Such a process is essentially *cultural*, in that it can be traced not only in what is normally thought of as 'political' activity (the discourses of party politics, or the rhetoric of electioneering) but also in a range of other public (and private) arenas, saturating the discourses, values and practices of social institutions and private relationships alike. At one level, the idea that Britain was a society that had succeeded in removing structural inequalities lay at the heart of the debates around the nature of social class throughout the decade and into the 1960s; affluence, it was argued, had removed the root causes of poverty, which was seen to lie at the heart of the political identity of the working class, and had also dissolved its cultural distinctiveness by opening up new patterns of consumption and leisure. At another level, a crucial part of the post-war settlement was the attempt to persuade women to return to traditional roles in the family, establishing a kind of 'domestic consensus', once their presence in the labour market was apparently no longer 'necessary' for the national economy; both of these themes will be returned to in subsequent chapters.

1953 AND 1956: A COMPARISON OF TWO CULTURAL MOMENTS

We noted earlier that hegemony was associated with attempts to interpret 'new' social experiences in terms of 'traditional' values, and that this was a project that sought to embrace the political and the everyday. A key moment in this process, as we also noted, was the moment of 1953, the 'moment' of the Coronation and the signification of the New Elizabethan Age. The year 1953 might be usefully contrasted with 1956, which, as a moment when cultural and political energies were released and focused towards change, was also a pivotal point in the decade – and, indeed, in the post-war period as a whole; however, if 1953 was a moment when a traditionalist hegemony and the consensus seemed at its most secure, 1956 saw the hegemonic project begin to falter.

In 1953, a number of events occurred which contributed to a new optimism; a British athlete, Roger Bannister, ran the first four-minute mile; a team led by a British mountaineer, Sir John Hunt, became the first to scale Mount Everest (although the two people who actually made the final assault on the summit were Edmund Hillary, a New Zealander, and Sherpa Tensing, his Tibetan guide); and the English cricket team regained the Ashes. Above all, it was the year of the Coronation of Queen Elizabeth II, who gave her name to the new age. None of these events were related, yet because they were independent of each other they confirmed a general impression – accentuated by the generally increasing prosperity – that Britain was advancing on all fronts. In 1956, too, a series of distinct events occurred, which were also related to each other to suggest a larger pattern and a different explanation. This was the year of *Look Back in Anger*, of Colin Wilson's *The Outsider, and of Brendan Behan's The Quare Fellow*; in another area of culture, it was also the year in which rock 'n' roll, Elvis Presley, James Dean and the teddy-boys appeared on the public stage, and in which cinema seats were ripped during showings of *Rock Around the Clock*. At the level of national and international politics, 1956 was the year of the Suez adventure and the Soviet invasion of Hungary. As Robert Hewison has observed, 'Retrospectively, 1956 has become an annus mirabilis . . . crudely, Suez and *Look Back in Anger* seem part of the same event' (Hewison 1981: 127).

The key symbolic event of 1953 was undoubtedly the Coronation. In certain important respects this Coronation was like no other, for, as Marwick noted, 'the new twist was that almost twenty-and-a-half million people, 56 per cent of the adult population, could watch, and did watch, the entire proceedings on television; a further 32 per cent, 11.7 million, listened on radio' (Marwick 1982: 109). The Coronation was the first modern media 'happening'; it helped to stimulate the sale of television sets and simultaneously helped to present television as the symbol of the new age. At the beginning of 1953 the number of licence holders stood at 693,000; a year later, it stood at 1,110,439. It was, therefore, not simply a family ritual that was being enacted, but rather a massive public spectacle, and the focus not just of traditionalist royalist sentiment but also of much speculation as to the current 'state of the nation'.

The new reign was presented both as a renewal of British traditions and as the dawning of a new age. The phrase 'The New Elizabethan Age', much in evidence in the decade, captures this fusion exactly. Britain's success, both at war and in creating the Welfare State, figured as the latest in a line of triumphant moments of 'national unity', its 'newness' – the rising tide of affluence, full employment and all that was distinctive about contemporary social experience – whilst being admitted and celebrated, was inserted into a view of history that emphasised a reassuring continuity and stability, which could keep the chaos of material advance at bay. The Coronation also occasioned speculation about Britain's position in relation to the rest of the world in the post-Imperial era. The concept of Britain as the head of the Commonwealth and the diplomatic – if not the military – centre of the Western Alliance, was of particular importance. The predominant image was that of the nation as family, with the royal family at its symbolic centre. As Shils and Young pointed out 'one family was knit together with another in one great national family through identification with the monarchy' (Shils and Young 1963: 73).

The key political event of 1956 was the Anglo-French invasion of the Suez Canal, which assumed considerable symbolic importance, both at the time and since. Furious at the nationalisation of the

15

Suez Canal Company by Egypt's President Nasser in July 1956 (which meant that effective control over the strategically important canal passed into Egyptian hands), the French and British governments engineered an invasion of the canal zone with the assistance of the Israelis, and seemed determined to stand firm against international unease. With only a week to go before the American presidential elections, however, Eisenhower engineered a condemnation of the invasion at the United Nations; Eden was exhausted and becoming ill; and there were rumours of Soviet intervention. The crucial factor, however, was a run on the pound necessitating an IMF loan, which needed American agreement; British compliance with the cease-fire arrangements was the price that Eisenhower extracted.

The Suez crisis had considerable effects on Britain's international standing; in particular, it exposed the delicate fiction that Britain was really 'running' the Western Alliance and had a foreign policy that could survive the displeasure of the USA. Of more concern in the present context, however, were its effects on the internal political geography of the country. After an initially uniform hostility to Nasser's nationalisation of the canal (at which time he was likened to Hitler and Mussolini by the Labour leader Hugh Gaitskell), opinion, particularly over the use of force, became divided. On the one hand, the feeling of those who favoured the invasion was summed up by a headline in the *Daily Express* – 'It's GREAT Britain Again!'. On the other, there were large public meetings (including an unexpectedly huge one in Trafalgar Square) held to protest against the action; 'Eden must go!' became a popular slogan.

The moment of 1953 offered images of coherence and stability, of a nation emerging from the vicissitudes of post-war recovery and pre-war class-struggle with its traditions intact. The moment of 1956, however, offered images of dissent, instability, fracture and powerlessness. It is not so much that the familiar landscape of early-fifties Britain was obliterated – indeed, it was towards the end of the decade that many of the ideologies that were discussed earlier assumed their most coherent expression – but rather that the contradictions and tensions that conservative explanations of change suppressed came to the surface; and for the first time in the decade, these emerged in the political as well as the cultural arenas, with implications both for the left generally (which, in the late fifties was advancing after a decade or more in retreat) and for a contemporary theatre.

16

A CONTEMPORARY THEATRE: LOOKING BACK
AT 'ANGER'

The break in intellectual and artistic culture that was signalled in 1956, however, did not initially assume political forms, but cut across existing boundaries between politics, culture and sensationalism; it also had a name, 'Anger', and a cast of instantly recognisable characters, the 'Angry Young Men'. *Look Back in Anger* was the archetypal 'angry' text – indeed, its appearance in May of that year helped to define the nature of 'Anger' for a contemporary public, much as its author became the quintessential 'Angry Young Man'. However, although the play may have propelled Anger into the headlines, it did not do so unaided. May 1956 also saw the publication of Colin Wilson's *The Outsider.* The book, which outlines the growth of the existentialist 'anti-hero', was written in a philosophic–literary discourse and received immediate and exceptional praise. At this stage, it was not so much the fictional creations that were the 'Angry Young Men' as Osborne and Wilson themselves, fixing Anger as a sociological as well as a literary/ theatrical phenomenon. Kingsley Amis – and the eponymous hero of *Lucky Jim,* Jim Dixon – resurfaced, not unexpectedly, as important figures as well.

In retrospect, the Angry Young Men had little in common, and the fact that they were treated as a coherent phenomenon (and were seen as 'news') is often attributed to the influence of the media, and especially the popular press, which were crucial in presenting Anger to a general public; as Colin Wilson noted, somewhat ruefully, 'the "new hero" of Amis and Wain had never got beyond the confines of the *New Statesman* and *Spectator,* but Osborne's Angry Young Man reached the *Daily Mirror* and the *Sunday Pictorial*' (Wilson 1959).The Angry Young Men were essentially the first literary/dramatic phenomenon to become a major media 'event', taking advantage of the new opportunities afforded by the expansion in popular journalism, television sales and the newly formed commercial television network. *Look Back in Anger,* especially, benefited considerably from exposure on television. An extract of the Royal Court production was shown on BBC on 16 October, reaching an audience estimated at 5 million. A month later, on 28 November, the play was televised in full at peak viewing time (this time by Granada for ITV). Why the play, and Anger generally, should have achieved such prominence is apparent from the critical context of its reception.

Look Back in Anger

As a major West End production from a new company, of which much was expected, *Look Back in Anger* was guaranteed a reviewing audience of all the national newspapers as well as the Sundays and the literary magazines. It might be expected that the reviews of *Look Back*, which the mythology would have us believe changed the face of British theatre, would have reflected the values of an established theatre culture and been uniformly hostile. Few of the reviews were actually 'favourable' in the sense that they were uniformly positive; but what is more important is that virtually all the reviews thought that the play was *significant*.

The critic from *The Times* defined the dominant terms in which the play was discussed in a vocabulary that reoccurred across all the initial reviews: 'The hero regards himself, and is clearly regarded by the author, as the spokesman for the younger post-war generation which looks round at the world and finds nothing right with it' (all quotations from the reviews are from Taylor 1968). Jimmy Porter was offered here as a spokesman for an experience that was essentially generational and specific to the post-war world – 'the younger post-war generation'. Porter's response to the post-war world was antagonistic and ungrateful, and, in Tynan's seminal review, left-wing. Tynan's review in the *Observer* was the most sympathetic – the most partisan – and was both a comment on other reviews and an articulation of his version of the play's basic premises. The review has since taken its place alongside *Look Back in Anger* itself as a characteristic representation of, to use Raymond Williams's phrase, an emerging 'structure of feeling'.

> All the qualities are there, qualities one had despaired of ever seeing on the stage – the drift towards anarchy, the instinctive leftishness, the automatic rejection of 'official' attitudes, the surrealist sense of humour ... the casual promiscuity, the sense of lacking a crusade worth fighting for. . . . The Porters of our time deplore the tyranny of good taste and refuse to accept 'emotional' as a term of abuse; they are classless, and they are also leaderless. Mr Osborne is their first spokesman in the London theatre.

Often, the emphasis on 'youth' dominated the reviews, operating as a kind of shorthand for contemporary experience and social change. John Barber (*Daily Express*) began his review in the following manner:

18

A first play by an exciting new English writer – 27-year-old John Osborne – burst on the London stage last night. It is intense, angry, feverish, undisciplined. It is even crazy. But it is young, young, young.

Later in the review the 'young' became socially specific – 'he [Porter] is like thousands of young Londoners today.' Several reviewers developed the generational definition of Porter's character from a more sympathetic point of view, particularly those who considered the play at some length and were writing for leftish papers/journals. T.C. Worsley, reviewing the play for the liberal/left *New Statesman*, not only accepted what had by this time become the main terms of the discussion, but also affirmed and elaborated upon them:

> His [Porter's] is genuinely the modern accent – one can hear it no doubt in every other Expresso bar, witty, relentless, pitiless and utterly without belief . . . don't miss this play. If you are young, it will speak for you. If you are middle-aged, it will tell you what the young are feeling.

Worsley was clearly drawing on an emerging social stereotype, which Porter exemplified, and which was built primarily around notions of youth and the distinctiveness of post-war social experience. It is perhaps Tynan's review that links the play, its protagonist and its author to an emerging discourse about the nature of post-war youth most decisively. The review concluded famously with the following:

> I agree that *Look Back in Anger* is likely to remain a minority taste. What matters, however, is the size of the minority. I estimate it at roughly 6,733,000, which is the number of people in this country between the ages of twenty and thirty. And this figure will doubtless be swelled by refugees from other age-groups who are curious to know precisely what the contemporary young pup is thinking and feeling. I doubt if I could love anyone who did not wish to see *Look Back in Anger.* It is the best young play of its decade.

There are several senses of 'youth' operating in the review. Early on, Porter is identified with the 'non-U intelligentsia' and given a more precise social location: the reference is to a post-war caste of intellectuals, removed by class origin and cultural orientation from the dominant, predominantly upper-class groupings that had survived from the pre-war years. However, elsewhere Tynan argued that this group was 'classless' as well as 'leaderless', and collapsed the category back into a socially amorphous 'everyone between the ages of twenty and thirty'. The slippage between different ideas of youth here is one that was common in the decade, particularly at the point where 'youth' is identified with the 'contemporary' ('life as it is lived at this very moment' as Worsley observed).

One of the most interesting elements in these reviews, therefore, is that they reveal a set of assumptions about the relationship of the play (and its author) to Britain in the mid-fifties, and that this is both shared and, to a significant degree, already in place. The fact that there was a remarkable unanimity about this amongst the reviewers was partly the result of the way that the play was marketed (a publicist at the Royal Court theatre has been credited with attaching the term 'angry young man' to the play and its author). However, this can only be part of the explanation. What this shorthand does is to connect a response to a particular production to much more general concerns about the nature of social change in the post-war world – concerns for which the idea of 'youth' and the 'contemporaryness' of contemporary experience are important. That these are not entirely 'new' concerns is also implied by the ease with which this interpretative framework is applied; *Look Back in Anger* was the point where these emerging explanations for post-war social change became focused around the theatre for the first time in the decade, placing the play at the centre of a distinctive socio-cultural moment.

The focus on the 'contemporary' in the reviews of *Look Back in Anger* is testimony to its structured absence from the theatre of the time. 'The contemporary' frequently functions as a synonym for social criticism, and against an unengaged, reactionary culture, the contemporary became a banner, behind which the oppositional forces in the theatre could (temporarily) gather.

The lack of the contemporary was not confined to theatre but was a feature of intellectual culture generally, and is related to the absence of sustained social criticism in the period. It is not so much that there were no oppositional or counter-hegemonic ideas in circulation, but rather that there were relatively few forums outside the main institutions of political power for initiation into political practice; as Miliband noted, one of the main differences between the thirties and the fifties was that the latter 'often appeared to lack the instrumentalities of radical change' (Miliband 1973: 347). Intellectuals – particularly literary intellectuals – acted largely as a 'subaltern' class, as Gramsci put it, forming an alliance with the ruling political caste, if not always actively, then often passively, by acquiescing to the status quo. Commenting on the docility of British intellectuals in 1955, Edward Shils wrote that 'in the main – scarcely anyone in Great Britain seems any longer to feel there is anything fundamentally wrong. . . . Never has an intellectual class found its society and its culture so much to its satisfaction' (quoted in Hill 1986: 21). Such acquiescence, or 'quietism' – a form of refusal to engage in the political or cultural process (in the wider sense) at all – did not necessarily imply contentment, however, nor was it right-wing in a simple sense; indeed, a cursory look at the output of the major intellectual and literary figures in the late forties and early fifties – T.S. Eliot, for example, or Evelyn Waugh – reveals anything but 'satisfaction'. In fact, although it would be wrong to write as if a single intellectual climate, a unified ideology, existed at the time, it is probably true to say that most forms of literary culture were imbued with a sense of loss, of disillusion with the immediate past and a loathing of the material priorities of affluent Britain.

One reason why quietism became so prevalent was that there seemed to be little opposition from the left to the emerging consensus. The Communist Party continued to exert an influence, particularly in the labour movement, in excess of its numerical strength despite the Cold War; however, this influence was being exercised largely without the energies of many of its intellectual fellow-travellers. Its fortunes, as well as its policies, always dependent on those of the Soviet Union, the Party suffered a haemorrhage of support even before the Second World War in the wake of the non-aggression pact between Stalin and Hitler, and the mounting evidence of an organised purge of dissidents. The disillusion that this engendered (which was only temporarily reversed during the war, when the Soviet Union became an ally) was articulated in a number of books that appeared in the late 1940s and early 1950s, one of the most influential of which was *The God That Failed* (1950) edited by Richard Crossman. It took the form of a series of contributions by writers who had been communists, or sympathisers with communism, but who had rejected their previous affiliations. Drawing on a parallel between communism and authoritarian Catholicism, the book described the attractions of communism to intellectuals 'wearied by the privileges of freedom' (Crossman 1950: 12). Arnold Wesker has written that reading *The God That Failed* was a key moment in his own disillusion with communism. 'That book disturbed me so profoundly', he told Walter Wager, 'that I wrote letters to Spender and Koestler and others to find out if the book was actually cold fact' (Wager 1969: 225).

The combination of consensus and the Cold War made what political writing there was on the left liable to misinterpretation. The fate of George Orwell's *1984* was an ominous example; conceived as a critique of totalitarianism in general (and Soviet totalitarianism in particular) the book was rapidly absorbed – especially after its appearance in the United States – into a pro-western conservative rhetoric.

The lack of engagement with the contemporary world was underscored, symbolically and actually, by the dominance of an earlier generation of writers and intellectuals whose formative years, politically and intellectually, were before the war; Stephen Spender, W.H. Auden, Evelyn Waugh, T.S. Eliot, J.B. Priestley and George Orwell, for example, had all established their reputations by 1939, and several of them had institutional power as well as literary influence (Spender's editorship of the right-wing cultural journal *Encounter*, for example). Most of the established – that is, most often performed and critically regarded – living playwrights, such as Noel Coward and Terrence Rattigan, were those that had made their reputations before 1950. Many of the most enduring stereotypes of British theatre in the early 1950s came from a perception that it was dominated by pre-war personnel and re-actionary social and aesthetic values, reflecting a wider cultural phenomenon (see Hewison 1981: 64).

It is no accident, then, that one of the most enduring metaphors of post-war theatre before 1956 concerns the 'country-house' drama. One of the most savage indictments of this kind of play was delivered by Kenneth Tynan, who helped both to establish and perpetuate the stereotype in a much-quoted critique of the genre:

> Its setting is a country house in what used to be called Loamshire but is now, as a heroic tribute to realism, some-times called Berkshire. Except when someone must sneeze, or be murdered, the sun invariably shines. Inhabitants belong to a social class derived partly from the playwright's vision of the leisured life he will lead after the play is a success – this

being the only effort of imagination he is called upon to make. Joys and sorrows are giggles and whimpers: the crash of denunciation dwindles into 'Oh, stuff Mummy!' and 'Oh, really Daddy!'. And so grim is the continuity of these things that the foregoing paragraph might have been written at any time during the last thirty years. (Tynan 1984: 148).

This was a partial, openly polemical view of the state of theatre in the early fifties and a great deal of what is interesting and valuable in the theatre of the time falls outside its ambit: 'Loamshire' was not an appropriate characterisation of much of the European drama or the American realism of Williams and Miller that could be seen in London in the early post-war period – nor even of the social milieu of Terrence Rattigan's plays, which were often more lower-middle-class in orientation. The significance of Tynan's account lies not so much in its accuracy as in the fact that it occurs in the context of a lament for the lack of the contemporary in British theatre. The article concludes with the observation that if audiences – 'people of passionate intellectual appetites' – are to be won back to the theatre then 'the theatre must widen its scope, broaden its horizon so that Loamshire appears merely as the play-pen, not the whole palace of drama. We need plays about cabmen and demi-gods, plays about warriors, politicians and grocers' (Tynan 1984: 149). This links some of the major concerns of the theatre in both halves of the decade – the search for new audiences, which is seen to be connected both to the social exclusivity of dominant forms of drama and the absence of representations of contemporary Britain.

The Movement: the Emergence of a Critical Context

It is significant that when a new literary movement did appear in the early part of the 1950s, its relationship to its immediate social and cultural context was central to the terms in which it was interpreted. This came in the form of a group of poets and novelists (and some who were both), who began to attract critical attention from about 1952 onwards and who were known collectively as the Movement: Philip Larkin, Kingsley Amis, Donald Davie, J.D. Enright, John Wain, Elizabeth Jennings and Thom Gunn[1]. The Movement had a well-publicised presence in the 1950s; in particular, it generated a series

1 For a full discussion of the Movement and its origins see Blake Morrison's *The Movement* (1980).

of stereotypes that were simultaneously literary and social, that were closely related to emerging explanations about post-war social change, and around which a critical context appeared that was to have considerable consequences for the way that *Look Back in Anger* was read. The key texts in this context were Kingsley Amis's *Lucky Jim* (1954) and Walter Allen's review of it in the *New Statesman*, which was regarded as having isolated some of the key elements in the Movement generally, as well as in the novel. Allen located a 'new hero' in contemporary fiction:

> A new hero has risen amongst us. . . . He is consciously, even conscientiously, graceless. . . . He has one skin too few, but his is not the sensitiveness of the young man in earlier twentieth-century fiction; it is the phoney to which his nerve-ends are tremblingly exposed, and the least suspicion of the phoney and he gets tough. He is at odds with his conventional University education . . . he has seen through the academic racket as he sees through all the others. . . . In life he has been with us for some little time. . . . In fiction, I think he first arrived last year as the central character of Mr John Wain's novel *Hurry on Down*. He turns up again in Mr Amis's *Lucky Jim*.
>
> (Allen 1973: 299)

'Lucky Jim' rapidly became a central figure in the discussion of post-war literature and social typology, and an available shorthand for a constellation of attitudes, values and backgrounds – much as Jimmy Porter did after 1956. Indeed, some of the key elements in Allen's review – the hostility to 'phoniness', the sense of a hero at odds with his university education, the comic attacks on an upper-middle-class cultural style, a prickly sensitivity – are all present in *Look Back in Anger* and the critical discussion that followed its first production. It is not only that Jim Dixon and Jimmy Porter are similar kinds of character, but rather that a critical context that emerged around the novel was deployed to interpret the play two years later.

The main elements in this common framework are apparent in the way Allen constructs a particular view of the relationship between the novel and the social world, one which is also adopted by the reviewers of *Look Back in Anger*. Dixon, a particular type of hero – what would, in the context of Anger, be termed an 'anti-hero' – is posited not only as a literary character but also as a representative figure on the post-war social landscape (where he was joined by Amis himself, in a conflation of author and character that also happened to Osborne/Porter). Much of the media attention that pursued the Angry Young Men discussed them in these terms, and this was as true of the tabloids as it was of the literary journals. Both the *Daily Mail* and the *Daily Express* ran articles that lined up Osborne, Wilson, Hastings and Amis as the 'post-war generation' in literature, who were asked to explain 'what they were angry about'. Despite the prurient interest that soon surrounded Osborne and Wilson (whose alleged sexual irregularities received considerable attention), the main concern of even the popular press was to see Anger as a phenomenon that was very much 'of its time'.

Elsewhere, the elements of which this new social archetype were formed were expanded upon to include the influence of the post-war expansion of higher education, the disillusion with the cultural style of the pre-war years – especially its politics – and a 'democratic' austerity that was perceived to be in harmony with Welfare-State Britain, and for which 'provincial' was a shorthand (the stereotype of the redbrick university lecturer or graduate is one that runs across much fiction and criticism in the period and is highlighted in the reviews of *Look Back in Anger*). Not only did the Movement, then, create a literature that was recognisably contemporary in a number of senses, it also led to the creation of a critical context, and a set of available symbols, that greeted *Look Back in Anger* when it appeared.

Anger and 'Youth'

That Jimmy Porter should be seen as a representative of post-war youth is, perhaps, not surprising, although, as Tynan's review suggests, 'youth' is a term that frequently lacks any precise social definition. The connection between the two seemed so self-evident as to go largely unexamined, yet there was nothing inevitable about the linking of what were two distinct social phenomena. Like Anger, the idea of Youth was itself an ideological construct, an essential part of the mythology of affluence, and the link between the Angry Young Men and youth described more than just a coincidence of age. Youth appeared as one of the most striking and visible manifestations of social change in the 1950s, 'the compressed imagery for a society which had crucially changed in terms of basic life-styles and values – changed in ways calculated to upset the official political framework, but in ways not yet calculable in traditional political terms' (Hall and Jefferson 1976: 9). Youth was the focus of moral outrage, of obsessive media attention, of government reports, of sociological analysis, of legislation and of cultural criticism throughout the decade and into the next. As Hopkins put it, 'to enter one's teens was to be inducted into an exclusive and privileged order, several million strong, which those outside it observed with an uncertain mixture of envy, awe, fascination and repulsion' (Hopkins 1963: 422). Youth was also a factor in national politics. During the 1955 General Election, the *Daily Mirror* had sought to promote the Labour Party as the party of 'youth' (a strategy that was hampered by the fact that the average age of the Labour Shadow Cabinet exceeded that of the government (see Smith 1975)).

Explanations as to why youth should occupy such a position in the social mythology of the period are not hard to find. Changes in the education system, for example, have a central role. The 1944 Education Act provided 'secondary education for all' in age-specific schools and ensured that an increasing number of young people were spending a large portion of their adolescent years in the company of their peers, removed from the responsibility of work (or the vicissitudes of unemployment) and could be more readily seen as a distinct social grouping.

Youth were also central to the debates about the effects of affluence on traditional moral and social values and allegiances. The general affluence seemed particularly available to teenagers; as one observer commented, 'the young were the outstanding financial beneficiaries of the post-war situation' (Hopkins 1963: 424). In 1959, Mark Abrams, one of the most influential exponents of the thesis, set the figure of the 'teenage consumer' on the post-war social landscape.

> As compared with 1938, their real earnings (i.e. after allowing for the fall in the value of money) have increased by 50 per cent (which is double the rate of expansion for adults), and their real 'discretionary' spending has probably risen by 100 per cent.
>
> (Abrams 1959: 9)

According to Abrams, 12s. 3d. out of an average weekly wage of 64s. was spent on clothing and footwear, the largest single item of expenditure. This revealed a pattern of 'distinctive teenage spending, for distinctive teenage ends in a distinctive teenage world' (Abrams 1959: 9).

That distinctively post-war phenomenon, the 'generation gap', has its origins here, for affluence was said to loosen the bonds between teenagers and the culture and values of their parents, rendering traditional class distinctions increasingly obsolete. As Colin MacInnes argued:

> The 'two nations' of our society may perhaps no longer be those of the 'rich' and the 'poor' (or, to use old-fashioned terms, the 'upper' and 'working' classes), but those of the teenagers on the one hand and, on the other, all those who have assumed the burdens of adult responsibility.
>
> (MacInnes 1966: 66)

The ease with which the Angry Young Men could be identified with youth resided partly in the fact that they were signified as a 'new generation', distinct from – and opposed to – the cultural and political establishment as teenagers were from their parent cultures and social values. Osborne, Wilson *et al.*, though clearly not products of the 1944 Education Act nor conspicuous beneficiaries of affluence, were characteristically lower-class, as well as being young and 'new' in the sense of being previously unpublished or unperformed.

Although the Angry Young Men as individuals were not directly 'products' of the Welfare State, Anger as a phenomenon was nonetheless seen as a result of the possibilities that it had created, and one that seemed clearly antagonistic towards the benefits it had bestowed. It was frequently the ingratitude of the angries that caused the most resentment, being simultaneously a mark of their lower-class origins and an inevitable result of the loosening of established values brought about by universal welfare and education; the generation gap always contained in its shadow a deep anxiety about the moral values of a socially detached youth.

The activities of working-class sub-cultures, especially the teddy-boys, were of particular concern. 'Deviancy', a term that originated in sociological discourse and rapidly became popularised, was applied to those aspects of behaviour that were most graphically anti-social, especially 'new' forms of crime such as the ripping of cinema seats. It represented a 'pathologising' of that behaviour, and had its roots, at one level, in anxieties about the effects of the Second World War, and at another, in the effects of post-war power-blocs, nuclear weaponry and the Cold War. The Angry Young Men were clearly not 'deviants' in the criminal sense (although some of the critical response to Anger sought to pathologise it, to reduce it to the outbursts of 'neurotic' personalities). However, the construction of Anger as a public event could be seen as a form of 'moral panic', a term coined by the sociologist Stanley Cohen in a seminal book on the evolution of youth cultures since the war.

> Societies appear to be subject, every now and then, to periods of moral panic. A condition, episode, person or group of persons emerges to become defined as a threat to societal values and interests; its nature is presented in a stylised and stereotypical fashion by the mass media; the moral barricades are manned by editors, bishops, politicians and other right-thinking people; socially accredited experts pronounce their diagnoses and solutions; ways of coping are evolved or (more often) resorted to.
>
> (Cohen 1973: 9)

Much of this is applicable to the way that Anger became defined as a symptom of social malaise. Indeed, in some ways it is those elements that seem so irrelevant to dramatic criticism now, that both provided key elements in the contemporary readings of the plays and propelled the theatre into a new position within British culture at the time; the 'scandal', Osborne's legendary rudeness to journalists and public alike, the assertion of 'emotion' over a crude and limiting reasonableness, the constant affront to 'good taste' – these were not political in any accepted contemporary sense, but nevertheless disturbing of the social status quo.

Look Back in Anger was not a passive recipient of the kinds of readings that were made of it, and if we were to ask the question why it should be *this* play and not, say, *Waiting for Godot* that was seen to break new ground, then the answer would lie at least partly in the familiarity of its dramatic and theatrical form. It has become a truism to say that the play was innovatory at the level of 'content' rather than 'form', and the issue here is partly to do with access-ibility. The play relies heavily upon, and works comfortably within, the kinds of plot devices that were familiar from the genre of the 'well-made play', a particularly British variant of the general natural-ist form (see Trussler 1969); neatly arranged act-endings and character entrances, carefully orchestrated, if obvious, repetition (the positioning of both Alison and Helena at the ironing board, for example) and even the use of a stock-device – the loss of a child – to develop the action, heighten the emotional impact and enable a reconciliation to occur between the two principal characters. The fact that the play's conventions were immediately readable meant that critical attention was more easily focused around the issues that it seemed to be raising. More importantly, the conventions of the play, which we may term broadly naturalist or realist, supported in quite precise ways the kinds of contextual readings that we have been examining.

To read Jimmy Porter as a representative social type, for example, is not simply to respond to the particular arguments of the play but to recognise that within realist drama the central protagonist embodies values, attitudes and a social experience that are not his or hers alone. Representativeness is, therefore, built into the dramatic conventions, and becomes a way in which characters escape their own specificity, a means by which the action takes on a significance beyond the immediate, offering a microcosm of the 'real world'.

Part of the immediate 'shock' of *Look Back in Anger* lay in the impact of its setting. The stage directions in the printed text locate the action in a specific and contemporary social setting and are quite specific about the way that the fictional space – a 'one-room flat in a large Midland town' – is laid out, delineating a living-space that contains the possibility of a full range of domestic activities; on view are a 'double bed', for example, as well as an ironing board, a 'heavy chest of drawers, covered with books, neckties and odds and ends' (Osborne 1957a: 9), a gas-stove and food cupboard. The realism of a set like this asks to be judged not only in relation to an observable social reality beyond the stage but also against other kinds of theatre; in both these senses the play was a considered provocation. The set was an act of semiotic vandalism, challenging almost point by point the iconography of the bourgeois living-room and the country-house drawing-room; here, the old 'chest of drawers' would be likely to be antique, and the profusion of books that covered it would be arranged in book-cases to denote a 'profession' or at least a general level of 'culture'. This strategy is continued through the opening image of the play, in which Alison is discovered at the ironing board, revealing the domestic labour that is normally concealed in the well-made play (but it is still performed by a woman, even though she is a wife rather than a servant). This opening also permits the audience a few moments of near-silence before the dialogue commences to absorb the visual information that confronts it. That this provocation did not go unremarked was clear from the reviews, nearly all of which noted the 'squalor' of a setting that carefully reproduced (in Allan Tagg's designs) the intentions of the text.

The conscious utilisation of contemporary references was present in other aspects of the play, too. Jimmy and Cliff are introduced to the audience from behind the Sunday papers, the contents of which – bishops, nuclear weapons and repressive sexual morality – become an object of Jimmy's satirical venom. A considerable part of the play consists of long set-pieces, angry, bitter and occasionally joyous tirades by Jimmy. These seem at times to stretch the conventions of the form, almost reaching across the footlights as direct address, and articulating opinions which were sometimes taken as statements of the central ideas of the play. However, their status is contradictory, for, as the stage directions reveal, they are not so much directed out to the audience, or even naturalised as 'political opinions', but are part of Jimmy's psychological warfare with Alison (and occasionally Cliff). The text is very clear about this: references to Jimmy being 'resentful at being dragged away from his pursuit of Alison' or 'scenting victory' provide a psychological context for an 'anger' that moves between the public and the social on the one hand, and the personal and the sexual on the other. From a viewpoint outside the immediate context, *Look Back in Anger* is a play less about a proto-political social rebellion and one that is more a protracted and painful exploration of a particular kind of post-war masculine identity.

That the Angry Young Men were men was self-evident, and worthy of considerably less critical attention than the fact that they were 'angry' and 'young'. Yet the kinds of dilemmas, hopes and possibilities for action that defined the central characters that dominated plays, films and novels, and which were read primarily in social, or sociological, terms, are also related to gender. This is not only a question of how women are represented in the period (although this is a large part of it) but also of how the relationship between class, politics and gender is constructed[2].

From this point of view, Walter Allen's 'new hero' is unambiguously male, and the opposition to a particular cultural style that Allen noted in Amis's *Lucky Jim* (pretentious, 'phoney', anachronistic and conformist) is identified with 'a rejection of what he sees

2 See Wandor 1987 for an extensive treatment of the construction of gender within a number of New Wave plays from a feminist viewpoint.

REPRESENTING CONTEMPORARY BRITAIN

as womanly. . . . He exudes a bullying contempt for women' (Segal 1990: 1). D.E. Cooper has sought to generalise the anti-women rhetoric of mid-fifties intellectuals by arguing that their real target was 'effeminacy', which is 'simply the sum of those qualities which are supposed traditionally . . . to exude from the worst in women: pettiness, snobbery, flippancy, voluptuousness, superficiality, materialism' (Cooper 1970: 257), and these are not peculiar to women. The argument is, however, a little elusive, for the characteristics of effeminacy are so closely aligned to how women were actually represented in the period, that an attempt to prise them apart looks doomed: 'voluptuousness, superficiality and materialism' delineate both effeminacy and some of the most common attributes of female characters, especially in New Wave novels and films. That this particular list should include the sexual and the social indicates not only (male) historical definitions of femininity but also the way that women were connected to fifties debates about consensus and the effects of affluence.

The connections between class/social positions and sexual insecurity are vividly clear in *Look Back in Anger*, where class resentment (struggle is too strong a word for it) is inseparable from an antagonism towards, and fear of, women. Osborne's portrayal of Alison's father is sympathetic, but Jimmy reserves his scorn for her mother, who would willingly 'kick you in the groin while you're handing your hat to the maid' (Osborne 1957a: 21): the linking of class snobbery with sexual emasculation is explicit. It is notable that one of the most oft-quoted remarks from the play, that 'There aren't any good, brave causes left', comes in the middle of a long and vituperative attack on women:

Why, why why do we let these women bleed us to death? Have you ever had a letter, and on it is franked 'Please give your blood generously'? Well, the Postmaster-General does that on behalf of all the women of the world. I suppose the people of our generation aren't able to die for good, brave causes any longer. . . . No, there's nothing for it, me boy, but to let yourself be butchered by the women.

(Osborne 1957a: 84–5)

The speech is symptomatic of the way that political and sexual impotency are interlinked in the play; if it was the former of these that attracted the most attention in the period, then that was partly because the problem of political commitment was already high on the agenda.

CONTESTING HEGEMONY: THEATRE AND
ANTI-CONSENSUAL POLITICS

In 1957, Kingsley Amis published a Fabian pamphlet entitled *Socialism and the Intellectuals*, which became a reference point for debate about the nature of political commitment. In it, Amis argued that the 'best and most trustworthy political instinct is self-interest' (Amis 1973: 260), a conclusion that was arrived at after a denunciation of the Labour Party as a willing partner in the consensus, and a castigation of the activities of the pre-war political generation. Amis's pragmatism was the result of what he saw as the closing down of the two main options available to intellectuals and artists to become involved in left politics – Communism and Labourism.

However, this kind of 'anti-political' politics was also a response to a sense of blockage in the system, a pushing against the limits of professional and social advance as well as political and artistic expression. Looking at the subsequent careers of several of those linked to Anger – Amis and Osborne spring not unexpectedly to mind – which have shown a remorseless drift to the political and cultural right, it would seem that professional advance was the main motive. From this point of view, the mid-decade cultural crisis was largely an institutional one that occurred at the point where the traditional arenas of cultural advance – the arts and communications especially – could not adapt fast enough to admit the next generation, particularly as it came from a different class background.

However, to argue that Anger was only this is to ignore the complexities of the cultural positions it represented. There are two ways of looking at this, and both are right in different ways: one can argue that the objects of derision – Jimmy Porter's assault on the upper-classes, the Sunday papers, and all things royal – reveal a curious parochialism at a time of profound social change, and proceed not so much from anger as from envy. However, it is also the case that it was precisely such traditional institutions that were being co-opted to define the terms in which the 'new' was to be interpreted. To attack these institutions of the establishment was to attack the symbolic centre of the hegemonic consensus, the essential terms in which mid-fifties Britain was being interpreted, often by subverting the traditionalist imagery, in which the 'New Elizabethan Age' sought to cloak itself. Osborne castigated the royal family at length in a variety of contexts, calling it 'the gold filling in a mouthful of decay', and accused the church of moral bankruptcy, arguing that 'It is precisely on this . . . level that people live' (Osborne 1957c: 70). Lindsay Anderson provided one of the clearest example of this in an account of Britain as a society locked into its own (irrelevant) past:

> Coming back to Britain is . . . in many respects like going back into the nursery. The outside world, the dangerous world is shut away; its sounds are muffled. Cretonne curtains are drawn, with a pretty pattern on them of the Queen and her fairy-tale Prince riding to Westminster in a golden coach.
>
> (L. Anderson 1957: 155)

In this context the opposition to censorship, which, apart from the opposition to nuclear weapons, was the political/cultural cause most likely to unite a wide spectrum of theatre activists after 1956, acquired a distinctive political logic. Pre-production censorship had existed since 1737, was reinforced in the Theatres Act of 1843, and was not abolished until 1968. Before any new play could be performed in public, the text had to be submitted to the Lord Chamberlain's Office for prior approval; if the Office did not approve, it had the power to impose amendments and substitutions, or cut any part – or even the whole – of an author's work under criteria that were laid down in 1909, but which could be applied at the discretion of the Chamberlain himself or members of his staff ('readers'). These criteria were not embodied in any statute, but were 'guidelines' established by a committee. In this way, the establishment was more than a distant abstraction to people working in the theatre; it wore a very particular and familiar face.

It was the character of the Office itself that so perfectly symbolised the persistence of traditional institutions in the post-war world. The Lord Chamberlain was – is – not simply a government-appointed civil servant but the head of the Queen's household; he is not, therefore, responsible to Parliament but only to the Queen herself and is paid for out of the Civil List. Censoring plays was only a small part of his job. The opposition to the Lord Chamberlain maintained its momentum as the fifties moved into the sixties, partly because the consensus against censorship in every cultural arena was becoming increasingly broad and its abolition was seen as an achievable political goal. Yet it retained its symbolic significance, too, as championing free speech embodied both a liberal defence of the freedom of the artist and a more radical attack on an establishment that was uncomfortably exposed in its nineteenth-century clothing.

A significant problem with the kind of anti-traditionalist rhetoric that characterised Anger was that it was essentially negative; it knew what it opposed, but the political values that underpinned this opposition were not always consistent or visible. However, very quickly, some of the most prominent New Wave theatre practitioners sought to rescue the vocabulary of socialism from the accretions of a decade of Cold War rhetoric. Osborne, Anderson and Tynan, in their contributions to *Declaration* (1957), a collection of essays edited by Tom Maschler, took the opportunity to call themselves socialist, offering, against the grain of contemporary intellectual usage, definitions of what that meant. For Osborne, 'Socialism is an experimental idea, not a dogma; an attitude to truth and liberty, the way people should live and treat each other' (Osborne 1957b: 83); for Tynan, 'To discover one is a socialist should be a liberating experience' (Tynan 1957: 121); and for Anderson, 'A socialism that cannot express itself in emotional terms, poetic terms is one that will never capture the imagination of the people' (L. Anderson 1957: 173).

Socialism defined in these terms is not about class-struggle, power or property relationships, but is rather an ethical and moral philosophy – and one that could be readily related to the situation of the writer. Such a moral/philosophical version of socialism, though within a humanist socialist tradition, existed in the border territory between liberalism, libertarianism and socialism, and, in avoiding suggestions of dogma and ideology, was a clear rejection of the perceived political positions of the thirties. This kind of humanism also followed the left generally in shifting the focus of enquiry away from the economic/political arenas to the cultural/personal ones, in which art traditionally had a central role to play.

One of the principal objectives of the New Left forces that gathered in the second half of the decade was to engage the young, post-war generation around a set of issues that recognised this kind of cultural agenda. The first issue of *Universities and Left Review* (1957), one of the first manifestations of a 'new' left politics, carried an editorial that recognised the degree to which this agenda was not going to be realisable within the terms of the 'old' (i.e. pre-1956) consensual politics. Recognising that Amis's pamphlet had raised 'in a somewhat disconnected and romantic manner the objections felt by most young intellectuals to participation in the Labour movement', the editorial blamed the process of politics itself. 'Given the feeble level of political controversy', it ran, 'who could argue with the young intellectuals when they said – they are still saying it – that politics was not "about them"'. However, Suez ensured that the situation had changed, and that 'much as we would like, we cannot think our way round Suez, back to that comfortable womb-world, in which Conservatives and Socialists still held hands' (*Universities and Left Review*, Vol.1, 1957; pp. 1–2). It was not the Labour Party – at least, not in its parliamentary guise – that spawned a 'new' politics of the left, but rather a new generation of activists with different priorities and histories, that found expression in the 'New Left' and the Campaign for Nuclear Disarmament (CND).

E.P. Thompson, one of the main figures in the New Left, argued that it arose out of the confluence of 'the dissident communist impulse with the left socialist tradition and with the post-war generation' (Thompson 1964: 104). The New Left was essentially a grouping of intellectuals around two journals, the *New Reasoner* (edited by E.P. Thompson and Philip Saville, who represented the first of these tendencies) and *Universities and Left Review* (which represented the second). In a broader usage, the term also referred to a larger group of intellectuals and radicals, based mainly in the universities and adult education. The main project of the New Left was to forge a radical socialism that was distinct from that offered either by the left-wing of the Labour Party, irretrievably locked into Labourism and the consensus, or by the Communist Party, wedded to Stalinism and Moscow. Many of the key figures supporting and contributing to the *New Reasoner* were intellectuals who were amongst the 7,000 members who deserted the Communist Party in the wake of the Soviet invasion of Hungary (the Party had supported the Soviet action). From the beginning their concerns marked them off from an earlier generation of apostates, who had adopted a rabid anti-communism; instead, they sought to 'develop the humane and libertarian features of the Communist tradition' (Thompson 1964: 104).

Universities and Left Review appeared at about the same time as the *New Reasoner* (in 1957). It was published from Oxford and edited by Stuart Hall, Gabriel Pierson, Raphael Samuel and Charles Taylor. The intellectual and political impulse motivating it was a rejection of the Labour Party and conventional British socialist politics, and a strong interest in opening up questions about culture at a political level. The concerns of the two groups were in practice almost identical, and the two journals merged to form the *New Left*

Review edited by Stuart Hall and with an editorial board drawn from those of its progenitors.

Parallel to the emergence of a New Left, and very much connected with it, was that of a new form of radical politics coalescing around the anti-nuclear movement, the most visible manifestation of which was the Campaign for Nuclear Disarmament (CND). There is not the space here to detail the origins of CND (see Driver 1964), but it is worth remarking that one of the main achievements of the campaign was to bring hitherto marginalised forms of political action – the march, the sit-in, the mass rally – into the mainstream of post-war protest. By 1960, the annual march drew over 75,000 people to Trafalgar Square, and in 1961 over 100,000 attended. These kinds of protest were successful partly because they came out of traditions of radical protest that were untainted by either Stalinist communism or the consensual games of established parliamentary politics (although CND always had one eye on mainstream politics, winning the Labour Party to a unilateralist position at the 1960 Party Conference – only to see its victory reversed a year later). CND was closely aligned to forms of pacifist and libertarian dissent, which went back to the pre-war pacifist organisations, and which was present in the active Quaker Fellowships and the many small anarchist groups after the war.

It is hard to avoid the presence of youth in contemporary accounts of the Campaign, and particularly in relation to its extraparliamentary activities. This is partly because the most distinctive feature of the Campaign was that it adopted forms of political action that could be seen, in Parkin's terms, as 'expressive activity' (Parkin 1968). That is, demonstrations and marches were not simply 'protests' designed to achieve specific and tangible goals, but were also means of expressing social and cultural values, were acts of celebration and affirmations of a communal identity, created and shaped by collective action. It is this aspect of CND's cultural politics, the long hair and duffel-coats of the marchers, the singing and playing of guitars, the alleged sexual promiscuity en route to Aldermaston, that enabled the media to generate another form of 'moral panic', and which attracted many young, middleclass people into its fold, as the fifties moved into the sixties.

The New Wave in theatre was closely involved in the activities of CND and its off-shoots; as Parkin has observed in the course of comparing the intellectual support for CND with that for radical political campaigns in the 1930s, 'one noticeable difference . . . was

that whereas poets seem to have been the chief creative representatives of the earlier period, the archetypal figures of the unilateralist
movement were actors and playwrights' (Parkin 1968: 99). The
commitment to the anti-nuclear movement took a variety of forms:
signing petitions, participating in demonstrations – and occasionally going to prison – and going on the annual Aldermaston march
(where the Royal Court banner was a familiar and regular sight).

Theatre practitioners – particularly writers, who were always the
most visible participants in anti-nuclear activities – were prominent
in the campaigns of civil disobedience that occurred towards the
end of the decade, and which were associated with the Committee
of 100 (an off-shoot of CND, committed to direct action and non-
violent disobedience). The Committee was a meeting point between the New Left and the New Wave. Lindsay Anderson, John
Osborne, John Arden, Arnold Wesker, and Bernard Kops were all
involved from its inception, and were later joined by David Mercer,
Robert Bolt and the actors Vanessa Redgrave and John Neville.
Their support was more than moral, and both Wesker and Bolt were
arrested in September 1961 during a demonstration in Whitehall.

Support for CND could be seen as 'non-ideological' and symbolic, embracing people with a range of political and philosophical
sympathies (this was partly true of even the more radical Committee of 100, which required a firmer political purpose). However,
if direct political activity, from whatever motive, was possible for
theatre radicals in the period, the creation of a more political, or
contemporary, theatre – and of thinking politically about theatre –
proved to be more difficult.

Politics and 'Vital Theatre'

It has become a truism to say that the theatre of the New Wave was
not political – although this is frequently a judgement that excepts
the plays of John Arden and some of the productions of Joan
Littlewood, and is made in relation to the more explicitly political
drama of the 1970s and 1980s. Dramatists may have sat down in
Trafalgar Square in protest against the Bomb, but rarely did this
emerge as a subject within the plays themselves (it is a theme in
David Mercer's trilogy *The Generations*, Robert Bolt's *The Tiger and
the Horse*, and Doris Lessing's *Each his Own Wilderness*). That there
was a mismatch between the political activities of playwrights and
the political ambitions of their plays is at least partly because of the

difficulty of finding an appropriate model of what a 'political' theatre might look like, or an appropriate language in which to formulate the relevant questions.

The problem surfaced in the way that questions about the nature of a contemporary theatre were posed, and answered, in *Encore* magazine. From its inception in 1956 until the mid-sixties, *Encore* was closely associated with the explosion of theatrical activity after 1956, helping to generate and shape critical debate about the New Wave. The magazine drew on a range of contributors, many of whom were prominent figures within the new theatre and, occasionally, the New Left (Raymond Williams and Stuart Hall were amongst them). However, the search for a new politics that was symptomatic of the New Left was frequently absent from *Encore*'s treatment of politics, even when such key ideas as 'commitment' were being debated. Anderson argued that the magazine should 'not be expressing every point of view, but the right one' (L. Anderson 1970a: 47). The editors replied by identifying *Encore* with the concerns of its audiences, who were sceptical of politics, equating commitment with conformity: 'It [the audience] recognises the need to face up to that old question What are you for? But it is also living in a time when the 'fors' have been shamelessly betrayed' (*Encore*, Jan./Feb. 1958).

Encore's concern with radical alternatives to mainstream theatre was focused through the idea of 'vital theatre'. The magazine's subtitle for most of its life was 'The Voice of Vital Theatre', and the term was a point of reference for many of its contributors in the late fifties. It was also the title of a symposium organised by the *Universities and Left Review*, extracts from which appeared in *Encore* in 1959. Vital theatre was a term which attracted a cluster of meanings, many of them social and cultural as well as theatrical, and the debates around it focused on a number of different concerns – to do with audiences and the nature of the social experience being represented in the theatre, for example – that will be considered in later chapters. Vital had a set of immediate and colloquial connotations – of youth and energy, as well as of being necessary and urgent – that place it on a landscape of fifties iconography. It also alluded to a possible social role for theatre, but one which was hard to define in the available languages.

George Devine, the first artistic director of the English Stage Company, attempted to locate vital theatre in a tradition of serious, yet popular, theatre ensembles in the twentieth century 'the theatres of Bertolt Brecht ... the Abbey Theatre, the Group Theatre, and coming nearer home, the Granville-Barker Theatre ... and the English Group Theatre of the Thirties'. What these theatres had in common, he argued, was that they were a 'true expression of, or a revelation about, certain deep feelings in a particular society' (Devine 1959: 24). The evasiveness of the language here is indicative of the difficulty many of the new practitioners had with both politics and the idea of political theatre, whilst being attracted to such possibilities in principle. The Royal Court may have had the reputation of being a theatre of the left, but, as one commentator acerbically noted,

> That the house was made to twitter at some titbit of dialectical reasoning was taken as evidence that the wedding of art and social commitment had in fact taken place. That Marx in the process had been made into a bourgeois humorist was either missed or ignored.
>
> (Goetschius 1966: 33)

Part of the difficulty was that the most available model of what a political – or 'committed', 'vital' or contemporary – theatre might look like was a theatre of propaganda, most easily recognised from the pre-war period. As Doris Lessing noted:

> The reaction is so powerful and so prompt that one only has to go up on a public platform ... for nine-tenths of the audience immediately to assume that one believes that novels should be simple tracts about factories or strikes or economic injustice.
>
> (Lessing 1957: 13)

With the idea of politics contaminated by its association with communism and the consensus, and with committed theatre identified with propaganda, it was in the discourses of realism that the project of creating a contemporary and anti-hegemonic theatre was pursued.

2

INSTITUTIONS AND AUDIENCES

If theatre seemed irredeemably conservative and unengaged in the immediate post-war period then this was partly because, as an institution and an industry, it was wedded to pre-war values and practices. These did not simply disappear at the arrival of the New Wave, but had their own trajectory; indeed, the subterranean patterns of funding and organisation that dominated theatre, especially metropolitan commercial theatre, helped to shape the possibilities for the new drama, how and in what circumstances it was produced, and the terms in which it was debated. It is particularly difficult to talk about one of the major objectives of much of the new theatre, the attempt to win new audiences, unless institutional factors are acknowledged.

THEATRE STRUCTURES

One reason why the theatre was so backward socially in the early 1950s was that it was backward economically. The commercial theatre (at this point the largest sector of the theatre industry by far) was the last bastion of unreconstructed capitalism in the post-war cultural professions, and operated in a context in which the intractable problems of the theatre industry were becoming increasingly apparent. Theatre managers were faced by a spiral of rising costs which could be neither deferred nor passed directly onto the consumer: the disproportionate rise in the costs of basic materials such as timber and canvas, the increasing need for a publicity budget, the unionisation of actors, which led to the granting of a minimum wage – these all conspired to make theatre a precarious commercial venture in the immediate post-war years. Richard Findlater observed that 'today [1952] it needs a much greater capital reserve to present plays than at any other time in the theatre's history. The freedom to produce plays is as limited as the freedom to start a national newspaper' (Findlater 1952: 124).

The response of most managements was to seek to consolidate their power by uniting the ownership of 'real estate' (it had long been the case that the point at which the most profits could be made was at the 'bricks and mortar' end of the production process) and production companies (as a means of ensuring the continuation of a product that brought them – occasionally – profit). This situation led to an unprecedented concentration of all the functions of production and distribution in a few hands (see Elsom 1976 and Findlater 1952) with a consequent narrowing of the range of plays on offer – in both London and the provinces – to those that were tried and tested (which usually meant plays by commercially successful, established and pre-war dramatists). As J.B. Priestley observed:

> The chances of a new and original play ever seeing the light depends in a vast degree upon its meeting the taste of one particular person. . . . The new piece they describe with enthusiasm at the Ivy Restaurant today will probably, within the next three years, be applauded from Torquay to Aberdeen'.
>
> (quoted Pick 1983: 88)

There were a few cracks in the edifice of this monopolistic commercialism. A loop-hole in the tax regulations, which allowed exemption from the Entertainments Tax for non-profit-making plays of 'educational merit', was exploited by several managements (notably H.M. Tennents and Henry Sherek), who used it to bring plays by established writers, such as Priestley, Rattigan, Bridie and Eliot, to the London stage. This was in addition to plays by continental writers, like Sartre, which might otherwise have received no major productions. Significantly, few new – that is, entirely post-war – dramatists found a platform in this way. In the provinces, companies such as the Shakespeare Memorial Theatre at Stratford and the Birmingham Repertory Theatre remained successfully independent, whilst in London small, independent theatre clubs (known collectively as 'little theatres', or arts theatres), operating precariously at the margins of the theatre industry, continued to bring new – and especially new European – theatre to this country (see Marshall 1947 and Elsom 1976). Significantly, it was the arts theatres that championed the new verse dramas of Eliot and Fry. The first production of *Waiting for Godot* was produced initially at a theatre club, the Arts (and was directed by Peter Hall), before transferring to the West End. However, the lack of permanence of many of the arts theatres, together with their financial and creative precariousness, made them ill-suited to the ambitions of many theatre professionals, who, looking to the much better-funded ensembles in Europe, sought a solution to the economic and institutional problems of the theatre, not in the market but in the State itself.

Theatre and the State: the Arts Council of Great Britain

By the time that *Look Back in Anger* appeared, state sponsorship for the theatre, distributed by the Arts Council of Great Britain (ACGB), had been available for ten years. Formed out of the Council for the Encouragement of Music and the Arts (CEMA), which had been established to take professional theatre ('serious', legitimate theatre, that is) and classical music and dance to both civilian and military populations during the war, the Arts Council was established in 1946, largely at the instigation of John Maynard Keynes, whose economic theories were to have such a decisive effect on the shape of post-war reconstruction. However, the Council had neither the resources nor the ideological will-power to effect immediate or significant change. In 1946, the Council had an initial budget of only £235,000, and by 1956, this had risen to only £820,000, nearly all of which was tied to specific projects.

Keynes believed that as public taste improved, then the arts should eventually become self-sufficient, democratised and supported by an educated and enthusiastic public; however, it is more helpful to think of the arts as having entered the era of the Keynesian 'mixed economy'. The economic rationale that permitted the State a role in the direction, and sometimes ownership, of sectors of the free market, was successfully mobilised by Keynes and others to justify State 'interference' in culture, at the same time as the arts were considered as the spiritual wing of the Welfare State, administering to the nation's psychic health as the NHS administered to its physical well-being. In this way, the Arts Council was a visible expression of consensual assumptions translated into the cultural sphere.

The Arts Council saw its function as being primarily to 'respond' to the needs and aspirations of those seeking its support, and in the ten years that followed the war, it withdrew into London (shutting its regional offices), shying clear of a more interventionist or radical role. The Council showed little enthusiasm for entering some of the more contentious areas of theatrical debate, having little to offer, in practical terms at least, the increasingly active campaign in the 1950s to secure a National Theatre, for example. In an open letter to the government entitled 'Mobilise the Theatre' and published in *New Theatre*, a number of prominent theatre practitioners of the day argued that for 'a sum no greater than that paid in Entertainment Tax in a year by a big West End musical show, we could put twenty decent companies on the road, going from hostel to miner's hall, from school to factory canteen' (Willis *et al.* 1947). This envisaged a much greater State direction of artistic activity than either the Arts Council or the government were willing to consider.

The Arts Council, then, had neither the will nor the resources to effect radical changes within the cultural professions. This represented a missed opportunity, especially for the theatre, the economics of which were in a parlous condition under private enterprise. The results of this, in terms of the ability of the system to allow the development of a specifically contemporary theatre, had, by 1956, become all too plain.

OPENING UP THE PROCESSES OF THEATRICAL PRODUCTION: THE ENGLISH STAGE COMPANY AND THEATRE WORKSHOP

By 1955, the relationship between the processes of theatrical production and the kind of theatre that was produced had become the subject of critical comment – particularly as even avowedly commercial plays were finding it increasingly hard to survive. As T.C. Worsley observed in March 1956, 'however genuinely anxious the commercial managements are to find new plays, the conditions under which they work operate against the original writer' (quoted Browne 1975: 4). Worsley was voicing an increasingly widely held belief that it was the system itself, rather than a lack of talent, that was responsible for the dearth of contemporary drama, and that what was needed was not only new writers, but also new companies.

The New Wave was associated primarily with two theatre companies, the English Stage Company (ESC), at the Royal Court, and Theatre Workshop at the Theatre Royal, Stratford East. Although much of this chapter will be concerned with these two companies, it is worth emphasising that they were not identical in their social and aesthetic ambitions, notwithstanding their importance for much of the new theatre; the English Stage Company was established as a writer's theatre with relatively loosely defined social ambitions, whilst Theatre Workshop was conceived as an acting/producing ensemble with shared political opinions and a commitment to popular forms and a working-class audience. Nor were they the only significant producers of new writing, if the period is taken as a whole; Pinter's early plays were produced by Michael Codron, a commercial producer, and, by the early sixties, the Royal Shakespeare Company was beginning to produce new contemporary drama (by Henry Livings for example) at its London base at the Aldwych. However, it is probable that the initial breakthrough was only possible because the ESC and Theatre Workshop, committed to new kinds of drama and operating in ways that were different from the prevailing commercial ethos, arose to promote them. Both companies were committed to working in distinctive ways outside the ideologies and practices of the commercial theatre system (although neither company was able to operate with any real freedom from commercial constraints). The partial opening up of the processes of theatrical production that followed were, in context, decisive in determining both the shape and development of a contemporary theatre.

The English Stage Company (ESC)

Unlike Theatre Workshop, the ESC was an entirely 'new' company. The history of the formation of the company has been detailed at length elsewhere (see, for example, Browne 1975), but it is worth noting that it drew on a range of existing theatrical interests (both professional and amateur), and, from the beginning, had some influential and experienced supporters (the Earl of Harewood, for example, who had strong connections with the world of opera, and Oscar Lewinstein, a veteran theatre manager associated with the pre-war worker's theatre movement). The ESC also succeeded in attracting the commitment of a businessman, Neville Blond, on whose insistence the company acquired a theatre and an artistic director, George Devine. Tony Richardson was appointed as his assistant.

The policy of the ESC rested on the desire to create a body of new drama by actively encouraging new writers and providing a management and a theatre that would put on their plays. Devine amplified this policy and gave it his own particular interpretation. In 1957, he contributed an article to the *International Theatre Annual* on the policy and achievements of the ESC after one year's operation. The article stands as a statement of the main aspects of the Company's policy at the time, and, incidentally, as a critique of the problems facing British theatre in the mid-fifties. Noting in passing the strengths of that theatre – which he suggests were largely in the realm of acting and production – Devine outlines three major areas of concern. The first of these was the need to encourage new writers for the theatre; the second was the lack of a proper context in which 'the contemporary dramatist could express himself without having to submit to the increasing hazards of the commercial theatre'; and the third was the divorce between the writer and the post-war world. 'The theatre in England', he wrote, 'tends to exist in a world of its own and not to be in touch with contemporary attitudes, with the contemporary search for new values, or, in any way with other branches of the arts' (Devine 1957: 152). This latter anxiety had both a formal and a social aspect; it was, on the one hand, suggestive of Devine's ambition to 'find a contemporary style in dramatic work, acting, decor and production' (Browne 1975: 12) and, on the other, an expression, albeit a tentative one, of his belief that new writers would bring 'new' themes onto the stage, and would explore hitherto uncharted areas of social experience.

Not surprisingly, it was this latter emphasis on contemporary themes and new opportunities for young writers that attracted the initial interest of the press, which was generally supportive of the new venture. *The Sunday Times* wrote: 'Modern English plays which concern themselves with current problems, political or social, are rare. It is for this reason that the debut . . . of the English Stage Company has become one of the most eagerly awaited events of the season.' Another critic, for *The Times*, clearly finding it hard to contain his enthusiasm, suggested that 'despairing young playwrights must have rubbed their eyes in astonishment when they read what are to be the aims of the new enterprise. Here . . . is a theatre formed to meet the desire and needs of the young writer' (Tschudin 1972: 27).

In fact, the emphasis on contemporary social realism that these responses suggest – and with which the ESC subsequently became largely associated – reflects only one aspect of the company's interests. This was inevitable, given the centrality of *Look Back in Anger* in contemporary critical accounts, and the increasingly anti-hegemonic role that the new drama came to play. However, the Court, and Devine in particular, were also interested in another kind of contemporary theatre, the Absurd, and from its inception, Devine had sought to promote this parallel strand in the ESC's work. He wrote that 'out of an annual programme of eight plays, the planned proportion was to be five English dramatists, two translations and one classical revival' (Devine 1957: 153). Although these proportions were not always adhered to, the work of Beckett and Ionesco had a distinct presence in the repertoire of the Court in its early years alongside other continental drama. Ionesco's *The Chairs* (1957), *The Lesson* (1958) and *The Rhinoceros* (1960) were produced, as were Beckett's *Endgame* (1958), *Krapp's Last Tape* (1958) and in French *Fin De Partie* and *Acte Sans Parole* (1957).[3]

There is a suggestion in the press reaction to the formation of the ESC that there were, in Devine's words, 'many good plays waiting to be produced if only there was a place for them to be done' (Devine 1962: 11). Devine himself did not believe this; indeed, part of the rationale behind the emphasis on foreign drama in the Company's programme was the desire to 'raise the general level of playwrighting' by exposing would-be British writers to work that was thought to be more ambitious. Devine approached the problem from two directions. First, he appealed directly to the writers. He approached a number of established novelists and asked them to consider writing for the theatre. This was an indication both of the difficulty of finding new playwrights at the time and of a general desire to raise the literary status of the theatre. Angus Wilson and Nigel Dennis both responded, and Wilson's *The Mulberry Bush* opened the first season at the Court. Dennis's *Cards of Identity* was the fifth production in the schedule. Devine also organised a

---

3 Despite Devine's undoubted commitment to Absurd drama, the ESC did not project itself as a company that wanted to be associated with this kind of experiment. In 1955, Beckett's *Waiting for Godot* was transferred to the West End, and was greeted with general bafflement, if not outright hostility, for its apparent formalism and obscurity. Devine was nervous of allowing the company to become too tainted with the avant garde brush. 'What we have been trying to create', he wrote, 'is, in fact, what was known at one time as an Art Theatre, but today such a term has a satiric connotation I am anxious to avoid' (Devine 1957: 154). An early press release proclaimed 'we are not avant garde, or highbrow, or a coterie set. We want to build a vital, living, popular theatre' (Browne 1975: 12).

playwrighting competition in conjunction with the *Observer*. Osborne's *Look Back in Anger* was received in reply; it was the only one submitted to be produced.

Second, Devine attempted to create a particular ambience at the Court, one which encouraged writers not only to write but to become involved in the production process itself, thereby increasing their experience of, and commitment to, the theatre. He established an ensemble of mainly young and unknown actors, attempted to run plays in repertory (a practice associated with admired continental theatres) and set all the initial productions against a permanent surround – a means, so Devine argued, of focusing attention onto the plays, rather than deflecting it onto the decor. In addition, all the plays were, at least initially, to be directed by either Devine or Tony Richardson.

As the ESC became established, new methods of attracting and assisting writers were introduced. A writer's workshop was set up in 1957, in which writers were encouraged to develop their craft by working with experienced teachers and directors to explore essential theatrical problems. The Company also instituted a system of Sunday night 'try-outs'; these were plays, hitherto unperformed, which were rehearsed with a full company and director but produced without costume or decor for one night only in front of an invited audience. In this way, plays which were deemed too risky for full production could nevertheless receive a public airing. The 'try-outs' were seen primarily as part of the learning process for the growing number of young writers who became associated with the Court. In addition, the ESC established links with provincial theatres whereby, on the one hand, such theatres could use the Court stage to mount London premieres of their productions, and, on the other, the ESC might set up a base in the regions. The 1959–60 season contained productions by three provincial theatres, and, in that same year, the ESC attempted to establish itself in Cambridge; the first experiment was not repeated, and the second foundered through lack of money.

Many of these innovations had, by the mid-1960s, been abandoned or modified, largely due to financial pressures. The importance of some of them was considerable, however, even though it was often subterranean and difficult to chart. The writer's group was particularly important to those who participated in it, giving writers with little direct experience of the theatre the opportunity to experiment with theatrical, as distinct from literary, form in workshops that encouraged experiment. At least two plays were written (and subsequently performed at the Court) directly out of the experience of being in the group, John Arden's *The Happy Haven* (1960) and Ann Jellicoe's *The Knack* (1962). Holland has argued that the group was important to the way that Brecht's theory and practice was assimilated into the work of writers such as Bond and Jellicoe (Holland 1978: 27).

Theatre Workshop

Unlike the ESC, Theatre Workshop was not a 'new' company, nor did it appear, in its structure and origins, like any other theatre of the period. The company arose out of the worker's theatre movement of the inter-war years, when its founders, Joan Littlewood and Ewan MacColl, ran a series of companies linked by a range of common concerns: a radical socialism, a commitment to performing for working-class audiences, and a voracious appetite for a variety of theatrical influences and methods. The plays performed were conceived by MacColl as 'dramatic metaphors about the political struggles of a society' and 'serious experiments in the theatre of expressionism' (Goorney and MacColl 1986: lvi), giving the company scope for the kind of exploration in non-naturalist performance styles (based on the meticulous study of theorists and practitioners such as Brecht and Stanislavsky) that had always been the hallmark of its work. In addition to performing to working-class audiences in their own communities, the company appeared at a number of foreign festivals, receiving the kind of critical attention that it rarely attracted in Britain, where, as a touring company playing largely out of London and away from the main theatres, it remained on the fringes of the theatre industry's consciousness.

By 1956, some three years after the move to London, Theatre Workshop had received critical acclaim for several of its productions of classics – which was the point at which its policy intersected with the interests of the literary critical establishment. Productions of Jonson's *Volpone* and Shakespeare's *Richard III* were favourably reviewed in 1955, and Brecht's *The Good Soldier Schweik* was transferred to the West End in that same year. It is ironic that one of the most experimental and politically motivated companies in the period – and one which was to become associated with the theatre of working-class social reality – should have come to prominence through its productions of the 'classics'. It was, however, the production of a new play, *The Quare Fellow* by Brendan Behan, a hitherto unperformed writer, that brought wider critical acclaim and a much higher public visibility. Bernard Levin wrote that the play 'dwarfs anything else to be seen at present in London, West or East' and that 'Brendan Behan is the most exciting new talent to enrich our theatre since the war' (Goorney 1981: 105). The first performance of *The Quare Fellow* was on 24 May 1956, sixteen days after the opening of *Look Back in Anger.*

The Quare Fellow transferred to the West End and then went on a short provincial tour. Behan did not follow up his success immediately, and his second play, *The Hostage*, did not appear until 1958, when, along with Shelagh Delaney's *A Taste of Honey*, it generated the kind of critical attention that the earlier play had done. Although Theatre Workshop was by now identified with the new theatre, its repertoire was still dominated by classical drama; only one entirely new play was produced between 1956 and 1958, Henry Chapman's *You Won't Always Be on Top* (1957). In 1959, following close on the success of *The Hostage* and *A Taste of Honey*, the Company produced Frank Norman's *Fings Ain't Wot They Used to Be* and Wolf Mankowitz's *Make Me an Offer* (both in 1959) and Stephen Lewis's *Sparrers Can't Sing* (1960).

Theatre Workshop was different from every other company operating in London in the mid-fifties, not simply because of the plays it produced, but also because of the processes it employed to produce them. The company was, in almost every area of its activities, an alternative to the then dominant forms of commercial theatre; instead of a clear division of labour between theatrical functions, the company valued critical discussion of texts and collaborative working methods; instead of *ad hoc* companies formed for particular productions, the Workshop was (at least until 1958) a permanent ensemble with a common training programme and a shared attitude towards their work; instead of performing for a known, middle-class audience in London's theatre belt, the company attempted to create a working-class audience in London's East End. The commitment to working in this way (albeit under the guidance of Littlewood, whose working methods were imprinted on every stage of the production process) plus the strong attachment to the exploration of theatrical language in its widest sense, ensured that a range of issues concerning the processes of theatrical production were addressed. The following are amongst the most important: the role of the actor in the creation of the theatrical, as distinct from the literary, text; the nature of the rehearsal process – in particular the ways in which a script might be reworked in rehearsal; the role of improvisation; the nature of theatrical realism (Littlewood argued that theatrical reality was the responsibility of the actors and their attitude towards their roles rather than residing in a set of scenic conventions); the relevance of the classical repertoire – particularly traditions of popular theatre – to contemporary audiences; the importance of training and theory; and the question of who the 'author' is of the theatrical production. Littlewood and the company were not, of course, the first people to recognise these issues – they were also addressed by many of the theorists and practitioners that they had so exhaustively studied over the years, for example Stanislavsky, Meyerhold and Brecht. However, Theatre Workshop's work from 1945 onwards is a record of probably the first sustained and practical attempt to address them in the post-war context.

It was not by chance that Theatre Workshop was one of the two companies associated with new writing. The working methods employed were particularly suited to working on new and perhaps unfinished scripts. Providing writers were willing to submit their work to the working practices that Littlewood established, they had the opportunity to learn about their craft in ways that were very difficult to replicate in other contexts. One irony was that these working practices – which included constant rewrites in rehearsal, often by the actors as well as the author, and the persistent criticism and support of both director and cast – frequently meant the writer relinquishing control of the text; it was the actor, not the writer, who was at the centre of Littlewood's rehearsal processes. Goorney reported that rehearsals of *The Quare Fellow* began with the actors improvising around the day-to-day routines of prison life, without having seen a script or knowing what parts they were to play. 'When the script was finally introduced', Goorney observed, 'the situation and the relationships had been well explored, the bulk of the work had been done and the groundwork had been laid for any cutting and shaping that was necessary' (Goorney 1981: 105).

Both Delaney and Behan submitted willingly to this process, but other writers, Mankowitz and Norman in particular, were much more critical of Littlewood's approach, being reluctant to release authorial control of the written text to the actors and director. By this stage, the necessity of transferring earlier successes to the West End had left Littlewood with actors unused to her working methods and sometimes as resistant and confused as Norman and Mankowitz had been. This may have a bearing on the fact that the two Behan plays, together with *A Taste of Honey* and the later *Oh What a Lovely War* (1963), were, and remain, the most successful and critically regarded of the Workshop's productions in this period.

By the late 1950s both Theatre Workshop and the ESC were obliged to transfer some of their most successful productions to the West End, where they could be seen by a larger audience over a longer period of time, and where there was at least some chance of making a profit. Far from signalling a 'take-over' of the commercial sector, as it has sometimes been argued, this policy was more correctly an accommodation by both companies to certain financial realities; moreover, it was an arrangement which benefited the West End itself by bringing in new audiences and by offering a relatively safe commercial deal. As John Pick has argued,

> It was in the interests of the West End managers to take some plays for which they did not have to pay rehearsal costs, which had an established reputation and for which there was already a known audience. Such transfers were often more in the interests of the West End establishments than of the 'revolutionary' theatres.
>
> (Pick 1983: 162)

Three decades further on, theatre economics ensure that West End transfer seems an entirely desirable occurrence, but the compromises that transfer imposed as a means of ensuring survival had a considerable impact on the most innovatory elements of the artistic policy of both companies.

At several points between 1958 and 1961, Theatre Workshop faced bankruptcy, despite the success of its productions with both audiences and critics. In 1958, it threatened to close until the Arts Council restored a cut in its grant. The original productions of *The Quare Fellow* and *The Hostage*, Delaney's *A Taste of Honey*, Mankowitz's *Make Me an Offer*, Norman's *Fings Ain't Wot They Used to Be*, Lewis's *Sparrers Can't Sing* and later *Oh What a Lovely War*, were all transferred with their original casts. This had the effect of ameliorating the financial problems that Theatre Workshop faced without actually solving them.

By 1961, the situation for Littlewood had become untenable, because the system of transfers had radically transformed the way the company worked. It meant, for example, the virtual destruction of the ensemble system, upon which much of the dynamic of the production process was predicated. Most of the experienced actors disappeared into the West End in the transfers, and new companies of generally inexperienced actors took their place at Stratford East. Unused to Littlewood's working methods and often drawn (according to Goorney) more by the mystique of the organisation or by the hope of getting into the West End, the new companies differed from the old in significant ways. The need to keep up a constant supply of productions meant that the emphasis on training discussion and collective methods of rehearsal gradually diminished. The very fact of being successful also brought problems; it was Ewan MacColl's jibe at the time that the local people couldn't get near the theatre for the Rolls Royces parked outside. Littlewood described the situation thus:

> For the past few years I have had dozens of West End managers breathing down my neck. The money from the West End was put into Stratford but we can pack the Theatre Royal to the roof and still cannot make it pay. I cannot accept a situation anymore where I am unable to work with a company freely.
>
> (Goorney 1981: 124)

The only alternative to West End transfers was a level of State subsidy that was commensurate with the company's ambitions, and this it never received. During the 1950s and 1960s Arts Council subsidy to Theatre Workshop fell far short of that offered the ESC. In 1961, Littlewood left the company to pursue other interests and the Theatre Royal was leased to Oscar Lewinstein; it was to be two years before Theatre Workshop once again took up residence at Stratford East.

The ESC was also affected by the need to work within the free-market system. Cushioned by the generosity of Neville Blond, the consistent, if not over-generous, Arts Council support, and the income from the sale of film rights of *Look Back in Anger* (plus royalties from the play's Broadway transfer), the accommodation of artistic policy to financial pressures was not as drastic as it had been at the Theatre Royal. Devine was faced, as Littlewood had been, with the problem that it was difficult, if not impossible, to balance the books even if the Court was full to capacity (which it rarely was). This expresses something of the dilemma that Devine faced (and exposes one of the myths that had grown up around the work of the new dramatists at the time); the Company was formed around a policy of producing new work, yet new work did not necessarily connect with either critics or audiences (see Browne 1975: Appendix B for statistics on this). Osborne's plays were generally sell-outs, and Wesker's did well (especially *Roots*); even Absurdist drama attracted good audiences (especially Ionesco). The work of other New Wave dramatists, notably John Arden's, was by contrast sparsely attended.

Devine believed it would take time to build audiences for new work; indeed, he told Neville Blond in 1955 that it would take a minimum of three years before the Company would even begin to break even. However, the difficulties of instituting a policy that was so avowedly anti-commercial forced Devine to tread the same path as Littlewood – towards West End transfers and the accommodation of cherished working practices to a necessarily more commercial policy. The repertory system was soon abandoned in favour of 'end-to-end' programming for limited runs, largely, it was argued, because the British theatre-going public found it too 'alien'. And even in the first season there were cracks in the ensemble system; Peggy Ashcroft was brought in to play the lead in Brecht's *The Good Person of Setzuan*. Devine was aware, too, that the financial success of the first season was *The Country Wife* – thus 'the new contemporary theatre was saved by a classical revival' (Devine 1962: 12). The following season contained a leavening of already successful plays, including at least one (Noel Coward's *Look After Lulu*) by a writer vilified by the New Wave. And as the Court became increasingly successful it attracted established theatrical figures, who were welcomed with alacrity; Laurence Olivier, at his own suggestion, was cast as Archie Rice, the central character in *The Entertainer*. Devine once argued that the ESC 'had to become part of the establishment, against whom our hearts, if not our faces, were set' (Devine 1962: 12), but the Court was never in real opposition to the theatrical establishment after 1956, but rather to a section of its commercial management, as the continuing support for the venture among critics and theatre personnel demonstrated.

Whatever 'revolution' occurred, then, at either Sloane Square or Stratford East in the wake of *Look Back in Anger* and *The Quare Fellow* it was not one which transformed institutional structures. Here, as in other areas of cultural and political life, the status quo proved far more resilient than the New Wave and its supporters noisily maintained.

THE NEW WAVE AND ITS AUDIENCES

The question of who the new theatre was for is one that surfaces in a number of contexts, and informs much of the thinking about the socio-political role of theatre in the period. That a new audience was central to the New Wave's sense of itself was recognised as early as 1957 by Lindsay Anderson, who observed that 'the development of a new kind of theatre ... is intimately bound up with the development of a new kind of audience' and that without it even the Royal Court, which should have been able to develop 'as a theatre with a permanent company, in pursuit of a definable and consistent tradition' was 'just a theatre run by the most progressive management in London' (Anderson 1970a: 46).

There was no shortage of speculation as to who that audience should be (and, indeed, actually was). For Littlewood and Theatre Workshop the new audience had a precise social identity, the working-class, and the search for it amongst London's East End was the continuation of an ambition that had shaped the company's policy throughout its long years on the road. The ambition was also shared (briefly) by many of the new dramatists, although for some (notably Osborne) it was more a genuflection towards the spirit of the times than a concrete objective.

The search for a new, non-metropolitan and non-bourgeois audience was intrinsic to the New Wave project to represent class experiences hitherto excluded from the theatre (and culture generally) in the post-war era, and aimed to complete the circle of play/production/public: it was also central to debates about the nature of social realism (see Chapter 3 below). However, as an ambition, it was fraught with problems that considerably pre-date the new drama, and which were enmeshed with long-term institutional and cultural changes. As Raymond Williams observed in *Encore*: 'The fact is that two or three generations of the working-class have grown up out of contact with the theatre, and the most enlightened programme of public support would not necessarily or quickly get them back' (Williams 1959: 6).

The ESC did not see its audiences in such class-specific terms, but nevertheless George Devine was constantly vexed by the problem of finding an audience for a particular play or dramatist, and was prepared to allow the work of certain writers (John Arden, notably) to play to nearly empty houses in the hope that it would eventually connect with a public. In 1959, he tacitly admitted that this rarely meant a decisively new audience that would thereafter remain loyal to the theatre. 'There is no regular audience', he observed, 'certainly at Theatre Workshop or the Royal Court'. Frequently the people who attended these theatres were those that could be found in any London theatre: 'If I present a big star in a play', he noted, 'the theatre would be full regardless of the play or its meaning' (Devine 1959: 25).

The problem was at root an institutional one; the Royal Court and Theatre Workshop were operating in a metropolitan context, at the fringes of the West End as 'minority' theatres, and as such could not hope to construct a new audience on their own terms – and certainly not a working-class one. This was a much more debilitating dilemma for Theatre Workshop than for the ESC, and, coupled with the crippling financial problems that the company was facing by the early 1960s, was central to its collapse and Littlewood's acrimonious departure.

However, another, newer audience does figure in accounts of the period – the audience of 'youth'. Devine characterised this audience not just as the public who attended the theatre, but also as a distinct social grouping for whom the Royal Court had a symbolic function.

> A new generation in art and literature was bursting out with us. And a new generation of public was there to receive them. Because of its nature, the Royal Court became the symbol of this new energetic and, to a great extent, provincial outburst. Products of the new Education Act, these young people came streaming into the tired metropolis, they woke up everything they touched. . . . For all these, the Royal Court became a symbol, even if they did not bother to patronise its plays.
>
> (Devine 1962: 12)

There is little hard evidence beyond personal anecdote as to how this young audience was constituted in any specific sense in the period. Devine is clearly drawing on a range of existing explanations about the relationships between the new intellectual classes, the provinces and the 1944 Education Act, which were by this point already familiar. In retrospect, this image of a theatre inhabited by a young public does correspond to real changes in audience composition, changes which were to become more apparent in the sixties and seventies and were related to the way that social mobility was made possible by the new, although still relatively limited, opportunities in higher education.

Drawing on audience surveys from the 1960s, Alan Sinfield has noted that between 55 per cent and 88 per cent of any given audience was likely to be under the age of 35, and that between 18 per cent and 35 per cent were likely to be students. Between 23 per cent and 48 per cent had completed higher education (the incidence of this in the population as a whole was no more that 3.7 per cent) (Sinfield 1983: 178). It is also important to note how a similar educational and social profile appears amongst theatre practitioners. Although the lower-class origins of many of the initial figures in the New Wave comes to dominate the way in which the movement as a whole is located as a social phenomenon, by the 1960s, when a much larger group had followed them into the theatres, the pattern looks very different. Using a sample of prominent writers and directors, Sinfield noted that 'only a quarter had not studied at University and of that quarter, a half had been at public schools (including Osborne, though he was expelled) and over half had been at Oxford or Cambridge' (Sinfield 1983: 179). This indicates that assumptions about the 'take-over' of the bourgeois theatre by a proletarian upsurge may have been premature.

Social mobility through education is clearly important here, and provides a framework for understanding the way that social change embraced not only theatre audiences but also theatre practitioners as well. These changes often gave rise to a sense of dislocation and anxiety (see Chapter 3 below), but were more often viewed optimistically as heralding an end to a society in which social divisions were based on inheritance and wealth. Education was, once more, of central importance to such explanations, being seen to operate as an 'open ladder', uncomplicated by factors of class or social geography. Such optimism was of a piece with conservative assumptions about the disappearance of class and class-conflict in the post-war world; as Charles Curran argued in *Encounter*, 'Britain, in fact, is now very close to the point where it will be true to say that there is a general correlation between social status and mental ability' (Curran 1956: 21). In 1959, Michael Young gave the new class that emerged a name in his ironically titled *The Rise of the Meritocracy*. It was – and is – a process that has been over-sold, and for which the evidence is inconclusive.

In the domain of culture, this optimism, which was by no means the property of the right alone, had an aggressive edge, for it could be seen as evidence of the replacement of an upper-middle-class mandarin cultural establishment with a new (initially) proletarian one. However, social mobility is a process that can be seen to operate in one of two ways. It can signify the 'take-over' by the articulate working-class of the cultural establishment: this inter-pretation lies behind the judgement of the American critic Leslie Fiedler, who argued that 'The young British writer has the in-estimable advantage of representing a new class on its way into a controlling position in the culture of his country. He is able to define himself against the class he replaces' (Fiedler 1958: 5). It might, however, just as easily signify that the new generation was engaged in a more familiar process – that of being co-opted into an existing middle-class, engaged in the process of transforming itself in new conditions.

John McGrath, who was himself a product of the new opportun-ities, has written a succinct, if acerbic, account of these processes in microcosm. Describing a typical night at the Royal Court 'a Sunday night production without decor of a new play in, say, 1960' (McGrath 1981: 12), McGrath describes the younger section of the audience, and argues that 'What these unprepossessing youths, of which I was one, were in fact doing was absorbing as many of the values of the middle class as possible'. Recognising that such people were indeed 'agents of change', he goes on to generalise the process:

> in true British fashion . . . the middle classes in the 50s and 60s absorbed and penetrated the bright young working-class youth, thrown up by the 1944 Education Act in appreciably large numbers, and . . . lo! after a short while, we were them. In other words, the 'new' audience for this kind of theatre was, if not in origin certainly in ultimate destination, merely a 'new' bourgeoisie, mingling in with the old, even indulging in miscegenation.
>
> (McGrath 1981: 12)

If 'embourgeoisement' occurred in British society in the fifties and sixties, then it is perhaps best to look for it not amongst the traditional and newly affluent working-classes but rather here, amongst the upwardly-mobile artists and their audiences. In this context, the Royal Court was not so much a bridgehead for

proletarian intellectuals but rather 'a theatre of middle-class transition' (Hirst 1985: 26).

THE METROPOLITANISING OF CULTURE

This process of middle-class renewal was overlain by another, which
may be referred to as the metropolitanising of culture. This refers
to a remorseless drift from the provinces to London, a process
commented on in the period, and present in different form in
novels, films and plays. This development was most visible amongst
intellectuals and artists, although it was observable amongst the
intelligentsia generally, and has been valued as a necessary 'unblock-
ing' of both institutions and cultural values, for which 'northern'
became a synonym. As Keith Waterhouse has recently commented,
'There were artists and writers coming in by the trainload. There
was so much energy. You could sell the film rights to a train ticket'
(*Guardian*, 20 January 1994).

The intelligentsia in this context should be understood in terms
outlined by Antonio Gramsci, who drew attention to its function,
defining it in terms of its organisational role rather than its
intellectual capacities.

> By 'intellectual' must be understood not those strata common-
> ly described by this term but in general the entire social
> stratum which exercises an organisational function in the
> wide sense – whether in the field of production, or in that of
> culture, or in that of political administration.
>
> (Gramsci 1971: 97)

In the post-war world, the structures of such occupations were
undergoing the kind of transformation and expansion that was
outlined earlier; the growth of the state, the creation of new cultural
professions around welfare and education (and the effects of these
on the older professions) are crucially important here, as is the
more general growth of a range of other organisational functions.
This is particularly apparent in education and the new communication industries – the media (especially television), advertising, all the arts, publishing – where many of the new opportunities
were suddenly appearing. Waterhouse was both an acute commentator on this cultural shift and, in his career, a typical product of it.
He was a novelist and playwright, who also worked across a range of
rapidly expanding media, such as journalism and cinema.

Given the renewed political and economic importance of London, it was perhaps inevitable that it should also be the site of new developments in culture and communication and become a magnet for social aspirations. Kumar has related the expansion of the cultural industries to longer-term shifts in the balance of power between London and the provinces, arising from the increasing involvement of the State in a variety of supporting, organising and regulating roles. Referring to this process as the 'nationalisation of culture', Kumar has noted that organisations such as the BBC (in 1926), the British Film Institute (in 1933) and the British Council (in 1934) were all established in London before the war. The process accelerated after 1945, and the Arts Council (in 1946), the Press Council (in 1953), and, in 1955, the Independent Television Authority, were all London-based and metropolitan in outlook (see Kumar 1981: 126). The effect of the Arts Council's policy in the fifties was to favour London at the expense of the provinces (it maintained strong formal and informal links with existing theatrical and operatic establishments), pursuing 'standards' (often a synonym for an emphasis on London at this time) instead of regional endeavour at a time of constrained resources; the Annual Report of 1951–2 concluded that it was 'wiser . . . to consolidate standards, rather than pursue a policy of wider dispersal' (Blaug 1976: 112).

For Kumar, cultural and economic centralisation of this order was damaging to the kind of deep-rooted localism that produced much of the great realist fiction and the reading publics of the nineteenth century. The issue then, as in the 1950s, was the interconnection between specific texts, audiences and the institutions that produced them, all of which were subject to long-term social and economic developments, which were not always easy to grasp from the limited viewpoint of the West End; to paraphrase Brecht, the problems of the theatre could not be solved in the theatre.

Institutional Alternatives

One option was to challenge the nature of theatre institutions themselves, not simply by creating a certain room for manoeuvre within the old constraints, but by trying to form new relationships between audiences, companies/institutions and economic realities. There is a way in which the history of post-war British theatre can be written at least partly in these terms; although it is beyond the limits of this study to consider this history in detail, it is worth noting that dissatisfaction with the metropolitan theatre system itself drove not only Joan Littlewood out of the theatre, but also John Arden and John McGrath as well.

Joan Littlewood's search for radical theatre forms and working-class audiences led her away from formal theatre entirely. She became increasingly interested in the community around the Theatre Royal and began to work with local groups in a workshop context. She was also associated with a proposal to establish a 'Fun Palace' of people's entertainment in the East End that eventually foundered through lack of money. In this way she prefigured a later generation of artists and theatre practitioners; the Fun Palace was a proletarian version of the multi-media Arts' Labs that sprang up in several cities in the late sixties, and the direct engagement with local communities was characteristic of the community arts movement that grew in the 1970s. For community artists, too, the range of questions that needed to be asked about theatre form, audience and politics could only be answered by radically reshaping the context in which they were posed, and by abandoning formal theatre structures entirely.

It is no accident that Arden and McGrath were amongst the most politically aware of dramatists, for whom the intractable problems of British theatre were as much ideological as they were organisational. Both attempted to create new production contexts, in new political conditions; Arden, after a brief spell in Yorkshire, went to Ireland, and now primarily writes novels. McGrath worked initially in television, and then formed two linked companies, 7:84 (Scotland) and 7:84 (England) committed to pursuing the objective of creating a contemporary theatre from a socialist perspective by touring to working-class venues and audiences, thereby contributing to – and benefiting from – the more politically aware culture of the 1970s and early 1980s. There are few examples of this in the fifties and early sixties, which, we should remind ourselves, was a period of dependence on commercial priorities; here, as in other ways, Centre 42 was an exception.

Centre 42

Centre 42 was launched in July 1961, and took its name from the number of a resolution passed by the annual TUC Conference in 1960 which affirmed the importance of the arts and asked 'the General Council to conduct a special examination and to make proposals to ensure a greater participation in the trades Union movement in all cultural activities' (Coppieter 1975: 39). Despite the opposition of the General Council itself, the resolution was adopted unanimously. The resolution was framed partly in response to a speech by Wesker at the *Sunday Times* student drama festival of that year, which became a pamphlet that was circulated to the general secretary of every union in the TUC. In it, Wesker had argued that the labour movement should become directly involved in supporting the arts. After the success of the resolution, Wesker was invited to join a group of writers – nearly all figures of the left – who were similarly looking for new ways of creating new audiences for the theatre. The group included John McGrath, Doris Lessing, Shelagh Delaney, Bernard Kops and Alun Owen – all of whom had been associated with the new theatre (and some of whom were participants in the debates around working-class realism). Wesker soon became the artistic director of the new organisation and its chief ideologue.

The hub of Centre 42's work was the organisation of a series of festivals, the first being in Wellingborough in 1961, which were organised in conjunction with local trades councils and partially financed by the unions. Five festivals were organised in 1962, but there was always a shortfall between the money generated by the festivals and their union sponsors and the actual costs involved. Centre 42 sought to remedy this by establishing a base – an old railway engine turning-shed in Camden which became known as the Round House. However, the financial problems that the organisation continually faced eventually overcame it, and to all intents and purposes Centre 42 had ceased functioning by the mid-sixties.

Centre 42 was established partly to create new institutions, to break the deadlock caused by the cultural and economic position of even the liberal minority theatres. 'The Royal Court and Theatre Workshop serve their purpose', he told *Encore* in 1962, 'but these are not organisations that are going to make a radical change in the total situation' (Wesker 1962a: 40). The organisation represented an attempt to by-pass the main structures of arts funding in Britain at the time, to circumvent both the strictures of the free market and the lukewarm patronage of the State. It also represented the first serious attempt to involve the labour movement in the funding of the arts, and if it failed in this then the labour movement itself must take much of the blame. The resolution, from which the organisation took its name, was remitted to the Education Office for a report; in 1961, this duly arrived and concluded that the only constructive role for the TUC was to pressurise local authorities to raise money for the arts through the rates (as they were entitled to do).

Centre 42 was, however, controversial, and though socialist in its aspirations and rhetoric it failed to take much of the left with it. The reasons for this are complex but may have something to do with the conception of art and culture that underpinned its activities, and to which we shall return in the following chapters. It is probable, however, that the most immediate – if not the main – reason for the failure of the project lay not in its attitude towards culture, but rather in its determination to move into the Round House. As soon as it became committed to a base in London, it was always going to be extremely difficult for the organisation (which was never very large) to maintain its original objective of mounting annual festivals away from the main centres of culture; it seems as if it, too, had succumbed to the allure of the metropolis with, in retrospect, predictable consequences.

3

REALISM, CLASS
AND CULTURE

The New Wave is often referred to as a realist theatre. The terms realism and 'social realism' are omnipresent in critical discussion of the period; and although 'realism', even in its most expansive definition, does not adequately describe every manifestation of the new drama, it is a term that resonates throughout the late fifties and early sixties, partly because it suggests a range of ambitions (in the plays, the writers and the companies) that are not simply theatrical but are political and social as well. Realism is a critical term that is used of other cultural forms, too, and the resurgence of realism in the cinema and the novel as well as the theatre testified not only to the existence of roughly comparable aesthetic strategies but also of a similar cultural politics. Realism usually becomes an issue in a culture when the representation, exploration and analysis of a society is on the agenda, and this is the principal reason why realism will have a significant presence in this book.

REALISM: PROBLEMS OF DEFINITION

The familiarity of realism, wherever we encounter it, seems to render its meaning uncontroversial and self-evident; the term is used so often, we must all know what it means. However, like many critical terms that have such a near-universal currency, realism is deployed in frequently ambiguous and confusing ways, concealing a complex history and a set of often contradictory positions; there is social realism, socialist realism, neo-realism in the cinema, surrealism and magical realism, and dramatists as different as Ibsen, Chekhov and Brecht have considered themselves, or have been considered, realist at some point in their development.

In the theatre, arguments about realism normally emerge

around 'content' rather than 'form'; as Raymond Williams has observed, realism has typically meant 'the injection of new content into an orthodox dramatic form' (Williams 1978: 498). In film, this emphasis has sometimes been reversed, and realism has been seen in terms of a specific filmic language, a particular construction of 'the real', to be defended or (more often) attacked in terms of its adequacy to the task (see MacCabe 1974). It is tempting to respond to this plethora of different usages by abandoning the term altogether and opting for a less comfortable but more precise vocabulary. Certainly, any attempt to arrive at a fixed and invariable definition will be a wasted journey; it is much more useful to think of realism not as a fixed category, but as a series of debates, which are historically variable, which operate differently across different cultural forms, but which have a set of common issues at their core.

One of the most comprehensive accounts of the historical development of realism in the theatre has been provided by Raymond Williams (Williams 1977). According to Williams, realism emerges as a fully constituted dramatic form only in the nineteenth century, and has, historically speaking, three defining characteristics: 'The three emphases which are then often consciously described as realism are the secular, the contemporary and the socially extended' (Williams 1977: 65). 'Secular' in this context means that 'elements of a metaphysical or a religious order' which 'directly or indirectly frame, or in the stronger cases determine, the human actions' within earlier forms of drama are dropped, 'and in [their] place a human action is played through in specifically human terms – exclusively human terms' (Williams 1977: 64). In this way, the encroaching rationalism of the nineteenth century, the development of science and 'historical attitudes towards society' begin radically to alter the sense of motivation in the drama, and to restructure dramatic logic to exclude the divine and the supernatural as agents in the narrative. The emphasis on 'the contemporary', derives from a 'siting of actions in the present' (Williams 1977: 64), which is related to an increasing reliance on colloquial speech, on dramatic language which approximates the everyday conversation of its audience. Lastly, social extension refers to the way that drama begins to represent an increasing range of social experience; specifically, there is 'a crucial argument in the early period of bourgeois tragedy about the need to extend the actions of tragedy from persons of rank . . . as it was put – "your equals, our equals" . . . "let not your equals move your pity less"'

(Williams 1977: 63). Social extension applies particularly to class experience, referring initially to the situation of the nineteenth-century bourgeoisie – the kinds of people who are the subject of Ibsen's plays – and then to the working-classes, especially in the twentieth century.

Considering the specific forms of contemporary realism, Williams added a fourth criterion to distinguish what might properly be called realism from other kinds of drama that share some of the territory marked out by the first three. This fourth criterion, that realism should be 'consciously interpretative from a particular political viewpoint' (Williams 1977: 68), makes it clear that realism in this sense is defined primarily by the ambition not only to represent but also to interpret the world politically, to show 'how things really are'.

These four criteria are extremely valuable descriptive and analytical categories, and will inform much of the argument that follows. Before commencing, however, there are several other issues that need to be considered in this general discussion of problems around definition, not the least of which is the relationship between the new post-war drama and what might be considered a realist tradition. Williams noted that one of the most significant 'moments' in the development of a fully contemporary, socially extended and secular drama was that of 'high naturalism' (the relationship between realism and naturalism is a thorny one, aspects of which will be considered in the following chapter). The term refers to the drama of Strindberg, Ibsen, Hauptmann and Chekhov from the nineteenth century and the early plays of Sean O'Casey and Eugene O'Neill from the twentieth (Williams 1981). One of the main ways in which drama of the late fifties and early sixties has been considered realist is that it had a clear relationship with this earlier theatrical moment. Katherine Worth has argued that the New Wave is best understood as 'a late – and possibly last – flowering of that [realist] tradition' (Worth 1972: vii). This connection is partly at the level of the position that each realist moment adopted in relation to dominant cultural values and theatre institutions. Like the progressive drama of the late nineteenth century, the New Wave was socially critical, attacking the values and opinions of the bourgeoisie from a position within the 'free' or independent theatres that operated with a degree of independence from the social and economic structures of dominant theatre practices – theatres such as the Moscow Art Theatre and the Freie Buhne.

However, the connection was also at the level of narrative structure and dramatic and theatrical method, and this opens up another front on which the struggles over realism have been fought.

Williams does not ally realism to any one artistic method, and is careful to avoid the suggestion that it is reducible – or that any dramatic form is reducible – to a particular set of dramatic or theatrical strategies. However, realism is frequently used as if it did apply to 'a particular artistic method' which is distinct from its usage as 'a particular attitude towards what is called "reality"' (Williams 1977: 61). In fact, in many subsequent historical periods these two senses of the term are often conflated – that is, a realist 'attitude' (political or social in origin, and embodied in a contemporary and socially extended narrative) is articulated through a particular 'method', which is also termed realist, and which offers itself in terms of its verisimilitude, its closeness to the outward forms of social reality. Perhaps the first thing that most people think of when they consider the term realism, is a play that 'reflects', or re-creates across the entire panoply of elements of dramatic form and theatrical representation, in as direct a way as possible an identifiable social world and asks to be judged in relation to it; this relationship is captured in the colloquial adjective 'realistic' in both its descriptive and evaluative senses. This is not entirely surprising, given the emphasis in realism on representing the contemporary world in a direct way, on dramatising experiences and environments and on utilising a language that are recognisably an audience's own.

This is not at all a simple process, and there are many ways in which the 'real' can be represented in drama and theatre, even within the general laws of verisimilitude: there is no single, immutable realist genre fixed in aspic for all time. Nor is the desire to represent reality in as direct a manner as possible solely the product of the realist tradition: as Stuart Hall has noted, 'the attempt to capture the rhythms and situations of real life has always been there' (Hall 1970: 214).

In the post-war period, our sense of what constitute 'realistic' conventions has been shaped partly by film. In the fifties, it was largely American film, particularly the new realism associated with the films of Elia Kazan, the screen adaptations of plays by Arthur Miller and Tennessee Williams, and the performances of actors such as Marlon Brando and James Dean that exercised a decisive influence. It was not simply that these films brought a new 'content' to the British screen (although this was also the case, as they were noted both for their representation of distinctively post-war young 'mis-fits' and for their treatment of issues, such as sex, which lay beyond the social and aesthetic boundaries of most British cinema); it was also the case that new performance styles, especially those originating from the 'Method', erected new criteria by which the realism of both cinema and theatre could be judged. *Encore* published several articles on both Stanislavsky and the Method, which were aimed both at informing readers and at carrying on a theoretical argument about the nature of acting, which centred on 'reality' and the need for a rigorous and consistent approach (all of which seemed absent from British acting, seen from *Encore*'s point of view). Certainly, the new performance styles seemed the very antithesis to the acting traditions that dominated both British cinema and theatre (the latter usually providing the framework in which the former was judged). In one sense, it is simply that the new American cinema exposed the artificiality of familiar British naturalism to a degree that made its conventions seem implausible and intolerable.

The artificiality of much established British acting was exposed in other ways, too, especially from the rising generation of actors. As with the American counterparts, the impact of the new actors who populated the Royal Court, the Theatre Royal and beyond, lay partly in their social background and the different experiences and values they brought with them. By the mid-sixties, there was a significantly larger proportion of actors of working-class origin in the profession, which Michael Sanderson has related to the increase in local authority grants for drama schools, the increased pool of potential recruits from the universities, and the new opportunities created by social realism in both the theatre and television (Sanderson 1984: 293). The result was a pool of actors who could respond to the demands of the new plays and, in doing so, shift the perameters around what was considered 'real' and 'authentic'.

The discussion of specific realist languages or methods is further complicated by the fact that we are frequently dealing with two distinct texts, the written play and its theatrical articulation, that play in performance. Narrative patterns (conventions for telling stories within the realist tradition) and methods of theatrical representation (the means by which meaning is created in theatre, including such non-linguistic elements as set, lighting, sound and costume) do not necessarily proceed in parallel, but have their own trajectories, their own particular histories; indeed, the rejection of realism (or naturalism, which is often the preferred term) that is so common in the post-war theatre is frequently a rejection of certain theatrical, as distinct from dramatic or narrative, conventions (some of these will be traced through the following chapters).

The dominant narrative form has been one that has centred on individuals, often with a single central character. A protagonist of this sort is not simply the hero/heroine in the sense of being the embodiment of the play's moral or political values, but is rather the structural centre of the narrative, whose dilemmas are the chief source of dramatic conflict, and who precipitates the significant action. Such a narrative generally leads towards a single crisis (flowing from the contradictions within, and the actions of, the protagonist), producing a central climax that unifies the different concerns and events of the work, and which has consequences that resolve the action at the structural, if not the thematic, level. Identification with the protagonist becomes the main 'point of entry' into the world of the narrative (although identification is never as complete or simple a process as critics of this kind of realism sometimes maintain) and one of the chief ways through which narrative 'point of view' is constructed.

Most New Wave plays utilised the structural device of a central, unifying protagonist. Indeed, the shift from the moment of 'Anger' to that of 'Working-Class Realism' was registered partly through the shifts in the critical responses to these central characters. For Anderson, Jo in *A Taste of Honey* was a new kind of heroine, formed by her class origins into someone very different from an Angry Young Man.

> She is [tough], with a common-sense, Lancashire working-class resilience that will always pull her through. And this makes her different . . . from the middle-class angry young man, the egocentric rebel. Josephine is not a rebel; she is a revolutionary.
>
> (Anderson 1970b: 79)

Similarly, many New Wave plays have narratives that are, like the plays of high naturalism, placed in a single fictional space, although in this case it was not the bourgeois drawing-room but rather a lower-class living-room: the 'comfortless flat in Manchester' of *A Taste of Honey*, the 'ramshackle house in Norfolk' of *Roots* and the living-room of a 'typical lower middle-class detached house in an industrial town in the North' of *Billy Liar*. Social realism was, like the plays of high naturalism, largely domestic in its orientation, situated within the 'private' as opposed to the 'public' domain; even when plays were not set within lower-class interiors, the action often utilised the semi-public settings of the street and immediate locality (Delaney's *Lion in Love*, for example, or Owen's *Progress to the Park* and Kops's *The Hamlet of Stepney Green*). This focus on the domestic and the everyday is both an aspect of the inherited realist tradition and very much part of the landscape of affluence, on which working-class culture was located and discussed.

Furthermore, these stage spaces were not simply backdrops to the action, nor was the 'photographic' detail, with which naturalist sets were traditionally realised, present simply to contribute to the 'reality effect' of theatrical realism, to authenticate its representations. One of the themes that runs through both high naturalism and post-war social realism is the way that social forces determine and shape the possibilities for change and growth. Indeed, whether rooted in positivist philosophy and empirical science (nineteenth-century naturalism) or in a more generalised recognition of the tangible constraints of a particular social and cultural order (post-war realism), environmental determinism was not only a theme but was made concrete in the stage space itself, which ceased to be simply a location for the action, and became a tangible representation of the oppressive force of a constraining social and natural order, limiting the possibilities for change and growth – 'the "stage as room": the room soaking into the lives of the persons as their lives had soaked into it' (Williams 1977: 64).

The intention to signify 'reality' rather than 'art' that accompanied this kind of narrative was also registered in realist theatrical conventions, which, in the nineteenth century, were achieved out of a struggle to suppress the essentially artificial nature of theatre, its 'constructedness'. This occurs (it should be placed in the present tense, as this kind of theatre is still recognisably present) across the full range of theatrical elements: lighting (largely 'naturalised' into the action, pulled into the fictional world); set design (the space being constructed as a recognisable approximation of the actual environments in which the characters that inhabit the action might reasonably live – typically a 'box-set', representing the domestic interior of the bourgeois family, framed within the architecture of the proscenium arch, the dominant form of architecture for the theatres utilised by post-war realists in the West End); sound, costume and make-up are likewise successful to the degree to which they support the general illusion of a plausible social reality. Perhaps most important of all, theatre of this sort has required the development of an approach to acting that has emphasised not the technical skills of the actor, but the degree to which he/she can become submerged in the character he/she is playing, and thus conceal his/her reality as signifier.

SOCIAL REALISM, SOCIAL EXTENSION AND HEGEMONY

Realism as both method and critical intention will be important in much of the analysis that follows. Initially, however, it is the key categories of the contemporary and social extension that are of especial interest, largely because they describe the terms in which the New Wave was seen as a distinctive (and 'new') development within post-war theatre.

The contemporary is, as we have seen, one of the critical categories mobilised to define and explain New Wave drama at the moment of its first appearance, and the desire to extend the range of British social experience – particularly class experience – represented in the drama is one of the central projects of several key writers and directors. It can be seen as an element in *Look Back in Anger*, and the terms in which the play was signified as being different from what had preceded it lay at least partly in its non-bourgeois, provincial setting. All the plays of Arnold Wesker in the period were concerned with the situation of the working-class, as were those of Bernard Kops (*The Hamlet of Stepney Green* (1958), for example). Shelagh Delaney's plays – *A Taste of Honey* (1958) and *The Lion in Love* (1960) – were also discussed in terms of their representation of working-class experience, with the added inflection that they were set in the North, a factor in the critical reception of Alun Owen's *Progress to the Park* (1961) and Keith Waterhouse's *Celebration* (1961) as well. John Arden's *Live Like Pigs* (1958) was seen as a semi-documentary account of the effect of a group of gypsies on a northern housing estate (although Arden himself was unhappy with this interpretation). Most of the output of Theatre Workshop in the period was concerned with a variety of working-class situations. Both *The Quare Fellow* (1956) and *The Hostage* (1958) by Brendan Behan could be seen as socially extensive, even though they were set in Ireland. The Workshop also produced several musicals set amongst London's 'low-life', notably Frank Norman's *Fings Ain't What They Used to Be* (1959) (with music by Lionel Bart), Wolf Mankowitz's *Make Me an Offer* (1959), and Stephen Lewis's *Sparrers Can't Sing* (1960).

A further reason why the class location of these plays should be such a factor in their critical reception was that many of the central figures associated with both the theatre and a wider intellectual culture were of working-class origin. Raymond Williams came from a working-class community in Wales, and much of his creative as well as theoretical work was heavily influenced by this experience; Richard Hoggart drew on his childhood in Leeds for the seminal *Uses of Literacy*. John Russell Taylor argued that one of the essential unifying elements amongst the otherwise disparate group of writers, of which the New Wave was comprised, was 'their predominantly working-class origin' (Taylor 1962: 15). Both Shelagh Delaney and Arnold Wesker were born into the working-class, John Osborne came from a lower-middle-class background and Brendan Behan was a working-class Irishman (with an IRA past). Similarly, the novelists David Storey, Alan Sillitoe and Stan Barstow came from northern (and midland) working-class backgrounds. In addition, several of the new generation of young actors who rose to prominence in realist plays and films – Albert Finney, Alan Bates and Tom Courtenay, for example – were from the working-classes.

In fact, what emerged at this time is not simply a particular kind of realism but a new cultural 'moment', in which representations of class would assume an importance not only for the theatre, but also for the way that the myths of affluence and consensus were contested in a range of cultural and artistic forms. The moment of Working-Class Realism, which superseded Anger, also embraced the novel and (as the fifties moved into the sixties) cinema and eventually television as well. The most important novels in this context were John Braine's *Room at the Top*, Alan Sillitoe's *Saturday Night and Sunday Morning*, David Storey's *This Sporting Life* and Stan Barstow's *A Kind of Loving*. And in the cinema, it was films based on these novels, plus a range of other adaptations from both plays and novels, including *Look Back in Anger*, *A Taste of Honey* and *The Kitchen* (see Chapter 6 below). As the fifties gave way to the sixties, television drama was also discussed in terms of its realism (and social extension in particular), notably ABC's *Armchair Theatre* series, and later the BBC's *The Wednesday Play* and *Play for Today*.

This extended to some of the most distinctive developments in small screen drama, such as the continuous serials (*Coronation Street* and *Z Cars* in particular). In addition, 'Working-Class Realism' was as much a critical as it was a creative moment, denoting a public language, a set of reference points and an interpretative framework, in which these texts were discussed and positioned in relation to wider debates about post-war change. In this sense, it can be compared to the moment of Anger, with which it clearly had affinities.

Returning specifically to the theatre, the critical language of social realism began to dominate accounts of the new theatre generally. This was indicated by John Mander, who wrote of 'the breakthrough of a new working-class drama on the West End stage', arguing that 'today there are a dozen working-class dramas as good as the standard fare of the West End playgoer' (Mander 1961: 189). A major reason for the centrality of social realism in contemporary accounts lay in the values and priorities of those figures – critics and writers (sometimes they were the same people) – who mediated the plays to a wider audience. Wesker in particular actively contributed to the debate about Working-Class Realism in a number of contexts – letters to the press and articles in *Encore*, which frequently drew other contributors into the debates.

One of the crucial mediators was, as in other contexts, Kenneth Tynan. In 1959, Tynan wrote a retrospective account of the decade's drama ('A Decade in Retrospect: 1959'). The article reflected the change in rhetoric between the moments of 'Anger' and 'Working-Class Realism'. Jimmy Porter is defined here not as a representative of youth but as a 'working-class hero', offending his critics by his brash self-confidence, yet making similar plays possible: 'Osborne's success breached the dam, and there followed a cascade of plays about impoverished people' (Tynan 1984: 272). Two years later, contemplating a moribund West End and the demise of Theatre Workshop, Tynan pointed to a crisis in the proletarian drama in its realist form: 'Dispassionately-eyed, the great proletarian upsurge of which we bragged so freely . . . looks very much like a frost' (Tynan 1984: 320). In this way, both the most significant achievements and the endemic problems of the New Wave were subsumed within definitions that identified the new theatre in general with a particular form of class-based realism.

One reason why social realism was so important to the way that the New Wave was understood in the decade lies in a more general interest in the nature of class identity in post-war Britain. It is ironic that at a time when cultural commentators were becoming increasingly concerned with the effects of affluence on accepted definitions of class, a great deal of the art of the period, especially literature, cinema and theatre, was concerned with the traditional working-class. It is, in fact, both paradoxical and entirely explicable that this should be so, for it is the situation and values of the 'older' ways of life that were felt to be most under threat from the 'newer' prosperity and the developments it brought in its wake.

The onslaught of affluence caused changes in patterns of consumption that, it was argued, crossed traditional class and economic barriers. In some of the most vociferous versions of the argument, Britain was not simply changing socially, rather the very notion of class itself was becoming obsolete under the impact of a new prosperity and the change in consumption patterns, habits and values that this entailed. What concerned social and cultural commentators in the fifties was the seepage of middle-class culture downwards into the working-classes, and this was noted, even before the war, by George Orwell. 'In tastes, habits and outlook, the working-class and middle-class are drawing together', Orwell argued: 'To an increasing extent the rich and the poor read the same books, and they also see the same films and listen to the same radio programmes' (Orwell 1980: 96). The cultural homogenisation that this suggests was the inevitable result of an increasingly common access to a shared and ubiquitous 'mass' culture. It also had considerable implications for the way that social class was traditionally analysed. If class was to be defined in terms of disposable income and consumption patterns, then 'Some working-class families have incomes as high as some white-collar families and there is little to choose between their styles of living and the goods and services they consume' (Abrams 1964: 57).

To discuss class in these terms was highly contentious, since it shifted the point at which class affiliations were defined from the moment of production to consumption, with a consequent masking of the distribution of power according to class origin. It did, however, put patterns of leisure and the working-class 'way of life' (what the fifties learned to call, in the wake of the New Left, its culture), in both its traditional and affluent forms, under the microscope – patterns which required new types of analysis, and a different kind of cultural response.

If social realist theatre can be seen as an anti-hegemonic force in the period, therefore, it is perhaps because of the particular force that social extension carried in a context where public discourses about the nature of 'what Britain is like' in the period were concerned primarily with the supposed disappearance of class in general, and of the working class in particular, and with the landscape of affluence. Social realist plays (and novels and films, too) offered an alternative imagery that could be mobilised against the mythology spawned by the new prosperity and 'embourgeoise-ment'; the working-class were reclaimed both for the theatre and more generally for a left-inclined intelligentsia, itself often of lower-class origin, and with a particular investment in the social ex-perience that preoccupied them.

Social realism did not need to have, in Williams's terms, an explicit and conscious political intention in order to be read in oppositional terms, and was always potentially anti-hegemonic, albeit in sometimes contradictory ways. To represent social ex-perience that has hitherto been largely unrepresented within dominant forms of post-war drama is to validate that experience, to argue that it is worthy of interest in itself and to remedy a significant absence. Andrew Higson, writing of realist films in the period, has related this to the humanist political values of the period and called it a 'moral realism [which] involves a particular construction of the social in terms of "universal human values"' and which is dependent on a 'surface realism, involving an icon-ographic commitment to the representation of ordinary people' (Higson 1984: 4).

Whatever the particular intentions of individual texts, a great deal of post-war art and culture that has concerned itself with working-class experience has carried a political and moral charge that animates both the work and critical responses to it. John Whiting may have claimed in the pages of *Encore* that 'the substi-tution in literature of the bed-sitting room for the drawing room, and the dustman for the duke is not an achievement for realism' (Whiting 1970: 109), but if we are to take the claims of social extension seriously then this is precisely what was argued at the time by the more politically active elements in the new theatre.

The politics of Working-Class Realism also embraced more than just class, of course. Part of the 'shock' of the New Wave lay in a general willingness to confront experiences and issues that could not be located in purely class terms, yet still lay beyond the boundaries of fifties culture. That this might be important to the

74

way that the 'contemporary' in contemporary Britain was perceived was sometimes recognised by reviewers. T.C. Worsley, for example, described *A Taste of Honey* as a play '"about" a tart, a black boy giving a white girl a baby, a queer. The whole contemporary lot, in short' (Worsley 1959: 252).

This anti-hegemonic impetus was not at all a simple matter, and to understand how it operated we must look both at the wider discourses that shaped the context of reception (and in particular at the way that the terms 'class' and 'culture' were understood in the period) and at the particular strategies of a range of texts themselves.

THE USES OF CULTURE: WORKING-CLASS REALISM AND SOCIAL SCIENCE

One of the most important and influential attempts both to define the nature of working-class culture and to question and assess the logic of affluence and classlessness was conducted by Richard Hoggart in *The Uses of Literacy* (1957); it was also closely connected to Working-Class Realism and its critical context. Part autobiography and part critical enquiry, the book is an account of working-class culture that draws heavily on Hoggart's own childhood in pre-war Leeds, and offers a working model (rather than an explicit theory) of working-class culture in a context where there was a perceived lack of any credible definitions. Hoggart offers a view of class that is essentially anthropological, in which it is primarily the sum of its cultural practices, its shared routines, values and habits, focused at the level of 'everyday life'. The chapter headings and sub-headings give a sense of how this dense, homogenous world is constructed; The Neighbourhood, 'Them' and 'Us', The Full Rich Life. It is an account that centres on the street, the home and the clubs, that evokes in a clear, direct and highly nuanced way, the 'common sense', the naturalness and the vitality of the particular 'way of life'. At one level, this is the book's major strength. The sense of a culture that is so manifestly 'present', so deeply rooted in everyday experience, is presented with such force and clarity that accounts of affluent, consumerist culture seem insipid by comparison. It is – at least in the first, and most influential part of the book – more a reflection of rather than a reflection on a class and its culture, and one in which such crucial arenas of social and cultural experience as the workplace, or forms of working-class politics have little place.

It was also a reflection of a class culture that could readily be seen as nostalgic, referring to a 'golden age' that was already disappearing by the time the book appeared. Although this was clearly not Hoggart's intention, it is certainly an element in the way that the book was read, and is a criticism that has been persistently levelled at it since.

There is no doubt that *The Uses of Literacy* was enormously influential in the late fifties and sixties, particularly when it could be related to other contributions to the debates about post-war culture. Terry Lovell has argued persuasively (Lovell 1990) that most working-class realist films of the early sixties reveal a 'structure of feeling' that comes almost directly from Hoggart's book – that is, a way of constructing a 'way of life' and an individual's relationship to it that was shaped by the concerns of *The Uses of Literacy*. Its influence was particularly marked in new forms of television, where the concern with working-class culture found a new home and a mass audience. The connections between the book and *Coronation Street*, which first appeared in 1961, have been noted by Richard Dyer:

> the emphasis on common sense, the absence of work and politics, the stress on women and the strength of women, and the perspective of nostalgia – inform *Coronation Street* and indeed come close to defining its fictional world.
>
> (Dyer *et al.* 1981: 4)

Apart from these specific influences, *The Uses of Literacy* was connected to Working-Class Realism at the level of its basic method and approach, for it was written in a 'literary' rather than a sociological style, reflecting Hoggart's own academic discipline, English literature. Laing has noted that the interest in the situation of the working-class in the period was often expressed through forms of sociology or 'social exploration' that either referred to literature (for example, Jackson and Marsden's *Education and the Working Class*) or used literary strategies (Clancy Sigal's *Weekend in Dinlock* is Laing's main example here; Laing 1986: 47). Indeed, as Sinfield has noted, 'left-inclined social sciences aspired to the condition of literature', often dwelling upon personal experience 'in the way that novels were understood to do' (Sinfield 1989: 245). This arose out of a concern to give value to the actual social experience of 'real' working-class people that was as much political as it was sociological, and to capture the dense reality of a class identity that was focused, as *Uses* made clear, at the level of everyday practices and rituals. From this perspective, carefully realised 'characters' and the evocative depiction of a particular social world were more important that statistical tables; they are also amongst the main generic features of contemporary realist theatre and fiction. Social science and Working-Class Realism existed, then, not in discrete areas of social criticism but as points on a continuum.

If sociology and social enquiry were becoming more 'literary', then theatre and literature were being increasingly understood in sociological terms, as documents about social reality, reflecting (if not reflecting on) a class experience directly. *A Taste of Honey*, for example, was described by Colin MacInnes as an authentic depiction of working-class experience, transcribed directly from social reality; 'It is . . . the first play that I can remember about working-class people that entirely escapes being a 'working-class' play: no patronage, no drama – just the thing as it is, taken straight' (MacInnes 1959: 70). Alan Brien made the anthropological reference explicit:

> *A Taste of Honey* still has the enormous advantage of being unlike almost any other working-class play in that it is not scholarly anthropology observed from the outside through pince-nez, but the inside story of a savage culture observed by a genuine cannibal.
>
> (Brien 1959a: 257)

This interpretative framework assumed not only that realist plays were 'about' the working-class but also constructed a particular relationship between author, text and the social experience being represented, seeing the plays as an unreconstructed 'reflection' of social reality, which relied on the personal situation of the writers to guarantee the 'truth' of the text, its sociological validity. The autobiographical origins of several of the plays was clearly important in this context. Delaney wrote about the kind of northern working-class background that she herself had come from, and, as a young woman writer, could be identified with Jo in *A Taste of Honey*. Wesker's *Trilogy* similarly drew heavily on the kind of politically conscious Jewish family in which he grew up, and he himself was sometimes identified with Ronnie Kahn. Within the sociologising discourse that interpreted them, the 'personal' story of the plays became a representative one, symptomatic of a general cultural phenomenon – the working-class writer as documentarist, or anthropologist: if Delaney's *A Taste of Honey* was, as Brien argued, 'the inside story of a savage culture observed by a genuine cannibal', then Delaney was an insider sending out messages to the rest of us, who are 'outsiders', secure by our own camp-fires.

The semi-anthropological language that pervades critical accounts of the new drama gains some of its validity from the ways in which class experience was linked to social geography, and in particular the connotations that the 'northernness' of the texts carried in the period. The 'North' evoked a reservoir of historical images and references, that were to do with its historical associations with capitalism and the working-class. In fact, relatively few social realist plays were set in the North (Wesker's *Trilogy*, for example, was set in Norfolk and London), although those that were (*A Taste of Honey* in particular) were important to the way that the moment was understood; many of the novels and films, however, were northern, and this helped to define the geographical as well as the class orientation of the genre as a whole. The North was the place that had given birth to the industrial revolution, and was associated with the kinds of heavy industries that had been the backbone of the Empire and the wellspring of economic prosperity until the early years of this century. It was also the home of the organised working-class, the Co-operative Movement and much of the Trade Union Movement. In this way, it was set against the South, the centre of the new industries of the inter- and post-war years, and the symbolic as well as the actual centre of affluence. The North connoted 'working-classness' in a very direct way, helping to define a particular social and cultural landscape and to fix a pervasive stereotype, implying an authenticity of experience and attitude that could be contrasted with the narrow, shallow concerns of the South. In this sense, it overlapped with, and to a degree replaced, the connotations of 'provincial' that also helped to shape the social meaning of post-war culture.

Dramas of Dislocation and Escape

In retrospect – and if we look closely at individual plays – the interpretative framework of Working-Class Realism only recognised certain elements within much of the social experience that was being dramatised (much as the critical context of Anger had been blind to the workings of misogyny). Although social extension was an important part of the realism of many New Wave plays, this did not always mean that such plays dealt with the *general* situation of the working-class, strictly defined. Wesker's *Chicken Soup with Barley* is located amongst a politically conscious Jewish family, a minority of a minority. And both *Epitaph for George Dillon* and *Billy Liar* are set specifically in lower-middle rather than working-class milieux.

Few New Wave plays either debate the nature of working-class life (Wesker's plays are important exceptions here) or seek to represent it in its 'typical' forms; we are not presented with central characters who can be seen as 'statistical averages'. Indeed, if the major plays of the period are considered, then it is apparent that few of the protagonists, whose social profiles permeate a variety of discourses, could be considered 'representative' of a central class experience; rather, they are often socially marginal (Jo and Helen in *A Taste of Honey*), metaphorically 'other' (the multi-racial cast of *The Kitchen* or the largely sub-proletarian cast of *The Hostage*) or bohemian (Jimmy Porter) in their social orientation, linked often by their youth as much as their position in the class structure.

In some respects, the central experience represented in many New Wave plays – and it is also present in the novels and films as well – is of characters who are dislocated from their origins, either removed by their education and experience from the class into which they were born (largely represented, in the theatre at least, as the family), or in conflict with it. The sense of rootlessness, of drifting, that is etched into these plays can also be traced to this experience. Class dislocation is one source of Jimmy Porter's crisis of identity; educated out of one class, he has found no place in another. Beattie Bryant in *Roots* is also in conflict with her class (and with herself), and this is one of the central themes of the play. In Beattie's case, it is not so much the formal processes of education – or, indeed, the allure of affluence – that are at the root (*sic*) of the conflict, but the exposure to a different set of moral and cultural values (through Ronnie Kahn) that are defined in the play as universal. In Alun Owen's *Progress to the Park*, which is set in a working-class area of Liverpool, the audience/reader is removed from the concerns (and class values) of most of the other characters because the protagonist, who provides a viewpoint on the events, is doubly marked as an outsider; first, despite having grown up on the street, he is Welsh, and secondly, he is now a writer in London (like Owen himself). The working-class youth of Anne Jellicoe's plays in this period (*The Sport of my Mad Mother* and *The Knack*) seem to have no cultural or social roots, by recourse to which we can explain or understand their actions or motivations.

The conflict between protagonists and their class background is sometimes resolved by escape. This is a motif within the narratives of the Movement novels of the early fifties, especially John Wain's *Hurry on Down* and Kingsley Amis's *Lucky Jim*, whose central characters (Charles Lumley and Jim Dixon respectively) are 'young men on the make' who flee the dour restrictions of the provinces and go to London, where new opportunities beckon; both, typically, take new jobs on the fringes of the media. In the theatre, it is Billy Fisher, the eponymous hero of Waterhouse and Hall's *Billy Liar*, who best embodies this social trajectory, although in Billy's case the move to London is imagined but never completed. Billy dreams of going to London to become a scriptwriter, and although this career aspiration is shown to be as much a fantasy as a great deal else in Billy's life, going South in the company of Liz is presented as a genuine freedom from the situation in which he is enmeshed. The term 'provincial' had, in this context, pejorative overtones that largely displaced the connotations of authenticity that were important elsewhere, and drew on a different set of stereotypes. Provincial – and northern – signified a grey, constricting drabness, that was the embodiment of limited ambitions and a philistine cultural outlook. In this equation, the South loses the associations of stale middle-class vacuity and becomes the site of a new freedom, a symbolic and actual territory where provincial refugees could make themselves anew. *Billy Liar*, more than many plays in the period, looks forward to the sixties, where London rather than the North is seen to be the wellspring of cultural opportunities.

'THE WORST SOCIAL INJUSTICE SINCE SLAVERY': SOCIAL REALISM AND 'CULTURAL DEPRIVATION'

The dominant readings of social realist plays in performance emphasised their 'otherness', their 'difference' from both the social experience of most metropolitan critics and the mythology of affluence. It was a difference that could be discussed not only in terms of its 'authentic' relationship to working-class experience, but also in quite other terms, as a manifestation of 'deprivation' – but not primarily of the familiar and pre-war economic kind. Walter Allen argued that in *Roots* Wesker was 'exposing the impoverishment of English working-class, no longer necessarily economic impoverishment but, in the deepest sense, cultural' (Elsom 1981: 94).

The idea of 'cultural deprivation' returns us to the debates about affluence and hegemony in a very particular form. Central to the consensus was the belief that the main economic problems of society had been solved, and that problems arising from structural poverty had been largely eradicated. Yet this optimistic version of post-war history was resisted by many on the New Left (and outside it), although their scepticism was connected to a partial acceptance of the mythology itself. From this position the realist intention to 'show how things really are' was pursued in terms of an interpretation of social change which emphasised a decline that could be registered at the cultural level. Yet what, in this context, might cultural mean? And what are the consequences of cultural deprivation for those to whom, like the Bryant family, the label was attached?

The definition and exploration of the concept of culture, in its differing senses, was an essential part of the project of the New Left, as we saw earlier. Hoggart's *The Uses of Literacy* made a distinctive contribution to the debate, linking the term to sociological/ anthropological notions of culture as a 'way of life'. Raymond Williams, however, whose writings on culture are sometimes thought – erroneously – to be identical to Hoggart's, pursued the idea of culture along different paths. Williams's *Culture and Society* (1958) and *The Long Revolution* (1965) were concerned with particular kinds of cultural practices and contain a sustained reflection on the nature and definition of culture itself. He moves across two usages of culture, the anthropological and the literary/ philosophical, insisting on their inseparability.

> We use the word culture in these two senses: to mean a whole way of life – the common meanings; to mean the arts and learning – the special processes of discovery and creative effort. Some writers reserve the word for one or other of these senses; I insist on both.
>
> (Williams 1958b: 76)

In practice, Williams's understanding of culture was always more ideological than that of many of his contemporaries. He argued that an understanding of working-class culture must make room for 'the basic collective idea' itself and its institutional expression – political parties and trade unions, for example, both noticeably absent from *The Uses of Literacy*. However, much of Williams's work in the fifties and early sixties was concerned with culture in its earlier usage, as literature, art and philosophy. *Culture and Society* was largely an attempt to trace the lineage of certain key terms in contemporary critical debate within a tradition of literary/cultural criticism that embraced Carlyle, Matthew Arnold and George Orwell, amongst others. For Williams, this tradition was classless, in the sense that it was 'necessarily, something more than the product of a single class' (Sinfield 1989: 242), and represented a unique, if sometimes fractured and contradictory critique of the main developments within industrial society. In arguing in these terms, Williams was developing – and radicalising – a form of criticism that had been championed by the formidable and highly influential literary critic, F.R. Leavis, who did more than almost any other critic in the mid-twentieth century to champion the idea of a 'great tradition' of literature, that embodied both aesthetic value and social/moral worth.

Culture as literature and art is one of the oldest, and most prevalent, conceptualisations of the term; it was also important to the analysis of culture in other ways, for it provided cultural critics not only with an object of enquiry but with a methodology as well. Both Sinfield (1989) and Shiach (1989) have argued that it was largely through the discourses of literary criticism that newer forms of cultural production – particularly those associated with twentieth century mass production, such as film and popular music – were analysed. One of the consequences of this reliance on literary models was that questions of moral/philosophical and social value were never far from the analysis; as Williams argued in *Culture and Society*, it was frequently the great literary artistic figures that engaged most fully with the processes of industrialisation and democracy.

The culture of which the working-class was being deprived, then, was frequently the enduring works of bourgeois art and literature. To champion 'Culture' against 'culture' was to make the 'best' available to all, and was entirely recoupable within a democratic humanist politics; in other words, because it was in literature that profound social questions were addressed and the habit of critical questioning could be engendered, its absence had a corollary – that a deprivation, which had its origins in economic inequality, was maintained by a passive acceptance of the status quo as 'inevitable' and the inability (or refusal) to make a significant challenge.

The activity of marking off what was 'good' or 'bad' in con-temporary culture occurred on the terrain of 'discrimination' or 'taste', which has never been simply a matter of aesthetics alone, nor has it been the province of any single discipline or discourse.

Matters of taste have always been explicitly to do with 'values' and therefore implicitly ideological; as Hebdige has written, 'the issue of taste – where to draw the line between good and bad, high and low, the ugly and the beautiful, the ephemeral and the substantial – emerges at certain points as a quite explicitly political one' (Hebdige 1982: 194). The politics of discrimination required an enemy, and in the fifties found it in 'mass culture', yet another conceptualisation of culture, this time referring to both the arte-facts and the means of communication characteristic of the age of mass production – magazines, pulp novels, popular music, as well as advertising and the newly available products of consumerism.

The hostility to mass culture and the consequent privileging of literature did not begin in the 1950s, nor was it only associated with anxieties about consumerist popular culture, but also embraced deep-rooted concerns about the processes of industrialisation itself. An antipathy towards mass culture saturates much of the writing of post-war conservative writers and thinkers (Evelyn Waugh's novels, for example, display an aggressive and blackly comic hostility towards not only popular culture, but also the entire post-war democratic era). Elsewhere, these anxieties can be traced in Leavis's work. He mounted a sustained critique of mass culture, both through his own work as a critic and through the journal *Scrutiny*, with which he was closely associated, and which appeared both before and after the war. To Leavis, mass-produced popular culture was meretricious, manipulative and intellectually, morally and ethically debasing, and Leavis gave intellectuals, especially literary intellectuals, a central role in the struggle to reverse its debilitating effects.

Added to this concern with the fate of literature were anxieties about the future of the 'authentic' working-class. In the second part of *The Uses of Literacy*, Hoggart mounted a polemic against the influence of a 'universal' mass culture, and especially popular literature. In a now much-quoted phrase, Hoggart described the process of cultural attrition that resulted from the mass con-sumption of popular culture as 'unbending the springs of action', maintaining that 'the strongest argument against modern mass entertainments is not that they debase taste – debasement can be alive and active – but that they over-excite it, eventually dull it, and finally kill it: that they "enervate" rather than "corrupt"' (Hoggart 1971: 196–7).

A similar anxiety (expressed in a more lurid form) can be found in an editorial in *Encore* that makes the connection between cultural deprivation and affluence explicit. Headed by a quotation from Matthew Arnold, the editorial contrasts the 'astonishing' material progress that has characterised the post-war period with the sterility of the national culture. 'The pleasures of the mind are unknown to the vast majority of the population', it notes, although 'things are not as bad as a swift look at the *Daily Mirror* and some television programmes might lead you to think.' The result of this is a 'trivialisation' that is 'the worst injustice since slavery' (*Encore*, May/June 1958). The solution to the problem is one that gained ground as the fifties moved into the sixties, the classically welfarist one of a 'middle-brow' culture based on government-sponsored theatres.

In the plays themselves, these positions were expressed in different forms. Judgements about the relationship between affluence, discrimination and political values, for example, were part of the encoding process of the realist *mise-en-scène*, particularly in plays that utilised a single fictional space. In *Epitaph for George Dillon* (Osborne/Creighton) the stage directions make it clear that the domestic setting is to be clearly marked as affluent, 'tasteless' and 'contemporary', containing a picture 'of a group of wild ducks in flight' (Osborne and Creighton 1960: 143). The ducks – a familiar indicator of lower-class kitsch – and a radiogram, television and cocktail cabinet function as signs not only of bad taste but also a restricted way of life; 'I've often marvelled at them from afar', says Dillon, 'But I never thought I'd see one in someone's house. I thought they just stood there like some sort of monstrous symbol' (Osborne and Creighton 1960: 184). In *Billy Liar*, the stage directions suggest that the interior of the Fisher household contains furniture 'that is quite new, but in dreadful taste – as are also the plastic ornaments and the wall plaques with which the room is overdressed.' This domestic space also contains the ubiquitous television set and 'flashy cocktail cabinet' (Waterhouse and Hall 1966: 211). Such sets require an audience that is able to interpret these intentions from the immediately available visual signs, one that is certain where the battle-lines around taste should be drawn – and which side of them they are on. At this point the specific ideologies that saturate the response to mass and working-class culture are registered in the particular conventions of the dominant forms of realist drama and theatre.

84

'AN ART THAT ESTABLISHES VALUES': WESKER'S *ROOTS* AND *CHIPS WITH EVERYTHING*

A central figure in these debates – indeed, probably *the* central figure – was Arnold Wesker. In his plays, his critical work and the activities of Centre 42, Wesker helped both to define the context for Working-Class Realism and relate it to wider political and cultural concerns. In particular, Wesker had a clear sense of the social role of theatre and its relationship to its audience. What was needed, Wesker asserted, was an art that aimed to 'fill the gap in education, that struggles to arouse interest in the world and persuade one to have faith in life. An art, in fact, that establishes values' (Wesker 1970: 98). That such an art would test itself against the corrosive effects of the mass-produced culture of affluence is a theme that runs throughout all his work at this time. It is, in particular, the main theme of *Roots* and part of the intellectual armature of *Chips with Everything*.

The benefits of affluence are not conspicuous in *Roots*; despite the references to Beattie's sister Susan's TV and radio, both the Bryant and Beales households are clearly beyond the prosperity and economic security that was supposed to have settled upon the British working-class. However, the issues the play posed connect it immediately to the central concerns of the New Left, and are registered at several levels, especially in the way that the play utilises its realist strategies.

The play's protagonist, Beattie, is set against the family, of which she is a part. Beattie is caught between the conflicting claims of her family and Ronnie, who, as an articulate member of the politically and culturally aware Kahn family, represents a set of values in which art has a central place. Beattie's dilemma is, however, an internal one as well; articulating his opinions as weapons in a war against the values and habits of her family, she continues to exhibit those values herself. Towards the end of the play, when Ronnie fails to appear, Beattie begins to find her own voice in a series of long speeches that validate her internal struggle and show her breaking through to a new consciousness. 'I'm beginning', she says in the last line of the play, 'on my own two feet – I'm beginning ...' (Wesker 1973: 148). The knowledge that she gains is initially that of the mastery of language, of words that can 'build bridges' as she says earlier in the play, which gives her an awareness of the general cultural situation that *Roots* explores and the power to name it; in doing so, Beattie also names the social forces that contain her family and determine their behaviour.

The problem that Beattie locates is one of cultural impoverishment, and this is not simply a contemporary phenomenon but has a long history. 'I'm telling you something's cut us off from the beginning. I'm telling you we've got no roots' (Wesker 1973: 146), Beattie says. It is at this point that the full resonance of the play's title is felt, for the lack of 'roots' is perceived by Beattie (and the play) as a lack of anything that connects her family (and, beyond them, society as a whole) to something that would both 'nourish' them and give them strength – would anchor them – in a contingent world. Beattie makes clear that the problem is essentially a cultural one (and the play draws on many senses of the word 'cultural', including the biological one), in which the mass of the population is cut off from the mainstream of intellectual and artistic development:

> Do you think when the really talented people in the country get to work they get to work for us? Hell if they do! . . . The writers don't write thinkin' we can understand, nor the painters don't paint expecting us to be interested. . . . 'Blust' they say, 'if they don't make no effort why should we bother?'
> (Wesker 1973: 147)

It is a meretricious and manipulative mass culture that fills the gap:

> So you know who come along? The slop singers and the pop writers and the film makers and women's magazines and the Sunday papers and the picture strip love stories – that's who come along, and you don't have to make no effort for them it come easy. 'We know where the money lie' they say, 'hell we do! The workers've got it so let's give them what they want. . . . Anything's good enough for them 'cos they don't ask for no more!' The whole stinkin' commercial world insults us and we don't care a damn. Well, Ronnie's right – it's our own bloody fault. We want the third rate – We got it!
> (Wesker 1973: 148)

This is an articulation of much that has been enacted in the rest of the play – of the sequence at the end of Act Two, for example, when Beattie attempts to teach her mother to appreciate a piece of music by Bizet. This also connects to many of the contemporary anxieties about the effects of mass culture and affluence, in Hoggart, *Encore* and elsewhere, and the role of high culture in opposing them. In some ways the ending of Act Two is a more persuasive illustration of Wesker's position, for it relies not on staging a didactic confrontation between Beattie and her family (as the final scene does, especially in performance) but instead gives a concrete demonstration of the power of art to transform social relationships. Beattie's enthusiasm animates not only her but also her mother, whom we are told in a final stage direction 'smiles and claps her hands' in one of the few genuinely shared moments in the play.

The role of language in both the perpetuation of cultural deprivation, and the resistance to it, is crucial. Words are bridges to Ronnie, they enable people to connect with each other, and language has the ability to transform the situation. The climactic moments in the play are generally those when the power of communication is at issue; Mr Bryant's problems at work, for example, are not defined so much as the result of unequal economic power, but rather as a problem of communication within the family. Language is not only used by characters, however, it also speaks through them. It is a means by which old cultural habits are continued and confirmed; language is both a metaphor for the ideologies that shape the characters' lives and one of the chief means of perpetuating those ideologies.

In this way, quotation is a motif that resonates through the play; characters seem to quote a language that is familiar and easy, yet expresses little of the complexity of their lives. The idea is made tangible in the way that Ronnie Kahn is present in the play largely through Beattie's recurrent quotations of him – he is metaphorically speaking through her.

These arguments about cultural attrition and the role of language are also at the centre of *Chips with Everything*. *Chips* is set in an Air Force training camp for National Service recruits, and follows the lives of the inmates of one hut during the period of basic training. Like *The Kitchen*, *Chips* is a play that is concerned with the activities of a group, yet – also like *The Kitchen* – there is a central protagonist, Pip Thompson, the son of a banker and general, who is determined at the start of the play to resist expectations and refuse officer training. The training camp is much more of a microcosm of the society of which it is a part than the restricted social world of the Bryants and Beales, and this is registered partly through language. The play is heavy with contrasting language styles, which have a class basis; the military argot and rhythms of

Corporal Hill, the NCO who governs the hut ('The last lot we 'ad here 'ad a good time, a right time, a right good scorching time'); the fractured colloquialism of the predominantly working-class recruits; the measured formality of the officers, at once professional and thoroughly bourgeois. Pip's sardonic eloquence marks him out as both educated and middle-class, and this places him both outside, and in opposition to, the culture and aspirations of his fellow recruits. The attention of the audience/reader is drawn to the centrality of language by the way that one particular character, Dickey, self-consciously plays with language, exhibiting an almost Baroque sense of linguistic ornamentation ('Good old Cannibal! He uttered a syllable of many dimensions. The circumlocution of his mouth has moved. Direct yourself to the bar, old son, and purchase for us some brown liquid').

One of the central problems that the play explores is that Pip has education and power, defined both by his background and the assumed self-confidence that goes with it, but has no politics to shape his professed rebelliousness. One of the climactic moments of the play has Pip tricked by the Pilot Officer, implausibly, into admitting that he merely wishes to lead those he actually despises, his fellow recruits. He is a flawed 'hero', central to the development of the narrative action, yet he is not a repository of its moral or political values. Instead, Wesker gives us a relationship that is a reworking of Beattie/Ronnie, setting Pip against Chas, a young working-class man, who places value on the education and power over language that Pip effects to despise. However, in *Chips* the relationship proceeds along different lines, for Chas, unlike Beattie, is desperate for knowledge and the power that he thinks it will bring, whilst Pip, faced with the kind of hero-worship that he has sought, rejects him. Here, though, Chas's hunger for education and escape also makes him willing to submit to a leader; 'I'll do what *you* want, Pip', he says. Thus, the relationship between educator and educated is a more ambiguous one in *Chips* than it is in *Roots*; power over language and culture can lead to personal transformation – but it may also lead, as Pip notes, to simply 'swapping masters'.

Power in *Chips* is exercised primarily through institutions (see Chapter 4), through the routines and values of the training camp. Yet even though we have moved away from the domestic setting of *Roots*, the model of cultural deprivation remains the same, and the villain is once again mass culture. The key scene here is the

Christmas Eve party (Act One, Scene Seven), where the Wing Commander, whose hatred for the lower-classes is explicit, demands that the recruits entertain each other with 'a dirty recitation or a pop song'; Pip's response is to persuade one of their number, a Scot, to recite a Burns poem, and the entire gathering, much less plausibly, to sing a traditional folk song of resistance, 'The Cutty Wren', which, we are told, has the boys 'gradually menacing the officers'.

That this seems a crude and didactic device is not simply to do with the choice of song, but rather the kind of cultural politics that underpins the crude opposition between contemporary pop and traditional ('authentic') folk culture. The problem is a symptomatic one, indicative of the difficulty of distinguishing between, and valuing, different cultural traditions, and of avoiding a collapse into a way of viewing mass culture as being simply manipulative. This was a problem both for Wesker and elements of the New Left generally; it also became one of the rocks on which Wesker's other main intervention into contemporary cultural politics, the arts organisation Centre 42, foundered.

In the pamphlet sent to trade unions prior to the Congress of 1960, which precipitated the founding of Centre 42 (see Chapter 2), Wesker commended the achievements of the labour movement in the economic sphere, but argued that culture had been neglected; the task was to 'break' the cultural habits of the working-class, as the achievements of the labour movement had broken the economic ones. 'The social and cultural habits of a group will continue', he argued, 'unless something is done to break them' (Wesker 1960b: 11). The habits referred to are not simply those of 'traditional' working-class culture, but also of 'mass' culture, against which many theatre activists had set their faces. At one level, this merely states in a stark and uncomfortable form what was being argued elsewhere on the New Left; that the only way to oppose the debilitating effects of mass culture was to intervene directly and attempt to shape the tastes of the audience. The tone of the argument, however, could be seen as patronising in a way that many others on the left – especially in the theatre – were anxious to avoid. In rejecting the culture of the traditional working-class in such a forthright manner, Wesker further alienated those who were working in its defence.

The festivals that Centre 42 organised consisted mainly of the products of high art – theatre, small-scale opera and dance, poetry readings (see Coppieter 1975). The exceptions to this were jazz and folk concerts (and Charles Parker's ground-breaking folk documentaries) – but both folk music and jazz were in some ways the acceptable and 'authentic' face of popular art. It was a constant criticism of the festivals that they promoted a culture that was essentially that of the organisers rather than of the audiences; there was little room for the kind of working-class entertainment that Hoggart describes in *The Uses of Literacy*, let alone for rock 'n' roll.

Although the preoccupation with culture at the expense of economics was shared across the left, in an important sense, New Left figures such as Williams were moving in the opposite direction to Wesker and many theatre activists. Far from drawing a line around high culture, the New Left began to construct links between different conceptions of culture and between different cultural arenas. Williams and Hoggart became increasingly concerned with television and popular culture, for example, giving evidence to the Pilkington Committee on the future of television in the early sixties; Hoggart, and later Stuart Hall, moved into the universities, establishing and then developing the Centre for Contemporary Cultural Studies in Birmingham, out of which a great deal of theoretical work in the area of cultural theory and popular culture emerged in the 1970s and after.

'ONLY IN HER OWN HOME IS SHE FREE': COUNTERING DOMESTIC CONSENSUS: *A TASTE OF HONEY* AND *EACH HIS OWN WILDERNESS*

Wandor (1986 and 1987) has noted that by being confined to the domestic in post-war drama, women have been restricted to/associated with the private and the non-political spheres, whilst men have been free to roam the wider world, acting on a public stage. However, as Wandor argues forcefully, it is not the case that the domestic must necessarily be unpolitical or non-ideological. That the domestic was the terrain of affluence and a Hoggartian view of culture, meant that the home, and women's role within it, were central to the hegemonic consensus in the period; as with other areas of culture and social life, the domestic was an arena where traditional identities and roles could be both confirmed and contested. The domestic was, potentially, the site of a kind of politics – one which was frequently marginalised in the context of the late fifties, but which has received more attention since – the politics of gender, where the 'personal' focus of realist forms might become politicised in distinctive ways.

After the war, women returned from the factories, as men returned from the forces and assumed many of the jobs they had previously occupied. This re-establishment of traditional gender patterns was hailed as a form of 'domestic' consensus (see Segal 1990) that echoed all its other forms; if, as Macmillan had claimed, the class war was over, then so too was the sex war for many people (including many women) and there was a remarkable degree of agreement about the lineaments of the new gender relationships.

The main aspect of domestic consensus was that women became defined overwhelmingly – publicly at least – in terms of their domestic roles. As one study noted:

> The writing and thinking on women in the fifties by feminists and non-feminists alike tends to take place within a framework which accepts the primacy of the woman's role as wife and mother and which assumes that other aspects of women's lives must be fitted into that.
>
> (Birmingham Feminist History Group: 1979)

Indeed, the home and the family attracted a considerable amount of sociological interest and the debate about its future as an institution was a very public one. Between 1942 and 1956, there were five government inquiries into the family and related issues, including a Royal Commission on Population (1949), and legislation sometimes followed (notably in the case of the Beveridge Report of 1942). The decline in the size of families, the younger age of marriage, the increased availability and use of contraceptives and the gradual but remorseless return of women to paid employment were all reasons for this concern (see Birmingham Feminist History Group 1979 and E. Wilson 1980).

There was no shortage of advice to women on how they should recognise and fulfil their domestic and familial responsibilities, much of it proceeding from concerns over the stability and identity of the family unit. John Bowlby's much-discussed research into the long-term effects of maternal deprivation (in *Child Care and the Growth of Love*, 1953) was used against working mothers and as support for the widely accepted argument that children required the attention of their mothers throughout their early years. Yet the role of wife and mother was itself undergoing change, not least because of 'new' expectations. The second Kinsey Report, *The*

91

Sexual Behaviour of the Human Female (1953), provided evidence of female sexual activity on a hitherto unacknowledged scale (which was duly publicised, often at length, in the press), one result of which was to focus attention on the need for pleasurable and guilt-free sex. Needless to say, sexual pleasure was only permissible within the bounds of marriage, and the anxiety over 'illicit' sex remained a constant preoccupation of both commentators and the press – an anxiety that found its way into the much-debated report of the Wolfenden Committee (1957) into homosexuality and prostitution. The Report, which advocated the decriminalisation of homosexuality and systems of 'moral welfare' for prostitutes (as well as increased penalties, should they be caught) was represented as a liberalising influence, yet the measures it advocated were argued in the context of increased moral censure and a concern over the effects of extra-marital and homosexual sex on the family unit.

As the guardians of the home, the place where most of the products of prosperity were enjoyed, women were the object of affluence, the target of advertisements and the drive towards the expansion of the market for consumer goods. However, women were producers as well as consumers, with the number of women in work rising by nearly one and a half million between 1947 and 1957 in response to shortages in the labour market in the late forties and the industrial expansion associated with the consumer boom (Hill 1986: 16). The importance of this to both the economy as a whole and to the income of individual families has been noted by Elizabeth Wilson (Wilson 1980: 62), who cites survey evidence to suggest that a woman's job was frequently the guarantee of her family's economic security (especially if that family was working-class). The economic significance of women's work was consistently underestimated in the fifties, with a woman's wages being written off as largely peripheral to her husband's income (it was only 'pin money') or as generating a market for 'luxuries', with all of the connotations of unrestrained hedonism that the word often carries.

In this way, women were seen to be both the main beneficiaries of affluence, and the repository of anxieties about the destabilising effects of the new consumer culture, and therefore occupied a specific symbolic place in the debates around mass culture outlined above. As Hopkins proclaimed, catching the tone of a recurrent rhetoric, 'the woman of the Fifties possessed at once the time, the resources, and the inclination to bring to perfection the new art of continuous consumption. She was the essential pivot of the People's Capitalism and its natural heroine' (quoted E. Wilson 1980: 61). In this kind of rhetoric, the distance between 'heroine' (champion of consumption) and 'fashion's eager slave' (the victim of consumption, unable to resist the allure of the new, 'meretricious' consumer culture) was not very great.

New Wave films systematically draw upon the kinds of associations that are represented here, between the domestic and consumerism in general, and between consumerism, mass culture and spiritual/social aridity, and this is encoded in the way that domestic interiors are delineated. There is an opposition, for example, between the authenticity of traditional working-class homes and 'the households that have adapted to the styles and values of mass consumerism' (Lovell 1990: 365). Within this opposition, women who accept the new values are represented as 'traps' for the male heroes (Barbara in *Billy Liar* and Doreen in *Saturday Night and Sunday Morning*) with marriage signifying a kind of prison and an accommodation to dominant (affluent) values. Although there are examples of plays that exploit the same connections, what are more interesting are those plays that actively *contest* them, that regard the domestic sphere, and women's roles within it, as an ideological battleground, where hegemonic assumptions can be actively explored and exposed.

A Taste of Honey

Motherhood, the family and gender politics are central to *A Taste of Honey*, which was one of relatively few plays in the period to explore women's concerns from a woman's perspective. As Wandor put it, 'the territory is largely domestic, and the dramatic action is controlled by women. The gender dynamics are female-centred, and women are centrally placed as subject matter' (Wandor 1987: 42–3). *A Taste of Honey* does this not by exploring a radically new dramatic language (as women writers have done more recently) but by subverting the conventions of the intensive dramatic mode of naturalism that Delaney had adopted. There is no attempt to connect the play to a wider social world, by 'argument' (characters do not debate the issues between themselves); nor does the play articulate a position on that world (there is no obvious authorial 'point of view' on display); nor, despite the contextual readings, does Delaney exploit the metonymic function of the characters, action or set, but rather the issues are visible in the texture of the personal relationships themselves. Stuart Hall noted this aspect of the play:

> Delaney is not at all self-conscious about her ability to portray Salford life but she accepts this as a framework for what she is really interested in communicating – her extraordinarily fine and subtle feel for personal relationships. No themes or ideas external to the play disturb its inner form: her values are all intensive.
>
> (Hall 1970: 215)

A Taste of Honey is remarkable partly because it breaks a number of racial and sexual taboos: Jo's lover is a black sailor and her flat-mate is homosexual, and the main action of the play is the journey into motherhood of a young, unmarried teenager. It is not simply that these things are represented, but that they are represented positively – that the form of the play elicits sympathy for characters that come to us heavy with connotations, who are part of a world that we 'read about every Sunday in the *News of the World*' (L. Anderson 1970b: 79). It is precisely such socially marginal and 'a-typical' characters with which the Wolfenden Report – and the press debate that followed it – was so concerned.

The action of the play is contained by a 'comfortless flat', and the stage space is clearly marked as domestic. It is, however, an interior in which all the domestic activities are potentially on display; the kitchen area, the double bed, the living and eating areas – these are all visible, delineating a whole 'way of life' in its routines and chores. Very little conventional domestic activity actually takes place in this space, though, and when it does, it is not performed by characters who inhabit traditional roles. This is part of a complex series of reversals and oppositions in the play, in which expected connections are severed. The mother figure, Helen, is very unlike a 'mother', having no domestic abilities, being feckless and sexually active. The caring role is taken initially by Jo, the daughter, and then by Geoff, a man who displays none of the conventional 'male' attributes. The nearest to a white, male, heterosexual gender norm in the play is to be found in Peter, Helen's lover and fiancé, who is presented as a lecher and a drunk.

The three central characters are all potentially sexually active, and the two women become so. However, sex is destructive to happiness in the world of the play – as it is in *Look Back in Anger.* It separates mother and daughter (Helen's marriage to Peter) and leaves Jo with a baby. Jo's relationship with Geoff is only possible because it is without sex. The only moments of genuine difficulty between them are when sex is involved; Jo's demand that Geoff tell her what he does with men nearly leads to his departure, and Geoff's attempt at a physical relationship with her is rejected as irrelevant. As a result of this, it is implicit that happiness can only be found in a 'family' that is constituted on a different basis to that of the traditional family, one which breaks all the rules, and in which the central role, that of mother, is detached from the biological mother and becomes the subject of negotiation. Geoff and Jo are as much mothers at different points in the play, in this sense. The problem that the play identifies is, as Wandor suggests, that 'motherhood is thrust upon some women, and some men are denied the chance to nurture' (Wandor 1987: 42). The main action of the play, which is Jo's transition from childhood to the adult world, is largely an accommodation to motherhood.

The ending of the play sees Jo and Helen reunited, and the mutually nurturing relationship of Jo and Geoff disrupted. The play, therefore, reinstates the biological mother/daughter relationship as the central one, completing the circle. Wandor sees this as the triumph of 'the old values, however dislocated' (Wandor 1987: 42). Lovell, however, places the relationship in two different contexts, seeing it as an alternative to both the mother/son relationship that was central to *The Uses of Literacy*, and to the father/child relationship that is 'at the centre of one of the most powerful interpretative devices of our culture, Freud's "family romance"' (Lovell 1990: 375). The parallels are useful; the play was performed a year after the appearance of Hoggart's book, and was received into a critical context that was partially shaped by it, as we have seen. And the exploration of the mother/daughter relationship – painful, ambivalent and full of rage though it may be in this instance – can be seen as a crucial story that has a central place in the development of women's writing.

Each His Own Wilderness

A play that can be usefully compared with *A Taste of Honey* is Doris Lessing's *Each His Own Wilderness* (1958). The play is ostensibly about the possibilities for political action in post-war Britain and presents a critical view of mid-fifties a-politicism. However, this theme is anchored by another, which redefines the political at the level of gender and sexuality. The action of the play is contemporary, and follows a familiar Ibsenite pattern. The events of the narrative occur over a two-day period and centre on a family party in the home of the Bolton family. The action concerns the crisis in the relationship between Myra Bolton and her son Tony (a crisis which also resonates for each of them individually, and which has broader significance). The generational opposition that is signalled here represents two contrasting attitudes to 'commitment' (Myra is politically active, a figure from a pre-war generation, whilst Tony is militantly unengaged). It is also an opposition between male and female, between mother and son. In these terms, the domestic is not simply a backdrop to the action, or a signifier of conservative 'ordinariness', but rather the main battleground, on which sexual and gender identities are struggled over in the play. Like *A Taste of Honey, Wilderness* sets its action in domestic interiors, but challenges expectations about what is appropriate activity within them.

There is little that is conventional about the Boltons' home. The action opens in the Hall, which is described in the following terms:

> Everything is extremely untidy; there are files, piles of newspapers ... posters lying about inscribed BAN THE BOMB, WE WANT LIFE NOT DEATH etc. A typewriter on the floor. The radio is playing tea-room music behind the war-noises from the tape-recorder.
>
> (Lessing 1959: 13)

The domestic space is, therefore, politicised. Furthermore, attitudes towards the domestic are at the centre of the significant oppositions and reversals of the play, in the sense that it is the son, Tony, rather than the mother, Myra, who assumes conventionally 'female' attitudes towards the home. Myra is untidy (we first see her looking 'slovenly') and undomesticated, uncomfortable about possessions and money, and wears trousers; Tony is obsessively neat, and attacks his mother for her tolerance of domestic squalor. Myra wants to sell the house; Tony wishes to remain in it. As Myra urges him to assume a more active male role, Tony becomes progressively more childlike, 'making machine-gun noises like a small boy' at one point. These oppositions are extended into the sexual sphere, for Myra is sexually active, whereas Tony appears a-sexual (despite a thwarted oedipal relationship with Myra's closest friend, who is also of her generation, and who, also like Myra, refuses to be a 'mother' to him). Most of the male characters in the play are present, past or would-be lovers of Myra's; sometimes this seems transgressive as well, as one of them, Sandy, is of comparable age to Tony.

The issues of the play, therefore, are both 'personal' and 'political', to do with the possibilities of political action on the one hand, and the way that these are rooted in personal, and especially gender identities on the other. Neither commitment nor a stable sexual identity is easily won, however, and the play explores the difficulties of achieving them both, and the contradictions that the struggle sometimes entails. It is possible to read the ending of the play, in which Myra walks out, leaving Tony to a member of his own generation, Rosemary, as an acceptance that it is impossible to be both a mother and pursue an independent life; Tony blames her for refusing to be a 'proper' mother, whilst Myra realises that, despite all her political activity, her priorities have been determined with reference to him. 'You may not think so', she tells him at the end of the play 'but the way I've lived, what I've done, my whole life has been governed by your needs' (Lessing 1959: 93). This level of the play's interests, though it is played out on familiar domestic territory, is not easily recoupable within the main concerns of late-fifties theatre, but then Lessing's own history gave her a particular viewpoint on contemporary debates. On the one hand, she was partly a figure from an earlier generation, whose political commitment did not evaporate in the early fifties as faith in communism collapsed and the contours of the Cold War hardened, and this position is represented in Myra. On the other, her subsequent writing became important for an emerging women's movement in the 1970s, where questions of the relationship between personal and political identities were framed in a different way. The kinds of issues that were later to emerge – and the consciousness that working them through gave rise to – are prefigured in *Wilderness*, yet have little resonance in the fifties. The play received one performance in a Sunday night production without decor at the Royal Court in 1959. Showing 'how things really are' may have been important to the realism of the New Wave, but the 'real' at this point had no space for a feminist interpretation of the politics of gender.

4

'BEYOND NATURALISM PURE'

Realism, naturalism and the New Wave

Stuart Hall, looking back at the new drama from the vantage point of 1961 in an article for *Encore* entitled 'Beyond Naturalism Pure', observed that 'the crude thesis is that what we have managed to do best is either a kind of pastiche (e.g. *The Hostage*) or a specially British brand of naturalism'. But this, he went on to argue, was not really an adequate summary of what was actually a much more complex picture: 'the pattern was never so clear-cut as the "kitchen-sink" school of critics would have had us imagine' and the decisive trend in contemporary theatre was that which evinced a movement 'beyond naturalism pure' (Hall 1970: 213). Hall's argument is important, not least because it challenged the idea of a single dominant methodology. In doing so, it also reproduced some of the confusions over the terminology – especially over naturalism itself – in a way that is symptomatic of the period.

We have used the term 'realism' in the analysis so far, but the kind of drama/theatre to which we have been referring has also been termed 'naturalism'. Hall outlined a variety of characteristics of the naturalist tradition, linking it to social extension and a radical politics along lines that are by now familiar: 'the desire to recreate working-class life, the preoccupation with humanist values and an interest in the attack upon the Establishment values through social criticism' (Hall 1970: 213). However, when Hall came to discuss the plays themselves, he drew on a sense of naturalism as an un-mediated transcription of reality to argue that Shelagh Delaney's *Lion in Love* was one of the few truly naturalist plays in the period. 'It was almost as if [the play] could be seen going on outside the window any time you chose to look', he observed. 'If you left at the end of the second act, you could be sure it would be there when you returned' (Hall 1970: 214). These two uses of naturalism are not identical, and the unconscious slippage between them is an indication that, like realism, naturalism was (and is) a term that has no fixed definition, yet is used freely and confidently in ways that are nonetheless confusing and contradictory. It is worth attempting to unravel some of the connections between these two terms, not only for the sake of theoretical clarity, but also because it is revealing of some of the central intentions underpinning certain methodological and critical developments in the new drama/theatre.

NATURALISM AND REALISM

In one usage, naturalism is virtually synonymous with realism. As Furst and Skrine have observed, naturalism 'was tied to the apron-strings of "Realism" from its first appearance' (Furst and Skrine 1971: 5). Even Emile Zola, one of the earliest and most vociferous champions of naturalism, often used the terms interchangeably. However, there was a strong sense amongst the protagonists of the New Wave that naturalism and realism were distinct, representing two impulses, if not two formal projects. The bases for the distinctions were not always clear or consistent, but within them, realism became identified with the new, contemporary, socially extended drama and theatre that we have been examining – or rather, it described the 'content' of that theatre, and the critical attitude towards contemporary society that informed it. Naturalism was connected to questions of method and used to describe the general mimetic tradition as a whole, the ambition towards veri-similitude that constituted part of the historical development of realism, as we noted in the previous chapter. This was most noticeable when it was theatrical representation, rather than dra-matic or literary form, that was being discussed. Naturalism has become, in much critical debate, a shorthand for a 'photographic' approach to theatre, one which attempts to construct a plausible illusion of social reality in all its outward forms, and does so across the entire means of theatrical communication (light, sound, *mise-en-scène*, acting). As such it is judged to be 'indiscriminate' and 'descriptive' in its all-inclusiveness, recording surface appearances, linked to a documentary and sociological impulse and generally accorded a low status.

In fact, the movement 'beyond' naturalism was also articulated as a clear rejection of naturalism as a particular tradition of theatrical practice – and this extended to directors and critics as well as writers. We need only to look at *Encore*'s main interests to get a sense of this. 'Vital theatre' was concerned with new audiences and a more diverse social experience in the theatre, but this was accompanied by a strong sense that these objectives would not be achieved by recourse to naturalism – this despite the fact that several of the central texts in the period have a clear relationship to the realist/naturalist tradition. *Encore* gave considerable space to the discussion of practitioners – theorists, writers and directors – who were associated with the main contemporary alternatives to naturalist theatre practice as it was understood; Brecht, for example, and other continental directors such as Planchon and Vilar, who could be seen as anti-naturalist in their approach to questions of theatrical form. Similarly, the writers that the magazine championed, John Arden for example, were frequently those at some distance from naturalism. The two figures most often regarded as the midwives of the new theatre, George Devine and Joan Littlewood, were both intellectually indebted to non- or anti-naturalist theatre, Devine to Copeau, Michel St Denis and the French tradition (see Wardle 1984), and Littlewood to a variety of European traditions.

In the post-war context, naturalism was, in one sense, simply a shorthand for the practices of the pre-1956 theatre, the chosen form of the directors, dramatists and critics associated with it. To reject 'naturalism' was to reject the creaky plots, artificially manipulated climaxes, the box-sets and lack of 'theatricality' that scarred the old theatre in the eyes of the new. There are social as well as formal characteristics at play here; the assault on 'Loamshire' was an assault on the social basis of the dominant genres. In this way naturalism was a term that focused the problems of an inherited tradition, and the assault on it was connected to the attempt to alter a theatre culture that was perceived to be institutionally and socially, as well as aesthetically, irrelevant.

The attack on naturalism was clearly a rejection of the tendency to equate the plays so described with documentary and unmediated transcription. Charles Marowitz defined naturalism in his 'Cynic's Glossary' as 'Like when the guy talks like everyone else like' (Marowitz 1961: 32) – a definition that probably owes as much to the new 'anti-theatrical' lower-class realism of Marlon Brando and contemporary American cinema as it does to British naturalism. Arnold Wesker, one of the writers most associated with naturalism in the fifties, rejected the naturalist label arguing that naturalism (although he also termed it realism) 'is a contradiction in terms, it doesn't exist, it's an impossibility, because reality is quite obviously every minute detail' (Leeming 1985: 50). Naturalism was, as a result, opposed to 'art', which was selective, transforming and interpreting the raw material of reality. Barry Reckford, in the introduction to his play *Skyvvers* (1963), went further, and juxtaposed not naturalism and art, but naturalism and realism, attaching the selective and transformative functions to the latter;

> naturalism . . . is the capturing of social reality. . . . Naturalistic speech is ordinary speech which is commonplace. Realistic speech sounds like ordinary speech but it has to be invented to convey an area of experience which is not on the surface.
>
> (Reckford 1963: 77)

One of the main objections to naturalism was that it marginalised questions of form and method; a theatre that asked to be measured in terms of its closeness to 'life' was successful to the degree to which it seemed 'transparent'. Naturalism, then, *suppressed theatricality*, and, given that much of the radicalism of British theatre in the fifties and sixties was an *aesthetic* radicalism, this emphasis did not find favour.

This kind of naturalism was also problematic for other reasons, for how, and to what effect, reality is represented is closely related to the claim of realism to represent 'how things really are' in a more analytical sense (as Reckford's comments suggest). The comparison with the drama of high naturalism is, once again, instructive. Strindberg (who actually used the terms to mean the opposite of their contemporary usages) railed against the dramatic method that was merely 'a simple photography which includes everything, even the speck of dust on the lens of the camera' and championed an approach that 'seeks out those points of life where the great conflicts occur, which rejoices in seeing what cannot be seen every day' (quoted in Williams 1980: 141). Chekhov protested vehemently to Stanislavsky about the latter's tendency to submerge his plays under a wealth of extraneous detail. And, by 1922, Stanislavsky was implicitly criticising his own earlier work in this defence of realism against naturalism:

> Realism in art is the method which helps to select only the typical from life. If at times we are Naturalistic in our stage

101

work, it only shows that we don't yet know enough to be able to penetrate into the historical and social essence of events and characters. We do not know how to separate the main from the secondary, and thus we bury the idea with details of the mode of life. That is my understanding of Naturalism.

(Bennedetti 1982: 12)

This is partly a question of dramatic method, but is largely a more important attempt to distinguish between two different epistemologies. The Marxist critic George Lukacs mounted a sustained attack on naturalism as part of a larger defence of realism on the grounds that the former simply represented 'the phenomenal forms' of reality, its surface appearances. Naturalism was concerned with the here and now, and with a causality that was immediate and self-evident. Realism, however, was able to see beneath 'whatever manifested itself immediately and on the surface' (Lukacs 1977: 33) to the laws that govern the inner workings of history. For Lukacs, it was the nineteenth-century novels in the tradition of critical realism – typified in the work of Tolstoy and Dickens – that offered a model for realism. Brecht, whilst rejecting Lukacs's view of the realist novel, nonetheless offered a similar critique of naturalism, noting, in *The Messingkauf Dialogues*, the limitations of 'descriptiveness' in an illuminating metaphor: 'The man who drops a pebble hasn't begun representing the laws of gravity . . . nor has the man who merely gives an exact description of its fall' (Brecht 1965: 25). Drawing on the metaphor of photography, Brecht goes on to contrast naturalism with realism:

The crux of the matter is that true realism has to do with more than just making reality recognisable in the theatre. One has to be able to see through it, too. One has to able to see the laws that decide how the processes of life develop. These laws can't be spotted by the camera.

(Brecht 1965: 27)

Brecht's antagonism towards naturalism was well known and explicitly ideological, embracing not only its epistemology but also the whole mimetic (or, as he somewhat misleadingly termed it, the Aristotelian) tradition. In doing so, Brecht opened up a way of redefining the links between naturalism and realism, between descriptiveness and analysis, and between method and intention in a decisive manner. Realism, for Brecht, 'is not only an issue for literature: it is a major political, philosophical and practical issue and must be handled and explained as such – as a matter of general human interest' (Brecht 1977: 76). Seen in these terms, realism must be conceived in terms that are 'wide and political and sovereign over all conventions' (Brecht 1977: 82); in other words, it is because realism has at its core the ambition to 'render reality to men in a form they can master' that new forms of representation are needed. Brecht summarised the position succinctly thus:

> Realism is not a mere question of form. Were we to copy the style of these realists, we would no longer be realists. . . . For time flows on, and if did not, it would be a bad prospect for those who do not sit at golden tables. Methods become exhausted; stimuli no longer work. New problems appear and demand new methods. Reality changes; in order to represent it, modes of representation must also change.
>
> (Brecht 1977: 82)

To be realist, then, might mean – and has frequently *has* meant in the twentieth century – that it is necessary to challenge the dominant theatrical and dramatic conventions associated, historically, with realism and naturalism.

REWORKING THE REALIST TRADITION FROM WITHIN: *THE ENTERTAINER, THE KITCHEN, CHIPS WITH EVERYTHING* AND *THE QUARE FELLOW*

The theatre after 1956 furnishes us with a variety of examples of plays and practices that begin to reshape – or replace – the established patterns, and this accelerates as the fifties moves into the sixties, although it follows different paths. Some writers, such as John Arden and Harold Pinter, whose early work was only initially – and only tangentially – related to social realism, need to be considered in other terms (and will be examined in a later chapter).

The lines of development are different, too, for dramatists than they are for other theatre practitioners, and it is largely the case that the movement 'beyond naturalism pure' was more apparent – and more radical – on the stage than on the page. The writers most closely associated with social realism do not so much reject the dominant conventions of realist drama as rework them from within, shifting them in apparently small, yet significant ways.

103

The impetus for change proceeded, on one level, from a recognition of one of the essential limitations of the inherited tradition. The tight narrative focus that realist plays adopted placed restrictions on their ability to represent directly the society they were trying to explore, for how much actual social reality can be *shown*, rather than simply be talked about, when the action is confined to a single location and a small group of characters? Some dramatists, such as Alun Owen, Willis Hall and Alan Plater, soon abandoned theatre for television, where the relative freedom granted by the camera to evolve new narrative patterns and move through the door of the box-set into the streets and communities that lay beyond, made the narrative limitations of naturalist theatre seem even more restrictive.

The work of individual dramatists revealed a variety of intentions. Osborne's plays seemed, after *Look Back in Anger* and *Epitaph for George Dillon*, to move effortlessly into new dramatic territory. *The Entertainer* signalled a partial move away from the single domestic interior, whilst his later plays rejected contemporary settings in favour of historical ones (*Luther, A Patriot for Me*); and *The World of Paul Slickey* was a musical; but there are continuities in this work that are partially concealed by the apparently radical break with naturalist dramatic patterns.

The Entertainer (1957) typified the shift away from a localised, domestic realism towards a more public drama, and is sometimes regarded as one of the more political plays in the decade. The political dimensions of the play lay mainly in the way it used the music-hall as a metaphor for the 'State of the Nation'. Music-hall also provided a framework for a systematic anti-naturalism in the play's theatrical languages, breaking the coherence of the fictional world, reminding its audience that they were in a theatre and acknowledging their presence by placing them in the role of the audience at one of Archie's tawdry rock 'n' roll shows. Even the central domestic scenes, which contain the thematic heart of the play, are played out against a background that makes no attempt to approximate a photographic representation of an actual social situation. Osborne specifies that 'swagging' should be used to 'break up the acting areas' and that 'Knee-high flats and a door frame will serve for a wall'. The setting, too, should be minimal: 'Furniture and props are as basic as they would be for a short sketch' (Osborne 1957b: 11–12). However, within this anti-naturalist theatrical framework, the concerns of the play connect it to those of earlier forms of naturalism; the possibilities of living a meaningful life in a social environment that is represented microcosmically in a constraining domestic situation, with the central conflicts played out largely in psychological terms. The effect of the music-hall interludes, then, was not so much to provide a metaphor for the nation as a context for the playing out of the primary emotional and psychological conflicts; when Archie Rice sings 'Why Should I Care', it is as easy to relate it to his own emotional despair as it is to the condition of England – a reading which Laurence Olivier's mesmerising performance in the central role in the 1957 Court production made more likely.

More than any other of the major dramatists of the late 1950s Arnold Wesker was considered a 'realist', writing plays that, both on the page and in the theatre, had a demonstrable affinity with the naturalist/realist tradition. Yet his plays, even in the earliest, and most 'realist' stage of his career, reveal Wesker wrestling with some of the essential problems of the form. The concept of a trilogy itself is, at one level, designed to overcome the limitations on themes and dramatic focus imposed by the three-act, single-set realist play. The action of *The Trilogy* covers twenty-three years and moves from one significant historical moment to another, from the routing of Mosley's fascists at Cable Street in 1936 to the election of Macmillan's Conservative Party in 1959. The trilogy form also allows the action to travel through different fictional locations, moving from the East End of London to rural Norfolk. In doing so it allows several narrative developments, which are nonetheless related at the level of character and theme. In addition, *The Trilogy* also overcomes the restricted viewpoint of the single protagonist by changing the central character from play to play. Interestingly, the character with the strongest autobiographical links to Wesker, Ronnie Kahn, is not in the strict sense a protagonist in any of the plays, although he is a literal presence in two of them, and a figurative presence in the third (*Roots*).

Wesker's most significant break from naturalist form came in his later plays, and has been termed 'modified naturalism' (Leeming and Trussler 1971: 40). What was modified initially was both the structure of the narratives and the location of the action, which was shifted away from the domestic and familial to other kinds of social institutions. Indeed, the movement away from the purely domestic became one of the more visible manifestations of the desire to break with the dominant forms of naturalist drama in the New Wave

105

as a whole, and proceeds from a variety of impulses, notably the intention to represent other kinds of 'reality' and admit a more developed political focus. Wesker's *The Kitchen* and *Chips with Everything*, and Brendan Behan's *The Quare Fellow* are of particular interest in this context.

The Kitchen is set within the kitchen of the Tivoli restaurant in London's West End, *Chips* within an RAF training camp for conscripts on National Service, and *The Quare Fellow* in a Dublin prison on the day and night before, and morning of, an execution. Initially, these different locations allowed both dramatists to broaden the focus of the action to include a greater range of characters. All three plays require casts that would make most professional companies blanch. *The Kitchen* contains no less than twenty-nine characters, all of whom were cast separately in the first production (doubling is not possible, given the structure of the play), whilst *Chips* requires nine conscripts and ten officers. *The Quare Fellow* lists twenty-eight characters (the first production was played with twenty-two characters, with only two actors doubling). This broadening of dramatic focus was also an attempt to avoid the limitations of the single protagonist. In fact, both the Wesker plays have strong central characters, Peter in *The Kitchen* and Pip in *Chips*, who are at the centre of dramatic interest, yet are still concerned with the situation of the larger group. Behan's play has no equivalent character (although one of the warders, Regan, appears to 'see more clearly' the issues of the play than the others). One of the major political points of all three plays is the way that human actions are structured by the institutional contexts in which they are placed, a theme that is best explored when a collective is actually represented.

These institutions are not simply backdrops to the actions and interactions of characters, but are always determining presences, defining and structuring the action; no matter what is happening between characters, work must go on in the kitchen, basic training must run its course, and the deadening routines of prison life grind remorselessly on. Indeed, the general narrative shape is determined by the situation of all the plays. The events of *The Kitchen* are contained within a single day, and are shaped by the cyclical routine of the preparation for the meal and the recovery from it; the stage directions inform us that one of the first tasks to be performed in the morning is the lighting of the ovens, which creates a noise that 'grows from a small to a loud ferocious roar' that will 'stay with us to the end' (Wesker 1960a: 19), acting as a constant reminder of, and metaphoric substitute for, alienated labour. The action of *Chips* is framed by the eight-week period of basic training and is structured into twenty-three scenes (itself a break from the familiar act–scene structure of Wesker's earlier plays), each of which can be seen as an episode, generally structured around an action (the stealing of coal, for example) which is generated by, or in response to, the demands of the RAF. The play begins with a long speech from Corporal Hill that establishes both the overall context and the relationships of power, of leaders and led, that will operate in it, and the play concludes with the passing-out parade. The main events in the narrative (for example Pip's refusal to engage in bayonet practice, which precipitates the central crisis of the play) similarly originate in the activities of the camp. The action of *The Quare Fellow* develops over twenty-four hours and is shaped by the preparations for the hanging seen from the viewpoint of both warders and prisoners. The quare fellow of the title, the prisoner awaiting death, is never seen. The larger part of the action follows from the interaction of groups of characters in public spaces engaged in routine activities; rarely are only one or two characters left on-stage, and even when they are, the presence of the others – especially the prisoners – is constantly felt through off-stage song and comment.

The fictional worlds of naturalism are essentially metonymic; that is, they represent a wider social reality by substituting something contiguent to it. They are also, to use another linguistic term that has entered theatre semiotics, synecdochal; that is they represent the 'part standing in for the whole', a selected instance of a wider social reality, and this is one of the principal ways in which naturalist plays overcome the limitations of space and dramatic focus. Both the Wesker plays draw attention to this function, often extending it. The kitchen was perceived not only as a metonym or synecdoche for other kitchens, but also as a metaphor for society at large. 'Mr. Wesker begins to imply' wrote Al Alvarez in the *New Statesman*, 'that the kitchen is not just a place of work, it is the whole condition of life, society, fate, what you will' (Alvarez 1959: 304). This is a reading that the play encouraged: as one character says, 'The world is filled with kitchens – only some they call offices and some they call factories' (Wesker 1960a: 43), and the same point could also be made of the training camp. Both metonymic and metaphoric functions are most clearly illustrated in the power relationships that each play explores. In *The Kitchen*, the distinctions between different kinds of chef, and between the chefs and the waitresses, is clear – indeed, Wesker draws attention to it in detailed explanatory notes that focus on the precise function of each character in relation to the governing hierarchy. These power relationships are particularly apparent in *Chips*, where they are on the surface and can be explored without breaking the fictional framework; the basic actions of the play – the parade, bayonet practice, even the Christmas party – reveal them in stark form.

The nature of the power relationships and how they operate is also the subject of the interviews between the upper-class protagonist, Pip, and the Pilot Officer, where the logic of a class power based on a patronising tolerance that glosses a naked control, is made clear. 'We listen but we do not hear', says the Pilot Officer in Scene Seven; 'we befriend but do not touch you, we applaud but do not act – to tolerate is to ignore' (Wesker 1990: 59). The political project of the play, then, is to use the specific location of the training camp – and of the armed forces – to provide an object lesson in the exercise of power. Wesker put it thus:

> Chips is a warning. It says . . . to the ruling class: you can no longer kid us. We know the way it happens. And to those who are ruled: look boys, this is the way it happens, and this is the way it will end if you continue not to recognise that you are very sweetly but very definitely being put in your place.
>
> (Leeming 1985: 25)

The terms in which Wesker's warnings were registered in the plays drew a certain amount of criticism from his contemporaries, which revealed not only an unease about his cultural and social positions, but also a perception of the problems that arise when forms of naturalism are allied to the realist ambition to comment directly upon, or analyse, society. This criticism has been formulated in different ways, but generally perceives an imbalance between 'character' and 'argument'. Albert Hunt noted a tension in Wesker's plays between 'faithful' representation of a particular social milieu and an over-arching set of ideas, too often set in the plays as unreconstructed authorial viewpoint. 'Roots is held in shape by the detailed observation of Norfolk life', he argued – that is, its 'opinion' is contained by its 'realism' – 'but isn't there less attention and more general argument in Jerusalem?' (Hunt 1961a: 12). Stuart Hall echoed the criticism, noting that 'Wesker . . . has had to do battle with his impulse to shift the naturalistic form, with which he is most comfortable, in the direction of "themes" and "ideas", with which he is less at home' (Hall 1970: 215). The problem is, in one sense, a formal one, in that it is perceived at the point where the desire to debate the situation ruptures the surface verisimilitude, where there is a conflict between the naturalist objective to depict a way of life and the realist objective to analyse it.

The Quare Fellow, however, adopts a rather different strategy. Whereas Wesker draws attention to the nature of the themes he is exploring and articulates a position on those themes through a particular character, Behan adopts a more observational stance, refusing to put into speech what the action should either make clear, or leave ambiguous. In some ways, the play was almost classically naturalist, maintaining the kind of distance from the situation, issues and characters that was associated with earlier representations of the underclass. This latter characteristic was particularly important, for, as Lovell has noted, the point of view in Zolaesque naturalism is of 'the uninvolved spectator' where the characters become the 'objects of observation rather than figures of identification' (Lovell 1980: 72), and this denied audiences both a privileged view of the events and a consistent focus for empathy. However, within this general approach, in which the essential grimness of the subject matter was accentuated by an obsessively detailed and anti-rhetorical acting style, the play also contains a consistent black humour that is located mainly in the comic interplay of the characters.

This combination of mordant humour and a serious subject matter is present in Behan's other play for Theatre Workshop, *The Hostage*; indeed it is a characteristic of many of the Workshop's productions at this time. In *The Quare Fellow*, humour is also a structural device, part of a general intention to distance the audience from the action and the basic situation, which both avoids the expected responses and denies the obvious channels of sympathy. There is no attempt, for example, to gain sympathy for the murderer, and no obvious device to allow the audience an emotional release. As one critic put it, 'There are no tears in the story, no complaints, no visible agonies; nor is there even suspense, since we know from the outset that there will be no reprieve' (Tynan 1984: 180). Instead, the prisoner's last walk to the gallows is narrated by a convict as if it were a commentary on the Grand

National; and the final image is of a group of prisoners squabbling over the dead man's effects above his grave. *The Quare Fellow* is clearly concerned with the issue of capital punishment, and in particular its effects on the rest of society. Yet society is not an abstract generalisation in the play, but a particular social institution, and the issues are not debated, but rather embedded in the routines and practices of the prison itself. The result is that it is not so much the quare fellow himself that is the focus of narrative interest, but the effects of judicial murder on the other inmates – and this includes warders and governor, as well as prisoners. It is, above all, an institutional process that is delineated in the play.

NATURALISM AND POETIC REALISM AT THE ROYAL COURT

We noted earlier that it was often in performance that the conventions of naturalist theatrical and dramatic practice were most obviously challenged, and this was true not only of Littlewood's productions at Theatre Workshop but also, perhaps ironically, at the temple of social realism, the Royal Court. As we have already seen, George Devine was as keen to promote theatre that was theatrically exciting and formally innovative as he was theatre that was socially relevant (within broad terms), and to do both without retreating into an avant garde ghetto. As a result, the repertoire of the Court was never, even in the late fifties, as dominated by social realism as is sometimes thought to be the case (in fact, although the Court staged all of Wesker's plays at this time, it did so despite persistent reservations on the part of both Devine and Richardson – see Wesker 1985: 5).

The Court's relationship to the realist project and naturalist stage practice was complex, and several tendencies were apparent, depending on the particular combination of director and designer that pertained in each production. Despite the widespread rejection of theatrical naturalism, productions at the Court could still be fundamentally naturalist, even when this produced a performance style that not only did not match the conventions of the play text, but contributed to a radical misreading of it. John Arden's *Live Like Pigs*, for example, was given a production (in 1958) that was predominantly naturalist in conception, locating it within a context of Working-Class Realism. This was not entirely fanciful, as the play bears some of the birthmarks of social realism, being contemporary in its theme and location (indeed, it was based on a real event that had occurred in Barnsley some years earlier), set in a lower-class milieu, and dealing with events and situations that could be read in terms of working-class 'squalor'. The set was designed by Alan Tagg, who had also designed *Look Back*, and consisted of an entire house in section. In his introductory note to the Penguin edition of the play, Arden writes that this 'had the effect of slowing down the action considerably' (Arden 1969: 102). His own preferences were for a more schematic layout: 'Distinctions between upstairs and downstairs can be made quite easily by arranging the upstairs rooms behind or beside the downstairs ones with only a foot or so difference in level' (Arden 1969: 102).

In fact, *Live Like Pigs* was written in a style that owed a lot to forms of popular theatre. Albert Hunt has convincingly argued that the play is patterned on the routines of music-hall, with an approach to characterisation that is likewise broad and anti-naturalistic (Hunt 1974). Little of this appeared in the first production, however. For example, ballads were used as an introduction to each scene. Devine, according to Arden, put the ballad singer, A.L. Lloyd, on-stage between the scenes to be 'quickly taken off again so that no-one was really clear whether he was in the action or out of it' (Arden 1969: 102). The production also failed to locate the music-hall structures in the play, and this encouraged a more conventional approach to the acting. In his introduction to the play, Arden revealed that he was alarmed by the production and the critical reaction to it, and felt the need to explain the position the play adopts. 'I was more concerned', he wrote, 'with the "poetic" rather than the "journalistic" structure of the play. The reception of the production at the Royal Court seemed to indicate that I had mis-calculated' (Arden 1969: 101).

Elsewhere in the repertoire of the Court, a tendency to rework or move out from naturalism can be found in the directing of Lindsay Anderson and John Dexter and in the designs of Jocelyn Herbert. Herbert designed all of Wesker's plays in this period, including all three parts of the *Trilogy*, and adopted, for these archetypically social realist plays, an approach that was resolutely anti-naturalist. *Roots*, for example, was set in the middle of an empty stage, the walls of the cottage only half constructed and open to the cyclorama at the rear of the theatre, onto which were projected scenes of the countryside. Projections were used for all three productions (in *Chicken Soup with Barley*, street scenes were projected

111

above the main playing space), and no attempt was made to construct a 'photographically' realised setting (see Herbert and Courtney 1993).

Anderson was a central figure in delineating an approach to what has been called (initially by Albert Hunt in *Encore*) 'poetic realism' (Hunt 1961b: 25). Although the term itself did not have the kind of currency that, say, vital theatre had, it nevertheless indicated both an ambition and a tension in certain productions and plays: Herbert described her design for *Roots* as 'my first attempt at poetic realism for a naturalist play' (Herbert and Courtney 1993: 32). The idea of poetic realism is one which attempted to overcome the 'descriptiveness' that attached to contemporary uses of naturalism and which focused on plays in performance. Hunt's article is also interesting in that he sees contemporary film as being an important influence, especially via the influence of Lindsay Anderson. The idea that realism could be 'poeticised' was one that had a particular resonance in British cinema in the mid to late fifties and early sixties, and Anderson was a key figure, in this as in much else.

During this period, Anderson was both a director at the Royal Court and, in the mid-fifties, a prominent figure in the Free Cinema documentary film movement (see Chapter 6 for a fuller discussion). Free Cinema documentaries owed more to Italian neo-realism and European art cinema than they did to the British documentary tradition (as represented by John Grierson). The emphasis of the film-makers (several of whom, like Anderson, went into print to expand on the rationale behind the films) was not only on contemporaryness of subject matter but also on their own personal vision and artistic 'style': 'Independent, poetic and personal – these may be defined as the necessary characteristics of the genre' (Hill 1986: 129). This parallels much of Anderson's theatre work at the Court, which, although it was clearly realist, could be seen as poetic as well. The culmination of this strand of both Anderson's and the Court's work was probably in the late 1960s, particularly in his productions of David Storey's plays (*The Dressing-Room* and *The Contractor*, for example) and in Peter Gill's productions of D.H. Lawrence's plays. Gaskell has written of this period of the Court's work:

> The Lawrence plays, with their detailed observation of working-class life, are the epitome of what would usually be called naturalism but in his productions Peter Gill had shown

us the underlying rituals that make up that life. The stage was full of images composed of the simplest tasks . . . Many of the Court's plays used a realistic sequence of people working to create metaphors of society.

(Gaskell 1988: 111–12)

The distinction here between 'detailed observation' and the composition of 'images' that could be read as metaphors indicated what the 'poetic' in poetic realism meant. Poetic meant, on the one hand, the crystallising of meaning in a moment in the dramatic action, in terms that both appealed to a sense of observed reality but also – and more importantly – revealed, in Strindberg's terms, what could not necessarily be seen every day. On the other hand, poetic also meant drawing attention to the form of the production, the aesthetic strategies employed – in particular, the use of actors as part of the creation of a *mise-en-scène* that was aware of its own 'constructedness'; this was to be contrasted with the main form of realism (invariably termed naturalism) that sought to hide its artifice, and maintain the appearance of a seamless and observed reality. In the cinema this poetic quality could be most readily seen in the work of the director and the cinematographer: in the theatre it was likewise evident in the work of the director and the designer.

A particularly good example of the way that this kind of 'poetic' quality was registered in the systems of a performance can be found in John Dexter's production of Wesker's *The Kitchen*. Produced initially on a Sunday night without decor in September 1959, the play was substantially extended and opened in June 1961 at the Belgrade Theatre, Coventry (by the English Stage Company), and then transferred later that same month to the Court. Wesker was present throughout rehearsals.

The Kitchen was in some ways already a problematical naturalistic play, as we have seen, and the terms in which it could be seen as 'modified' naturalism lay not only in the self-consciousness of the central metaphor of the kitchen, but also in Wesker's stage directions; 'it must be understood', he wrote, 'that at no time is food ever used . . . the waitresses will carry empty dishes and the cooks will mime their cooking' (Wesker 1960a: 14). This instruction was obeyed in Dexter's production, and is an indicator of the general approach that was adopted. Jocelyn Herbert's set similarly drew attention to itself as a 'set' as well as denoting a 'kitchen':

we used the bare stage for the first time with the back wall and

113

all the pipes showing . . . it was also the first time we put the
lighting-rig above the set and allowed everything to be seen.
. . . For the first Sunday performance we used trestle tables for
the stoves and we put tins on top of them so they made the
right noise. The boxes set round the stoves created a passage
way; the cook stood in between the boxes and the stoves, and
the waitresses came round outside the boxes with their orders.
I remember arriving that Sunday and thinking that the tables
for the salads and the sweets should be white, so I went home
and got my sheets and pinned them round. We never changed
the main idea [for the full production] we just made it better.

(Herbert and Courtney 1993: 38)

The colour scheme was carried over into the design for the
costumes as well, which were uniformly black and white. This
created a visual context, in which the actors were mobilised in ways
that were simultaneously 'realistic' (the actions were those indicated by the text and were plausible within the fictional situation)
and 'stylised' (a favourite word in the reviews, indicating that the
qualities of the movements themselves were emphasised). As one
critic put it: 'John Dexter . . . has convinced us that we are watching
absolute naturalism while imposing on his almost universally bril-
liant cast of 30 a highly individual formalism' (Tschudin 1972: 174).

This 'aestheticising' of an essential realism in the production style
drew a generally warm critical response. Tschudin has noted that a
recurrent adjective referring to the organisation of the actors was
'balletic': hence 'Dexter's production has an almost balletic control
over the swirling movement'; and 'highly commendable was the
manner in which . . . Dexter kept the huge kitchen staff weaving in
and out like busy ants in a sort of frenzied ballet'. As another
reviewer commented, this 'almost . . . balletic ritual' was the means
by which 'Dexter's production emphasised the symbolic elements
in the play' (Tschudin 1972: 177). The sections of the production
being referred to here are the lunchtime rush, where the meals
were served at great speed to an off-stage audience, and the
'interlude' of relative peace that followed it. These were also the
moments whose shape and effects were decided in the rehearsal
process itself, and over which Dexter had the most influence and
direct control. The general movement pattern of the rush is
indicated in the text through the dialogue, yet it is clearly a sequence
that needs to be realised in theatrical terms for its full effect. And

Wesker has said that the interlude was written at Dexter's suggestion because 'some quiet period was necessary between the morning service and the afternoon service' (Tschudin 1972: 176).

Poetic realism of this sort was clearly a way of challenging the dominant languages of naturalist performance, and one that met with general approval. The gains appeared to be self-evident and arose out of the way that the working practices at the Court at this time allowed writers to form close links with particular directors, which in turn allowed the text to be modified in rehearsal and the production to be developed in conjunction with the author. All of Wesker's plays at the Court were directed by John Dexter. A potential problem, however – and it was a problem that has been noted in relation to New Wave films especially – is that the aestheticising of a situation or action could mask its significance – that the 'poetry' could contradict the 'realism'. It is arguable that part of the theatrical force and thematic resonance of *The Kitchen* lies in the fact that the routines of the kitchen are oppressive and inhuman. In this sense, the play is almost classically naturalist in its delineation of an environment that determines and shapes the lives of those that inhabit it. These forces are registered, as with *Roots*, not only in the set itself but also in the activities that are meticulously played out within it, detailed in carefully realistic terms. This sense of realist detail is particularly important if the climax of the play, the severing of the gas pipe, is to have more than a 'theatrical' meaning. Peter's assault on the pipe is not only an arresting theatrical device but also an ultimately futile gesture; it is integral to the pessimism of the play, a pessimism that has its origins in the naturalist room-as-trap, that it should be read not as a solution to the problems that the play explores, but as a symptom of them. Some critics found the ending, in Tynan's words, 'melodramatic and deplorably unmotivated' (Tynan 1984: 180). This may have been because the central fact of alienating physical labour had been blurred by the choreography – that the play had become, in fact, less about work than about the work of actors.

REALISM AGAINST NATURALISM: THE CASE OF TELEVISION

Social realism took different paths as it entered television. There was no real proliferation of televised versions of stage successes (this kind of relationship between the original theatre text and the new media was not nearly as important as it was for New Wave cinema). However, television successfully lured writers from the theatre, some of whom, like Pinter (whose *A Night Out* was transmitted in 1960), continued to work in both media. Others, such as Alun Owen, Clive Exton and Alan Plater, transferred almost entirely to television, generating plays specifically for the new medium, which shared the realist agenda – the concern with contemporary society and social extension, in particular. Several new plays – Owen's *Lena Oh My Lena*, for example – were very much on the domestic terrain of northern Working-Class Realism.

Theatre writers, particularly new writers, were able to find work on the television networks, because much television drama continued to think of itself in terms of theatre (the 'single play' was the form of drama that often attracted the most kudos), and this found institutional expression in both the commercial network and the BBC. ATV's *Armchair Theatre*, under the influence of its Canadian head of drama, Sidney Newman, provided a weekly series of single plays (which included the work of Pinter and Owen). After Newman moved to the BBC in 1963, *The Wednesday Play*, also organised around weekly, one-off plays, continued and developed the process, bringing a number of seminal texts to the small screen during the six years of its run (1964–1970), including *Cathy Come Home* (Loach, Garnett and Seabrook 1966). The success of these initiatives (audiences were measured in millions, and the plays often had a critical impact that went beyond this) demonstrated the inter-relationship of institutional and political/aesthetic factors. Newman gave his producers and directors considerable freedom to generate and make projects, justifying the policy in terms that were essentially realist; 'I said I want you to concentrate on the turning points of English society', he once remarked of the instructions he gave his producers at the BBC. 'I gave them the money and left them alone. And so *Cathy Come Home* and *Up the Junction* – all those real breakthroughs' (quoted Gardner and Wyver 1986: 47).

It is not surprising that, given the inherited dependence of the new, fledgling television drama on the theatre, that the debates around aesthetic form should be couched in terms that are similar to those we have already encountered, and which often centre on 'naturalism'. It is often argued that naturalism is the habitual mode of television drama (and even film), by which is usually meant a kind of scenic literalism, a use of location to authenticate the 'reality' depicted, or the use (over-use, as 'naturalist' is generally a term of abuse) of studio shooting. Up until the early 1960s television drama was naturalist – and, indeed, 'theatrical' – in a more specific sense for a number of reasons, not the least of which were technological constraints, which ensured that it was impossible radically to open up the inherited forms of single-set naturalist drama. Until the early to mid-sixties, television drama went out live and was studio-bound for a range of aesthetic and technical/economic reasons. On the one hand, the lack of a cheap and effective means of editing onto tape meant that pre-recorded material (except when it could be incorporated into a 'live' transmission) and the use of retakes were all but impossible within the financial constraints imposed by the television companies (see Laing 1986). On the other, there was a strong feeling that live drama was aesthetically superior in terms of its 'look' and because it guaranteed a continuity within the actor's performance (and was contrasted favourably with film, where the reliance on takes, retakes and out-of-sequence shooting was said to make the actor's work much harder and less successful). These constraints were both the cause and effect of the deep-rooted reliance on single-set naturalist drama.

The situation began to change in the early sixties when the use of 16 mm film and cheap videotape made it possible to both pre-record and edit material relatively cheaply and – more important – to free writer and director from the constraints of the studio. The result was that it became possible to reposition television drama in relation to both film and documentary, with the consequence that developments in the forms and methods of television drama (as well as its intentions) were largely away from 'naturalism' as it was understood, whilst maintaining a realist impulse, and this can be tracked along several paths.

Social realism was important to the new forms that were originated on television, the drama series and the continuous serial. *Coronation Street*, which has been a constant presence on British television since its first appearance in 1960, was conceived in relation to a specifically Hoggartian agenda, as we saw earlier. Its 'realism' was the subject of considerable comment. It was clearly on the terrain of social realist texts in other media, providing, as Marion Jordan has noted, 'narratives of personal events' peopled by characters who were 'working-class or of the classes immediately visible to the working-classes . . . and . . . credibly accounted for in terms of the ordinariness of their homes, families, friends' within a northern, urban location that was 'the present'. It was also shot in a style that did not foreground its own artifice, but seemed an 'unmediated, unprejudiced and complete view of reality' (Jordan 1981: 28) – i.e. naturalist.

Coronation Street – and the continuous serial generally – offered the possibility of solving some of the problems associated with the dominant forms of realism/naturalism. Although very much on the domestic terrain of all forms of social realism in the period, *Coronation Street* had the potential to take advantage of the more fluid narrative structures that television (even studio-based television) permitted; the interiors of several domestic spaces were represented, as well as the street and public spaces, such as the Rover's Return, with the action cutting between them. Also, the form of the continuous serial allowed no 'closure', no imposed or false 'climax', to the narrative; the life of the community could proceed in a story that, like 'reality' rather than art, had no final resolution. Yet the serial was always conceived as 'entertainment' as well as a 'realistic' portrayal of the North, and *Coronation Street* has always had a strain of comedy running through it focused largely around the idiosyncrasies of particular character types. Of the original cast, both Pat Phoenix, who played Elsie Tanner, and Violet Carson, who played Mrs Sharples, were from the music-halls rather than from the legitimate theatre.

That the Street itself (and the community of which it was an indexical sign) was the subject of the serial, was both a guarantee of its authenticity as a piece of contemporary social realism (it was about 'society' and a culture focused at the level of the everyday) and a stimulus to debate about what 'community' might mean in affluent Britain. Tony Warren, the serial originator, defined its appeal in terms that echoed the anthropological framework common elsewhere: *Coronation Street* provided a window on 'A fascinating freemasonry, a volume of unwritten rules. These are the driving forces behind life in a working-class street in the North of England' (Warren 1969: 58). Derek Hill, however, suggested that the appeal of the serial was not so much that it reflected the here-and-now of working-class social existence but that it embodied an 'almost nostalgic sense of group interdependence . . . at a time when community feeling is rapidly disappearing' (quoted Laing 1986: 188).

Coronation Street's version of working-class culture could be read, like Hoggart's, as nostalgic and sentimental. Sigal, himself a commentator on the cultural mores of the contemporary working-class, expressed this forcefully: '*Coronation Street* is a lie from start to finish if it is supposed to represent any recognisable aspect of life.' It was also a representation that suppressed internal class divisions ('It is false in its avoidance of class tensions . . . that I know . . . to be alive between shop-keepers and residents in the north' (Sigal 1962: 63)) and which refused to recognise the increased prosperity that was such a factor in many accounts of the post-war working-class. In the seventies, the serial was also criticised for its lack of a specifically political dimension and its refusal to dramatise the world of work – criticisms that were also levelled at *The Uses of Literacy* and New Wave cinema. In the eighties, *Coronation Street* was rescued by a generation of critics more alert to gender politics for the seriousness with which it represents women's concerns (see Dyer *et al.* 1981).

The early episodes of *Coronation Street* were bound entirely by the Street itself; no such inhibition affected the other major carrier of social realism amongst the series/serials, *Z Cars*. Like *Coronation Street*, *Z Cars*, set in Liverpool, was a considerable popular success, and, from its inception, was discussed largely in terms of its relationship to ideas of realism. The first episodes were shot in 1961 (and screened in 1962), at the same time (and in the same geographical area) that *A Kind of Loving* was being filmed, and the series could readily be seen in relation to 'authentic' depictions of the northern working-class. *Z Cars* was not, however, limited by the domestic and the everyday – utilising the genre of the police series precluded that. John McGrath, who along with Troy Kennedy Martin was one of the originators of the series, saw the police as a way of 'getting into a whole society . . . the series was going to be a kind of documentary about people's lives in these areas [of Liverpool] and the cops were incidental – they were the means of finding out about people's lives' (McGrath 1975: 42–3). *Z Cars* was also set against that other seminal depiction of the police, *Dixon of Dock Green*. The comparisons that were made between the two series generally favoured the realism of the former, by which was usually meant that the police were seen in a less than favourable light, depicted (in a favourite formulation) as 'real people'.

The 'realism' of *Z Cars*, however, was also connected to the way it began to break away from the dominant conventions of television drama. As in the theatre, debates about form were, for the participants, focused around the rejection of naturalism. Both Kennedy Martin and McGrath inveighed against naturalism, which

119

stood in for the inherited tradition of single-set, psychologically based theatre and mainstream (i.e. Hollywood) film. Naturalist television drama was a 'makeshift bastard born of the theatre and photographed with film techniques' (Kennedy Martin 1964: 20). The allusion to cinema was in some ways misleading, since the main features of the kind of naturalism Kennedy Martin was attacking were predominantly theatrical: the over-reliance on dialogue ('Naturalism deals with people's verbal relationships with each other'); the subservience to 'natural' time ('studio-time equals drama-time equals Greenwich Mean Time' (Kennedy Martin 1964: 20)); scenic literalism and the dominance of the studio ('we wanted to get away from box-sets and general lighting, the whole pseudo-theatrical approach to television' (McGrath 1977: 103). The result was a drama that was both aesthetically barren and, in terms of the potential for realism, crucially limiting. 'Naturalism contains everything within a closed system of relationships', argued McGrath. 'Every statement is mediated through the situation of the character speaking. . . . In terms of presenting a picture of society, it can reveal a small cluster of subjective consciousnesses, rarely anything more' (McGrath 1977: 101).

What was required was a style that freed the drama from these debilitating physical and ideological limitations. The key term for McGrath was narrative, used not with reference to theatre but rather American television and cinema, where the model was of a story that was told through incident, events, through a complexity of action and a multiplicity of locations and characters. One model was an American police series, *Highway Patrol*, which, whilst being 'cheap, nasty and American' had 'action, pace [and] narrative drive' (McGrath 1977: 103). The first series of *Z Cars* was transmitted live, utilising both film inserts and pre-recorded scenes on videotape, and its production team were granted a freedom that is rare in these more cost-conscious times (see McGrath 1977). Analysing the narrative structure of one episode in the first series, Laing noted that 'there were 83 scenes (a change of scene on average every 36 seconds) and 254 camera shots on the script' (Laing 1986: 171). McGrath linked this sense of rapid narrative movement in *Z Cars*, of a drama defined by situation and action rather than language and psychology, directly to its realism: 'We placed a conscious emphasis on narrative – society, real and recognisable [and] *in motion*. No slick tie-ups. No reassuring endings' (McGrath 1977: 104).

The issues that concerned both Martin and McGrath were not finally resolved in the series, however, and institutional and formal pressures combined to draw *Z Cars* back onto more familiar territory; 'The series rapidly became a lot of naturalistic dramas about how difficult is the policeman's lot' (McGrath 1977: 104). The dominance of characters, of 'personalities' followed through time, which has become one of the chief characteristics of drama series and the continuous serial (and *Z Cars* had aspects of both), is one of the more contentious issues when questions of realism are being considered, and an indication that one aspect, at least, of the inherited naturalist theatre tradition was remarkably persistent.

The movement beyond studio-based drama can also be found in the development of the single play. On the one hand, it is possible to trace a kind of aesthetic radicalism in the works of such writers as Dennis Potter and David Mercer, which, although often contemporary in their concerns, became increasingly distanced from both the formal and social characteristics of social realism. *Where the Difference Begins . . .* (1961), for example, the first part of David Mercer's trilogy *Generations*, is set in the house of a Yorkshire railwayman, and focuses on the by now familiar themes of class and class-dislocation across generations; the final part, *The Birth of a Private Man* (1963) moves between Yorkshire, London, Berlin and Warsaw and incorporates documentary footage. On the other hand, one singular and influential development has been the bringing together of documentary and fiction techniques in what is now generally called documentary drama, which is of particular interest here.

Documentary in this context is both a kind of 'reality status', a way of signifying a particular, and 'objective', relationship between a text and social reality (in the way that the term documentary was sometimes used in the discussion of working-class realist theatre), and a body of specific techniques derived largely from television documentary. One of the initial intentions of the originators of *Z Cars* was that it should be a semi-documentary account of the reality of police work (see McGrath 1977 and Laing 1986). A more consistent and elaborated example of the way that fiction and documentary can be combined within a realist (and explicitly political) framework can be found in the work of Ken Loach and Tony Garnett, who directed and produced a range of seminal television plays in the period, including *Cathy Come Home* (1966), written by Jeremy Sandford, *The Lump* (1967) and *The Big Flame* (1969), both scripted by Jim Allen.

Documentary enters the plays/films of Loach and Garnett largely through what John Caughie has called the 'documentary look', which is a specific set of filmic strategies ('hand-held camera, the cramped shot, natural lighting and inaudible sound') that have 'a prior association with truth and neutrality' (Caughie 1981: 343) and which create a 'system of looks which constructs the social space of the fiction, a social space which is more than simply a background, but which, in a sense, constitutes what the documentary drama wishes to be about' (Caughie 1981: 342). Documentary drama of this sort is a long way from the formal rhetoric of stage naturalism, but its objectives, which include an 'attention to the social environment and to the community' connect documentary with the ideology of naturalism. Like the naturalist fiction of Zola, documentary drama aspires towards the objective status of science: 'documentary drama seems to produce its analysis by setting in motion a dramatic experiment within the world observed' (Caughie 1981: 342).

The ideological limitations of this naturalist 'experiment' were explored in the 1970s as part of a project to define the limits and possibilities of 'progressive' texts (see MacCabe 1974). Another Loach/Garnett/Allen text, *Days of Hope*, was the centre of interest here. A proper consideration of these debates is beyond the scope of this analysis, but it is worth remarking that the criticism of naturalism (which, *pace* Brecht, was expanded to include the entire illusionist/mimetic tradition of representation) echoed that of descriptive naturalism that we encountered earlier via Lukacs, Strindberg and Stanislavsky. Naturalism and documentary drama, or the 'classic realist text', is guilty of empiricism, of being seduced by the surface of things, of assuming that reality is bound by what can be seen and immediately represented. From this perspective, the documentary look refuses to distinguish between phenomena, and whilst claiming to 'reveal' or capture the world, merely conceals it. This criticism never entirely described the complexity of the texts themselves (any more than it entirely described the operations of nineteenth-century naturalism), and it is interesting that it is another Loach/Garnett/Allen collaboration, *The Big Flame*, that is the principal example analysed by Williams in his account of the development of realism (Williams 1977) on which much of the preceding two chapters have drawn. Williams sought to rescue the realist project, as represented in its contemporary form by *The Big Flame*, from the all-embracing dismissal of realism/ naturalism that had begun to colonise cultural politics in the mid-seventies. In defending realism (in its critical rather than formal sense) Williams reminds us that possibly the most debilitating problem of naturalist/realist drama was not so much its specific methods as its 'structure of feeling'. Naturalism, even the drama of high naturalism, portrayed its characters as essentially 'trapped' by the society in which they existed: 'showing a man or woman making an effort to live a much fuller life and encountering the objective limits of a particular social order' (Williams 1979: 221). *Transforming*, or working through, these limits was not possible for either high naturalism or the New Wave.

5

REDEFINING REALISM

POPULAR THEATRE AND REALISM

Another way in which the theatrical languages of realism/natural-
ism could be contested – although it goes beyond this – was
connected to the renewed interest in popular, 'illegitimate' and
non-literary theatre forms. In some ways, 'vital theatre' was a
synonym for popular theatre. Looking back to the nineteenth
century for appropriate models, Ted Willis argued (at the *Universities and Left Review* symposium on vital theatre) that 'the only real
vitality . . . lay in the music-halls' (Willis 1959: 22), a point of view
endorsed by Devine in relation to contemporary theatre: 'My own
thought is that the use of music, song and dance in the so-called
straight theatre is the direction in which we must go' (Devine 1959:
23). *Encore*'s interest in practitioners working outside dominant
forms was often focused around those who had a relationship with
an idea of the popular – Brecht, for example, or Planchon. The
journal ran a series of articles on the subject at about the time that
the vital theatre debates were taking shape, which drew in contributions from Michel St Denis amongst others. And the influence of
popular forms on several plays in the period – on Osborne's *The
Entertainer* and *The World of Paul Slickey*, for example, and all the
plays of John Arden – has been frequently noted (see, for example,
Davison 1982 and Hunt 1974).

'Popular' is another term that, like realism, has been used in a
variety of ways, and has both specific and general meanings,
referring to both particular performance genres (music-hall, cir-
cus) and to the appeal to a broadest possible audience at a given
theatrical and historical moment. Louis James has observed that
there are, broadly speaking, four different kinds of theatre/drama
which have been termed popular:

The first, which we may call folk drama, is related to a pre-literate, rural society. It is traditional, close to ritual and the everyday life of the common people. Industrialism and the growth of cities in the nineteenth century broke up the older genre. Large theatres were built to entertain the masses, exploiting possibilities of spectacle and sensation, and the star actor. This was the area of the commercial working-class theatre, music-hall and melodrama. But the division of theatre along lines of the class of the audience was always uncertain, and with the development of film and then television we arrive at the period of mass media. In reaction to this, the radical elite created agit-prop theatre, attempting to restore drama to the people as part of the class struggle.

(James 1981: 1)

As James goes on to suggest, this schema is a problematic one, imposing a rough chronology on a diverse and overlapping history. Most of these senses of popular theatre have a presence in the late fifties and early sixties (and beyond). From this perspective, these different kinds of popular drama (with the possible exception of that produced by the radical elite) are linked by virtue of being largely 'illegitimate' – that is, they do not belong to the traditions of the literary drama, although they may intersect with it – and by an appeal to the broadest possible audience within a given historical period, whether for commercial or political reasons.

In the late 1950s, popular forms were also of interest initially because they could be used to oppose the conventions of the dominant realist/naturalist tradition. This is a challenge to the aesthetics of theatre that does not belong to the post-war period alone, but can be located as a major tendency within twentieth century drama. Davison has argued that the main line of development within serious 'legitimate' theatre (particularly in its anti-naturalist, or modernist forms) from Pirandello through Brecht to Beckett, Osborne and Pinter, has absorbed popular genres (particularly music-hall), allowing their specific languages to redefine literary conventions (Davison 1982). To those with the more general cultural ambitions of vital theatre, however, popular forms suggested a more fundamental attack on established structures. Against a naturalism that was linked to the 'old', bourgeois theatre of the West End, popular forms allowed the possibility that theatre could, once again, not only be about the working-class but also address that class in ways that were accessible to it. The popular, with its implicit suggestion of a broad, socially extended audience, was therefore seen as a way out of the impasse created by the social isolation of the theatre – hence its centrality in the vital theatre debates.

This way of viewing the popular suggested the terms in which an interest in popular genres could be related to realism. This was partly because of the charge that particular forms carried in the context. The main model of a popular theatre with a broad appeal was music-hall. The appeal of music-hall was multi-layered. On the one hand, it provided a particular performance vocabulary, a repertoire of specific 'routines' that could be used to determine an acting style (Theatre Workshop's productions provide evidence of this); on the other, it fulfilled a complex symbolic role, or roles, in the struggle to create a contemporary realist drama.

The music-hall was important because of its specific connections to an 'authentic' working-class. This linkage did not only occur in the theatre, for, as Innes has pointed out (Innes 1992: 105), a popular radio programme of 1956, *The Boy in the Gallery* (scripted by Colin MacInnes and Charles Hilton) presented a view of the halls as the authentic expression of a traditional, warm and gregarious working-class culture, much as Richard Hoggart had done in *The Uses of Literacy*. Linked frequently to the North, and appearing as a point of reference in the reviews of such central texts as *A Taste of Honey*, the music-hall had a significant place in the imagery of Working-Class Realism.

Another sense of realism is important here, as well. Realism, we should remind ourselves, has been used to denote a particular attitude towards reality, one which is concerned to explain and analyse a given society. From this point of view, as Brecht wrote, 'the terms popular art and realism become natural allies'; if it is 'in the interests of the people . . . to receive a faithful image of life from literature', he argued, then realism should be 'absolutely comprehensible and profitable to them – in other words, popular' (Brecht 1977: 80). This did not imply a simple capitulation to existing popular genres, but rather a critical appropriation of them, a reworking of forms according to the demands of the situation; it did, however, suggest that popular traditions could become a means of achieving realist objectives, could be utilised to 'show how things really are'. Brecht framed his argument within a particular Marxist aesthetic, one that was in turn shaped by a sense of the

126

urgent demands of the historical moment. A different way of arguing for the radical potential of popular forms – and one which relies on a different politics – can be found in the late fifties.

POPULAR THEATRE AND LIBERTARIANISM: THE POLITICAL AESTHETIC OF JOHN ARDEN

The political expression of left-wing libertarianism (or anarchism) was civil disobedience and the activities of the Committee of 100; one of its main aesthetic expressions was an interest in popular artistic traditions. This position was shared by many socialists as well (the line between 'socialists' and 'libertarians' being particularly fluid at this time). Looking back at this period from the late 1970s, the veteran anarchist George Woodcock noted an unexpected resurgence in the support for anarchist and libertarian ideas and arguments. This could be found in the increased readership of the journal *Anarchy*, which commented on a range of contemporary issues (particularly nuclear ones) from a position that managed to draw on the familiar tenets of anarchism without being bound by the 'old ideological disputes' (Woodcock 1979: 27). *Anarchy* was interested in cultural matters, publishing several articles on the new theatre, as well as reviews and articles by Arden and Wesker (Arden also wrote regularly for *Peace News*; see Arden 1979). It was also read by those people who had been drawn into politics by the anti-nuclear movement, and who were also one of the main audiences for the new theatre. Woodcock cites evidence from a readership survey conducted by a parallel anarchist magazine, *Freedom*, to argue that the new anarchists were predominantly professional or white-collar and young; 'the new anarchists . . . are a movement of dissident middle-class youth' (Woodcock 1979: 30), which are exactly the terms in which Thompson and others characterised the constituency of the New Left generally. The kind of left-wing libertarianism that *Anarchy*, CND and the Committee for 100 represented was, in some senses, a more radical form of the more general humanism that in the pages of *Declaration* was defined as socialism. It contained, as Woodcock argues, a strong commitment to a politics that had its roots in morality as much as economics, embodying 'a vision of society in which every relation would have moral rather than political characteristics' (Woodcock 1979: 31). It was also a philosophy that was resolutely anti-materialist, and by extension anti-affluence, seeing in such consumerist materialism the chains of a new dependency. The apex of this rejection of post-war prosperity was the counter-cultural movements that swept Europe and North America in the late 1960s, and which were similarly located amongst middle-class youth. One of the crucial elements in libertarianism is the rejection of the centralised state and a deep and instinctive distrust of systems of power and authority. This has led, on the one hand, to experiments in democratic decentralisation, to an emphasis on locally based, self-organising communities (of the type that Ghandi propounded), and, on the other hand, to a model for political activity that privileged direct action (as in the activities of the Committee of 100) rather than the representative democracy favoured by the British labour movement. Closely connected to this, libertarianism favoured freedom and personal responsibility, conceived in communal as well as individual terms, and stressing 'the natural, the spontaneous [and] the unsystematic' (Woodcock 1979: 32). Within this political perspective, the popular tradition, which was conceived often in the singular, was viewed as the authentic voice of a suppressed culture, a voice that was instinctively oppositional and subversive. One of the most articulate exponents of this view was John Arden.

Arden has frequently been referred to as a socialist. Whilst this is undoubtedly true of his politics post-1968, the term needs some qualifications if it is to stand as a judgement of his earlier position, as Michael Cohen has pointed out (Cohen 1985). Arden referred to the 1960s as a period when he (along with his wife, Margaretta D'Arcy) put his faith in non-violent anarchism. He did not belong to any anarchist organisations, but clearly the 'neo-anarchism' that Woodcock located in the early sixties was a considerable influence on both his plays and his thinking about the nature and role of popular art. Arden has commented on how he views the tradition of popular theatre in several contexts. In a letter written in response to Ted Willis's comments on vital theatre, Arden argued that the aim of theatre was to 'activate and excite' its audience, in a formulation that avoids the more propagandist formulation of 'convert' or 'persuade'. 'Apart from the pantomime and the music hall', he observed, 'it is quite a long time since the mass of English people could find anything in the theatre to produce this effect' (Arden 1959: 42). The model of a truly popular drama, from which many of these popular genres are a debasement, is the Elizabethan and Jacobean theatre, which not only had an audience that cut across social class, but also united the literary and popular, the legitimate and the illegitimate, dramatic traditions. This latter tradition had its roots in the Dionysiac comedy of Aristophanes and could be traced forward through Roman mimes to the mummers' plays and the morality plays before arriving at the theatres of Shakespeare and Ben Jonson. The tradition is also represented in street ballads, popular fayres and spectacles and latterly pantomime and music-hall. This was a version of theatrical history that was not only radically different from that which appeared when only the 'legitimate' literary drama was considered, but also connected to other aspects of popular entertainment and celebration. Arden's plays at this time are all written with reference to this tradition (see Hunt 1974 and Gray 1982). *The Waters of Babylon* (1957) was a satire on the premium bond scheme which draws on the conventions of stand-up comedy, quick-change acts and music-hall; *Serjeant Musgrave's Dance* (1959) is infused with the imagery of nineteenth-century street ballads; *Live Like Pigs* (1958) contains characters that are direct descendants of nineteenth-century vagabonds, and uses music hall to pattern its dialogue; *A Happy Haven* (1960) was conceived as a Jonsonian comedy of humours, using masks; and *The Workhouse Donkey* (1963) was a celebration of the Dionysiac virtues of anarchy, licentiousness and disorder.

The subversive potential of the popular tradition was two-fold. First, it contained, when viewed as a whole, an image of the lower- and working-classes that official culture rigorously suppressed. Seen through the eyes of the writers of this tradition, Arden argued, 'the English prove to be an extra-ordinarily passionate people, as violent as they are amorous, and quite astonishingly hostile to good government and order' (Arden 1970: 126). This version of the popular could be seen as curiously nostalgic and a-historical, sharing much of the concern for the decline of working-class cultural forms that Richard Hoggart and others articulated (Arden suggested that the tradition, though still in existence, was buried under 'several hundred years of puritanical falsification, the sad remains of it. . . traced in *The Uses of Literacy*'; Arden 1959: 42). But it also allowed a different set of questions to appear on the agenda. Arden's view of the popular theatrical tradition, and the theatrical languages associated with it, has also been articulated by the Soviet critic, Bakhtin, who has been the focus of interest in the nineties. Bakhtin gave a particular emphasis to the subversive potential of popular comedy and communal celebration, which, as

John McGrath has argued, embodied 'The concept of an unofficial, Rabelasian merry-making which is licensed to mock, parody and create obscene versions of the church and state' (McGrath 1990: 153). Secondly, the popular dramatic tradition articulated universal poetic truths, of which the 'social problems of 1959 (or 1600 or 400 BC) are but a part' (Arden 1970: 126). This suggests the potential for a radical theatre that was significantly different from social realism.

In fact, many of Arden's plays occupy the thematic territory of social realism, dealing with contemporary issues and socially extended characters/social situations (*Waters of Babylon, Live Like Pigs* and *The Workhouse Donkey* in particular). These plays have a much more direct relationship with the texture of popular life in fifties and early-sixties Britain than almost any others; *The Waters of Babylon* represents a premium bond scandal, at a time not long after the first appearance of the scheme; *Live Like Pigs* was based on a contemporary newspaper account of an incident on a northern housing estate; and *The Workhouse Donkey* deals directly with corruption within the political system, even though it is local rather than national government that is subjected to scrutiny. The expectation amongst critics that his plays should therefore be judged in the same terms as social realism frequently blinded them both to their theatrical and political potential. The plays were clearly 'anti-naturalist' in their use of the formal devices of the popular genres, to which Arden was indebted. However, the ideologies of traditional realism and naturalism ran deeper than this, and the expectation that Arden should create central characters who embody, or at least elucidate, the values of the play (which he refused to do) led to a reading of his plays as 'non-political'. The denial of empathy with his protagonists led Taylor to comment that 'Arden permits himself in his treatment of characters and situations in his plays to be less influenced by moral pre-conceptions than any other writer in British theatre today' (Taylor 1962: 84). However, from a different political and aesthetic viewpoint it is difficult to see how the plays could be read as 'neutral'. Arden himself was clear why his plays should not be subsumed within a notion of realism that was identified with contemporary naturalism:

> To use the material of the contemporary world and present it on the public stage is the commonly accepted purpose of playwrights. . . . What I am deeply concerned with is the

problem of translating the common life of today into terms
of poetry that shall at the one time both illustrate that life and
set it within the historical and legendary tradition of our
culture.... Social realism ... tends in the theatre to be
dangerously ephemeral and therefore disappointing after the
fall of the curtain. But if it is expressed within the framework
of the traditional poetic truths it can have a weight and impact
derived from something more than contemporary documentary facility.

(Arden 1970: 125–6)

The specificity of social and political concerns, of the 'contemporary' in contemporary theatre, is in this way blurred by an
emphasis on the 'universal', which reveals an instinctively oppositional politics that is bound neither to a particular time or place
nor to a narrow definition of the political. The opposition between
the 'poetic' and 'documentary' is one that we have encountered
before, but is given a rather different inflection here; the crucial
opposition is not primarily between an unmediated transcription
of reality and the 'aesthetic', but rather between the immediate/
local and the historical/mythical. The 'traditional poetic truths' of
the popular tradition are the means by which Arden can insert
contemporary concerns into a view of history that is essentially
anarchist and libertarian, rather than Marxist, and in which the
essential and reoccurring conflicts are between the instinctive
anarchy of the people and the repressive order of 'good' government of whatever complexion. In this sense, Arden's plays are a
libertarian critique of hegemony.

From this political perspective, the operation of consensus,
which, as we saw earlier, was so essential to a reading of post-war
politics and culture, is the latest manifestation of a much older and
intractable process, whereby all those who participate in a system
necessarily become committed to its survival. The social system,
whoever administers it, both absorbs dissent and marginalises –
even organises against – those who remain outside it. Arden's plays
of this period contain characters and groups who are 'outsiders',
when measured against the typology of traditional social classes; for
example, the different kinds of immigrant in *Waters of Babylon* and
the Sawneys in *Live Like Pigs*, whom Arden described as 'the direct
descendants of the "sturdy beggars" of the sixteenth century'
(Arden 1969: 101). The disorder that these groups create is a fact

131

of their social existence (and not a product of 'personality'), which both challenges certain stereotypes about the 'Englishness' of contemporary social life, and relates to a tradition of dissent and exclusion.

Live Like Pigs is, in Arden's words, 'a study of differing ways of life brought sharply into conflict and both losing their own particular virtues under the stress of intolerance and misunderstanding' (Arden 1969: 101). The Sawneys represent one way of life, and the other is embodied in the Jackson family, who are, at least initially, familiar figures on the post-war landscape, being newly affluent and 'respectable'. The opposition between the two families is represented in the contrast between two types of family unit. The Jacksons are a conventional social unit of mother, father and child; the Sawneys, however, are a dysfunctional family that nevertheless seems to survive, where the central relationship is between two people who are not married (Rachel and Sailor) and where lines of paternity do not follow straight paths. The action occurs not amongst the familiar nineteenth-century terraces of New Wave films, but on a post-war council estate, which is regarded by everyone except the Sawneys as a 'step up'. The value accorded the estate by those who live there is represented metonymically by the two houses that provide the setting of the action. To the Jacksons, their neighbours and a wider society represented by the housing official, the house is highly desirable ('a lovely house, I'd call it', as the official says); but to the Sawneys it is a trap, a constraint on their freedom, which they have no choice but to accept. 'We have no choice, have we?' says Rachel near the beginning of the play 'So what if we *don't* like it? We've no bloody choice' (all quotations from Arden 1969). The action of the play is structured around reversals; the Sawneys, who arrive at the beginning of the play, are the chief agents of disruption, challenging the values and habits of their conventional neighbours, yet by the end it is they who are destroyed as a viable unit. The family is fragmented, with Rachel taking to the road and Sailor metaphorically and literally disabled by a broken leg. In this clash of ways of living in the post-war world, it is the dominant order that wins, represented in the final scene by the policeman and housing official. The dominant order wins in another sense, too, in that the Sawneys are eventually contained by the violent actions of Mrs Jackson and her neighbours, suggesting a reaction to the 'other' that is disturbing and irrational in its ferociousness. Violence, the play suggests, is a response that is not far below the surface of an 'everyday' affluent existence when it is the central elements of social existence that are under threat – the lynchpins of traditional family and communal life.

In *The Workhouse Donkey*, the consensus also emerges victorious at the end of the play, only this time it is a consensus that mirrors the national consensus between the major political parties. As in *Live Like Pigs* (and other of Arden's plays), the action consists of a reversal of expectations. The opening scenes establish an opposition between the local party machines, Tory and Labour, which by the end of the play are unified against the threat to the existing order (shabby and compromised though it is). This is represented by Charlie Butterthwaite (the donkey of the play's title, and its dominating character) and Inspector Feng. These two threats signify the contradiction between order and anarchy translated into the densely realised and highly structured political life of a northern town. Butterthwaite represents chaos and disorder, allied to creativity and spontaneity, whilst Feng represents its opposite, an order that is so rigid that it becomes brittle, shattering under the double impact of the compromises that constitute political life in the town and of falling in love. The consensus is one that by definition abhors extremes, expelling Charlie (who is threatened with prison at the end of the play) and Feng (who returns to London). Yet it is a consensus that also denies the possibility of real change, partly because it does not command the assent of those it claims to represent; finally bereft of the power that he has so assiduously acquired and facing gaol, Charlie addresses his fellow councillors: 'Look at 'em. . . . You ruled them, *I* ruled them, and we never knew who they were! . . . We piped to them and they did not dance, we sang them our songs and they spat into t'gutter' (Arden 1971: 129). In the final sequence of the play, Arden presents the audience with a formal summing up of the terms of the status quo, with both political groups closing ranks against not only Charlie and Feng but also the audience. The last speech is delivered by all who remain on stage (the representatives of the political establishment of both parties) and confronts the (southern) audience with a belligerent defence not of their actions but of their identity: 'We stand alone to the north of the Trent/ You leave us alone and we'll leave you alone/ We take no offence where none has been meant/ But you hit us with your fist, we'll bash *you* with a stone!' (Arden 1971: 132). In some ways this assertion of the 'otherness' of the North works against another reading of the conclusion to the narrative – that the status quo established in this one northern town is a mirror of a political process that is not only local but national in its operation.

Arden's political aesthetic had two further aspects, which embraced the nature of the theatrical event that he wished to create. First, he emphasised the celebratory aspects of theatre, particularly comedy, which aimed to put the audience in contact with the inherently subversive virtues of the Dionysiac (and Aristophanic) tradition. Arden summarised this in his introduction to *The Workhouse Donkey*: '[the theatre] never will be catholic if we do not grant pride of place to the old essential attributes of Dionysus: noise / disorder / drunkenness / lasciviousness / nudity / generosity/corruption/fertility/and ease' (Arden 1971: 9).

Secondly, this kind of aesthetic implied that theatre should become a very different kind of social, as well as aesthetic, event. Anarchist oriented theatre of the late 1960s frequently sought to dissolve the distinction between stage and audience, moving towards the participatory happenings of the American Living Theatre, in which theatre was intended to 'enact', and hence precipitate, the revolution. Such an approach was also apparent in the surrealist inspired Happenings that evolved in the United States from the fifties onwards, in which audience and actors shared in communal celebrations of creativity that were transformations of everyday living. Arden and D'Arcy staged a form of anarchist event at their home in Kirbymoorside in 1964, in which they invited anyone who wanted to come along to participate in a festival of creativity. Although such activities were peripheral to Arden's main theatre work, the thinking that lay behind them led him to look for a different model for the theatrical event. Of *The Workhouse Donkey* Arden wrote

> I would have been happy had it been possible for [the play] to have lasted, say, six or seven or thirteen hours (excluding intervals), and for the audience to come and go throughout the performance, assisted perhaps by a printed synopsis of the play from which they could deduce those scenes or episodes which would be of interest to them particularly, and those which they could afford to miss.
>
> (Arden 1971: 8)

This in turn implied a kind of theatre that was one part of a larger event that would 'offer rival attractions as well, and would take on some of the characteristics of a fairground or amusement park'. The model here is not so much the alternative theatre of the late sixties but a more traditional working-class communal celebration, involving 'restaurants, bars, side-shows, bandstands and so forth, all grouped around a central playhouse' (Arden 1971: 8). Arden was not alone in offering such radical ideas for transforming the social and cultural nature of theatre, for reintegrating it into popular entertainment: Littlewood's concept of the 'Fun Palace' was, from this point of view, a logical extension of the experiments with popular theatrical form that had characterised the work of Theatre Workshop since its inception. Indeed, it is probably the output of Theatre Workshop at this time that provides the most consistent example of an attempt to integrate the popular into contemporary performance in the period.

THEATRE WORKSHOP AND THE POPULAR

The routines of music-hall constructed a relationship between stage and audience that was fundamentally different from that permitted by realist drama; as Davison has suggested, 'the audience has once again become a part of the theatrical experience'. In the music-halls, the audience was 'directly addressed, conversed with, cajoled, even insulted; it was never forgotten' (Davison 1982: 105). This attempt to use the forms of music-hall (and other popular genres) to redefine the relationship between actors and spectators was most clearly evident in Littlewood's productions at Stratford East. Goorney noted that in *The Hostage* (1958) there was 'no "fourth wall" between the actors and the audience, and the music-hall style of production made it easy to involve anything untoward that happened in the auditorium' (Goorney 1981: 115) (when the play transferred to the West End, this often meant the drunken inter-ruptions of the author). The *New Statesman* commented that in Stephen Lewis's *Sparrers Can't Sing* 'you could almost be out in the street again; the protecting, invisible fourth stage wall seems gone' (Lewis 1960: 302). Tynan (on *The Hostage*) commented that some of the acting was 'sheer vaudeville' (Mikhail 1979: 125) and likened the play to the *commedia delle'arte*, whilst Robert Brustein called it a 'roaring vaudeville . . . its substance taped together with burlesque routines'. He concluded that it was 'open to doubt whether *The Hostage* belongs on the legitimate stage at all' (Mikhail 1979: 128).

In Littlewood's work, the return to popular forms arose naturally out of both the working practices and the political and cultural ambitions of Theatre Workshop. For Littlewood, the music-hall provided a set of concrete theatrical practices, a means of replacing the traditional codes of realism in acting and design, that sprang as much from an ideological impulse (to replace outmoded representations on the stage and to reach a working-class audience) as it did from aesthetic ones. The critical response to her productions was partly one of reaction to the appearance of 'illegitimate' forms on the 'legitimate' stage. But more importantly it was an indication of the way that popular forms were actually used – in particular, the way that they co-existed with elements that were more recognisably part of a realist tradition.

It was noted earlier that virtually all Theatre Workshop's productions of contemporary plays in the period were realist in the sense that they were set within a specific lower- or working-class milieu and were recognisably contemporary, as well as drawing on working-class cultural forms. Indeed, the improvisatory approach to rehearsal and performance meant that the plays were frequently contemporary in a very immediate sense, with the script changing night by night (the attentions of the Lord Chamberlain's Office permitting). The focus on ensemble playing and collective responsibility in rehearsal and performance meant that plays (that were also musicals) like *Sparrers Can't Sing* and *Fings Ain't Wot They Used To Be* emphasised a tangible and highly localised 'way of life'. For example, the *New Statesman* wrote that the plot of *Sparrers* concerned:

> the truth of the Stepney life itself. . . . Three generations of an East End family come out on their neighbouring doorsteps; the older bicker and gossip, the younger ones mooch, go courting, hope to borrow five bob. Anything west of Aldgate doesn't exist.
>
> (Lewis 1960: 302)

It is also a way of life that was imbued with some of the concerns that are present in other forms of working-class realism (and not only in the theatre). There is a sense, for example, of loss within the representation of the East End communities in both these plays: 'Do we sense a wistful regret' wrote Lewis of *Sparrers*, 'that the East End scene is not today what it was?' And *Fings* embodied in its title the tension between past and present, with the former seeming preferable to the latter. As Stuart Laing has observed, 'the title song was a direct comparison between "then" and "now" in working-class life-styles (Southend against Paris as resorts; local palais v. bowling alley)' (Laing 1986: 160).

It is not simply a matter of a realism of content versus an 'anti-realism' or naturalism of form, however, although this is partly the case. The text of *A Taste of Honey* suggests that a jazz band is visible on stage, and notes several moments when characters (especially Helen) turn and address their remarks to the audience. The dialogue in the play is frequently structured like music-hall 'patter'. Anderson noted 'The abandoning of the fourth wall, the sudden patches of pure music-hall' and commended the acting style, which allowed 'no sloppy identification', but combined (in Avis Bunnage's Helen) 'the broadest eye-on-the-gallery caricature with straight-forward, detailed naturalism' (L. Anderson 1970b: 80). This indicates the presence of *several* styles of performance, suggesting that part of the appeal of the production lay in the way that it combined music-hall with a more straightforwardly 'realist' acting style. In an article discussing Littlewood's working methods in *Encore*, Milne and Goodwin commented on the way that this worked:

> At the beginning of *A Taste of Honey* . . . a more or less naturalistic sequence shows the mother and daughter to-gether. Jo goes out to make some coffee, while the mother goes on talking to her. She turns her head quite casually, and suddenly you find she is talking directly to the audience. . . . This sort of thing sometimes puzzled but always entertained, and it certainly made you think about the play instead of the next interval.
>
> (Milne and Goodwin 1960: 10)

A similar point can be made about *The Hostage*, and in this case the broadening of the range of performance styles was accompanied by an 'opening out' of the narrative itself. Behan adapted and translated the play from his own original, entitled *An Giall*, which was performed in Dublin in June 1958. This was in all respects a more traditional play, closer in its form to familiar patterns of realism. Richard Wall, who has compared the two texts, called *An Giall* a 'restrained . . . tragi-comedy' (Wall 1979: 138). The published text of *The Hostage* is of the reworked version, but the shape of the original is still occasionally visible. Indeed, the appeal of the play lies partly in the tension between those elements of its form that draw on the conventions of an intensive, broadly naturalist narrative mode, and those that come from the music-hall and other popular forms.

The Hostage is set in a brothel in a run-down part of Dublin, which also doubles as a safe house for the IRA. The hostage of the title is a young British soldier, Leslie Williams, who is taken in reprisal against the sentencing to death of an IRA 'martyr'; if the latter dies, so will Leslie. Indeed, the climax of the play occurs when the brothel is invaded by the security services and Leslie is killed – not executed in revenge, but accidentally shot. At one level, *The Hostage* has a tightly structured narrative. The events of the play occur over one night and a morning and the location of the play is the same throughout, consisting of a single room and corridor. It has a single plot line (the kidnapping of the soldier), with a familiar pattern of cause-and-effect embedded in a recognisable dramatic conflict/ tension (will he be murdered), leading to a single climax and resolution (his death). Described in this way, it bears a strong resemblance to dominant forms of naturalism. Yet, the elements that were added in the Workshop production, and which were most easily registered in performance, transformed these narrative conventions, not by ignoring them, but by consciously interrupting them. Much of what happens on the stage bears no necessary relationship to the central narrative line (although some of it does at the thematic level); characters burst into song, tell jokes, argue and fight with each other and harangue the audience in ways that gain their effect partly in relation to the 'real' story of the hostage, redefining the conventions through which this story is told in the process. The space, for example, loses its specificity, changing in purpose and even shape as events demand. The corridor is described in the stage directions as being also 'a landing, or another room in the house and also serves as an extension of the room when the characters need room to dance and fight in' (Behan 1978: 129). The inclusion of direct address to the audience, of songs, and of self-contained comic routines cuts across the narrative line, creating a 'theatrical' narrative that constantly interrupts the 'dramatic' one, without finally losing it. The concerns of the play are explored, then, not only through dialogue and the unravelling of the basic dramatic situation, but also through song, anecdote and jokes. This approach also allowed a variety of modes of characterisation. The soldier, Leslie, and the young girl who attends him, Teresa, had strong roots in a consistent psychology, whilst several of the inhabitants of the brothel were comic types.

The Hostage, then, can hardly be described as naturalist. It is, however, a play that has certain realist intentions, especially in relation to the way that the past is presented, with the largely popular conventions of performance becoming the means by which these intentions are articulated. One of *The Hostage*'s prime intentions is to de-bunk much of the mythology surrounding twentieth-century Irish history, especially the 'troubles'.

The brothel is at one level a place of escape from history, peopled with characters attempting to follow, largely unsuccessfully, their own idiosyncratic and often sexual paths. The play constructs an opposition between past and present, between a 'then' and 'now', with Leslie and the young maid, Teresa, with whom he has a relationship, represented both as victims of that history and as representative of an experience that is outside it. Both characters are only vaguely aware of the events that loom so large for the others, and their relationship is conducted in terms that echo not the certainties of Irish history but more familiar romantic patterns. This central relationship belongs to a more 'poetic' core to the play, in the sense that Arden used the term, evoking an archetypal situation of two lovers doomed by the forces of an impersonal society ranged against them. A relevant parallel, as some reviewers pointed out, was with *Romeo and Juliet*. This universalising of their relationship is connected to a politics that is predominantly libertarian, in the sense that the central conflicts are, as in Arden's plays of the period, between order and creative disorder, 'politics' and love, spontaneity and cold rigidity. Leslie's death is therefore a waste, demonstrating not only the absurdity of IRA fundamentalism but of politics *per se*. This was a popular and accessible version of contemporary politics, as the largely favourable reviews suggested. The danger of the approach was that it could also be seen as an 'anglicising' of Irish history (see Wall 1979: 140) that was comfortable for English audiences at a time when the IRA was largely dormant, and which could be said merely to indulge (as its author did) the English proclivity for stereotyping the Irish and exoticising the lower-classes.

HAROLD PINTER AND SOCIAL REALISM

Pinter's plays, though of the moment of the New Wave, clearly have an oblique relationship to its main concerns, political and formal. Little of the subsequent critical attention that the plays have attracted – which, as Michael Scott has pointed out, has 'reached industrial proportions' (Scott 1991: 12) – has thought this relationship worth exploring. It is not difficult to see why.

John Russell Taylor gave Pinter a chapter all to himself in *Anger and After*, which is both an indication of the critical status that was, even at this early stage (1962), being afforded the plays, and of the difficulty of relating them to the main positions and developments. 'The assignment of writers to various sections of this book has been at best a rather arbitrary business', wrote Taylor in the opening sentence of the chapter: 'with Harold Pinter the system just breaks down' (Taylor 1962: 323). The difficulty of categorising the plays (which has not eased over the years) arose initially because Pinter was not associated with either the Royal Court or Stratford East. Indeed, the fact that the plays surfaced at all owes a lot to a commercial producer, Michael Codron. *The Room* and *The Dumb Waiter* were produced at the Hampstead Theatre Club (which had a reputation for experimental drama) in 1960, although they subsequently transferred to the Royal Court as a double bill in the same year. *The Birthday Party* (1958) was produced by Codron and first performed in Cambridge before being transferred to the Lyric in Hammersmith, whilst *The Caretaker* (1960) was performed at the Duchess in the West End.

The Birthday Party was the first of the plays to receive a London production, and was therefore the first to be substantially reviewed. That those reviews were uniformly hostile (with the exception of Harold Hobson's) has often been noted – hostile enough to close the play after a few days. However, critical opinion shifted quite quickly. Wardle produced a positive review of the production later in the year in *Encore*, which distanced itself from the prevailing critical incomprehension. By the time *The Caretaker* appeared, Pinter's intentions were (apparently) better understood. Tynan wrote that 'With *The Caretaker* Harold Pinter has begun to fulfil the promise that I signally failed to see in *The Birthday Party* two years ago' (Tynan 1984: 278). The comparison has been made, perhaps inevitably, with the critical reception of *Look Back in Anger*, although the calumny heaped upon *Waiting for Godot* is perhaps a better point of reference. The response to Osborne's play was primarily an ideological one; the form, at least, was familiar. The response to both *Godot* and *The Birthday Party*, however, showed a radical unease about the kind of play that was being offered, about the nature of the forms being employed.

Ironically, perhaps, Godot/Beckett (and what critics were learning to call the Absurd generally) provided one possible interpretative framework, in which the plays could be discussed – or rather dismissed, as was largely the case: Wardle noted that 'there are two ways of saying that you don't understand a play; the first is to bowl it out with that word "obscurity" . . . the second way is to say that the seminal influence of Ionesco can be detected' (Scott 1991: 111). Certainly Ionesco, whose name at this time functioned as a sign for foreign, absurdist and philosophical drama, was a point of reference. 'If the author can forget Beckett, Ionesco and Simpson', wrote the *Manchester Guardian* 'he may do much better next time'. *The Times* argued that *The Birthday Party* was a 'surrealistic drama' which 'gives the impression of deriving from an Ionesco play which M. Ionesco has not yet written' (Elsom 1981: 83).

A second interpretative framework – although one much less present in the immediate reviews – was that provided by some elements in social realism. This is not surprising given the surface similarities between Pinter's plays and the characteristics of New Wave realism that were most often used to define the form. The settings of the plays were uniformly lower-class and contemporary, and although much criticism since has focused on the metaphorical significance or theatrical function of these locations, some reviewers connected them directly to a specific social experience. Tynan, for example, argued in the course of a review of *The Caretaker*, that 'London is unique in the déclassé decrepitude of its Western suburbs, with their floating population . . . their prevalent dry rot – moral as well as structural – and their frequent casual suicides. Mr Pinter captures all this with the most chilling economy' (Tynan 1984: 280). A similar point may be made in relation to the language of the plays, which is recognisably of a lower-class idiom. Even the narratives themselves could, from one point of view, be seen as the familiar territory of realist writers. John Arden, in a perceptive account of Pinter's plays in 1960, noted that *The Caretaker* was 'a perfectly straightforward story that might almost have been overheard in a public bar'. Such a story could be easily assimilated into a tradition of realism:

> The conventional treatment of this sort of story is not difficult to imagine – it might make a Willis Hall or Ted Willis TV piece – and the interesting thing is the closeness with which Mr Pinter's writing in fact does approach such a treatment.
>
> (Scott 1991: 117)

The plays also suggest a method of presentation that is similarly realist. However, although all the markers of theatrical naturalism are present in performance – the box-sets, curtains, fourth-wall illusionism, the 'realistic' lights and costumes – the plays simply do not signify as naturalism, even the 'realism' of the general mimetic tradition. One critical response to this disruption of the signification process has been to see the systems in which the plays operate in terms of symbolism and metaphor – to assume that Pinter has gone along the same path as the later Ibsen, in which specific social settings and actions are drained of their particularity, their symbolic possibilities emphasised instead. These are approaches that Pinter has explicitly rejected. In fact, Pinter's challenge to realism is a fundamental one, for it attacks the epistemological basis of the tradition.

A premise of all of the realism that has been discussed so far is that reality is knowable, and that the objective of realism is to show 'how things really are' – to 'know' reality better; and if our understanding of the world is incomplete, then this is because we simply do not yet have the analytical tools to master its complexities. These tools may be found within the disciplines of positivist science (the basis of much nineteenth-century naturalism), or within an analysis of social and economic conditions (the basis for much Marxist-inspired realism in the twentieth century). Wherever they come from, there is, as Lovell notes, a 'basic realist belief that there is an external knowable reality which can be made accessible through the construction of works of art' (Lovell 1980: 84). Pinter, however, challenges both the degree to which reality is indeed capable of being defined and understood with the precision that realists claim, and the belief that the function of theatre is to provide representations – and experiences – that are themselves fixed and 'knowable' and that collude with the myth that the world is likewise. For Pinter, at least at this time, reality is problematic and uncertain, and the meanings that can be deduced from it ambiguous and transitory. He expressed this position in the following way in a lecture given in 1962:

> The desire for verification on the part of all of us, with regard to our own experience and the experience of others, is understandable but cannot always be satisfied. I suggest that there can be no hard distinctions between what is real and what is unreal, nor between what is true and what is false; it

can be both true and false. ... Because 'reality' is quite a
strong, firm word, we tend to think, or to hope, that the state
to which it refers is equally firm, settled and unequivocal. It
doesn't seem to be, and in my opinion, it's no worse or better
for that.

(Pinter 1976: 11–12)

The kind of theatre that proceeds from this view of reality is
necessarily different from the dominant forms of realism, not least
because Pinter does not appear to have a realist 'project', and this
makes his writing the antithesis of Wesker's; that is, he has no
discernible critical or political ambition for his plays that is carried
on outside the theatre, and which can be related to wider political
or cultural concerns. This does not mean that Pinter was, as a man,
'a-political' – indeed, he was actively involved in the Committee of
100 and is one of the few dramatists of the period whose left-wing
opinions have not deserted him in the ensuing years (witness his
support for CND and the campaigns in defence of Nicaragua in the
1980s). It does mean, however, that he could see no political or
educational role for his theatre. 'Beware of the writer who puts
forward his concern for you to embrace', he wrote in 1962, 'who
leaves you in no doubt as to his worthiness, his usefulness, his
altruism, who declares that his heart is in the right place, and
ensures that it can be seen, in full view, a pulsating mass where his
characters ought to be' (Pinter 1976: 9). This is, on one level, a
caricature of the 'commitment' of other New Wave dramatists, but
it also suggests a severing of the expected connections between
writer and play, as well as between play and political ideology; a play
is not a vehicle for ideas, but a distinctive experience, the meaning
of which is inseparable from the event itself; and the writer is not
the privileged authority about his work, but may be just as unclear
as his audience about the precise meanings that are to be deduced
from them (indeed, 'deduction' has no place in this model of how
theatre works). 'I can sum up none of my plays', Pinter has written,
'I can describe none of them, except to say: That is what happened.
This is what they say. That is what they did' (Pinter 1976: 9).

We have already noted that this redefinition of the nature and
purpose of theatre is accomplished with realism's own methods,
and this may be one reason for the initial hostility to them. For
what Pinter effects is a radical reworking of the main conventions of
realist theatrical and narrative form, largely by fracturing the logic

that holds them together, a point noted by Arden.

> Hitherto, plays we can call Realist have tended to follow the
> Ibsen model: in other words, a series of events was developed,
> connected by a strictly logical progression of fact, and we
> could be sure that anything done or said on the stage had its
> place in the concrete structure of the plot. . . . But Mr Pinter
> does not work like this . . . he leaves his corners never quite
> joined up.
>
> (Scott 1991: 117)

Like many plays within the realist tradition, the fictional territory
of the plays is the domestic, the everyday, realised theatrically in
concrete, naturalistic detail. Both *The Room* and *The Birthday Party*
begin with that most ordinary of domestic routines, breakfast. These
domestic spaces also become the sites of terror and fear, often when
familiar, comfortable routines are wrenched from their associations
and invested with newer, darker possibilities – the eponymous
birthday party, for example. Rooms can also be protected spaces,
safe havens against a threatening outside world. The off-stage space,
which in realist drama becomes an extension of the on-stage world,
representing what is felt and known of the wider world, but which
cannot be realised directly, becomes in Pinter's plays a frequent
source of undefined threat. In *The Dumb Waiter*, the connections
between the characters and the outside world are disturbed and
defamiliarised, the action controlled by whoever sits at the other
end of the dumb waiter, their identity uncertain and motives
unexplained. Stage props and set are stripped of their expected
functions. Objects are not simply signs of observable reality, part of
the realist appeal to lifelikeness, nor, when they are activated in the
texts, are they invested with narrative significance or incorporated
into a structure of ideas. Instead, objects are set free from their
connotative tasks and take on other, less tangible significances. The
set of *The Caretaker* is full of objects, some of which, the Buddha
being the clearest example, are clearly 'out of place', their very
implausibility in such a densely realised world being the source of
their theatrical power. Familiar objects can also become threatening; a vacuum cleaner is used to terrify the Tramp in *The Caretaker*,
for example. Language is, similarly, stripped of its function to define
concrete reality. In realist drama, language is used to denote
character and situation; characters reveal themselves through what
they say, pinning down their social, cultural and personal identities.

Yet in Pinter's plays, language explains nothing with any certainty. It does not reveal personality or explain the situation, nor does it necessarily clarify the 'themes' of the play – the last being a particular sin in a logocentric theatre culture, where the main theatrical traditions are those that represent ideas in language. Characters, too, are uncertain about those things that provide much of the solidity of realist drama. As Arden says, 'there is a deliberate haze about the past, and indeed the present, of all his characters, which never becomes so opaque that we are bewildered. ... We never quite catch a complete view of them' (Scott 1991: 117).

Enabling us to form a complete view of a central character is one of the main objectives of the realist writer, yet, in Pinter's plays, central elements in the construction of theatrical characterisation are absent; a character's presence in the situation is frequently unexplained, and his/her actions may or may not be 'motivated' in terms of either narrative consistency or what we may agree is plausible human behaviour. Where, for example, do Goldberg and McCann come from in *The Birthday Party*, and why do they destroy Stanley so thoroughly? Stanley himself is uncertain about his past, and it is not possible to 'explain' his current behaviour in terms of what we are told about that past. In this way, the chain of cause-and-effect that holds the realist narrative together is severed, and when these connections are broken, the 'reality' that they construct loses its definition.

Pinter's refusal to explain his plays is also one manifestation of a more widespread development in post-war theatre, which is the focus on the performance as the moment where the meaning of the play is defined, rather than the play text. On occasion, the meeting of play and audience became a confrontation, which could, as in the case of several of the early plays of Edward Bond, challenge not only conventions of post-1956 realism but also the dominant theatre culture and the social values that supported it.

THE WASTELANDS OF AFFLUENCE: EDWARD BOND'S *THE POPE'S WEDDING* AND *SAVED*

Edward Bond owed much to the explosion of theatre activity after 1956. It is not that he was obviously influenced by the plays that he saw, but that he took advantage of the new opportunities that were created. Like several other new writers of working-class origin, he was a beneficiary of George Devine's determined support of young talent at the Royal Court. He became a member of the writer's group, and, in the manner of an emerging pattern at the theatre, formed a close working relationship with the new artistic director of the ESC, William Gaskell. Both *The Pope's Wedding* and *Saved* were performed at the Court (in 1962 and 1965 respectively). 'I couldn't have worked at any other theatre', he once said; 'there's no other English theatre that would have produced my plays' (Bond 1972: 10). This association with the theatre was one reason why both plays were interpreted, at least partly, within the critical context of social realism.

In certain respects, the critical response to Bond's plays followed the same path as that accorded Pinter's, and, seen from the viewpoint of the early sixties, rather than thirty years later, there are considerable similarities between their plays of this period, as Jenny Spencer has recently observed (Spencer 1992). Like Pinter, Bond seems to give us all the expected ingredients of dominant forms of realism, yet produces very different effects. Both writers utilise a language that is militantly unrhetorical and elliptical, and create recognisable characters (and character types) that exist in an 'everyday' reality that is nonetheless sodden with violence. There is also no authorial point of view on open display to interpret and provide a context for the action.

It is not surprising, then, that *The Pope's Wedding* was read mainly in relation to the concerns of contemporary realism, and in particular as a semi-documentary depiction of a segment of the young working-class, in classically naturalist terms, 'a photographic portrayal of rural life' (Spencer 1992: 14). As such, the play was valued for the meticulousness of its observation and Bond was applauded for his ability to evoke 'mood'. Although it may not appear so, a similar interpretative framework was in evidence in the response to *Saved*. The events surrounding the first production of *Saved*, Bond and Gaskell's wranglings with the censor and the court case that followed, the fist fights in the auditorium and the verbal punch-ups in the press, have been detailed elsewhere, and will not be rehearsed here (see Browne 1975, Elsom 1981 and Hay and Roberts 1978). The critical furore that rapidly enveloped the play was in one sense a focus for a more general anxiety about the limits of the new realism and centred largely on Scene Six, which includes the stoning of a baby on-stage. As one critic put it, 'It is peopled by characters who, almost without exception, are foul-mouthed, dirty-minded, illiterate, and barely to be judged on any recognisable human level at all' (Elsom 1981: 180), whilst another called it 'a concocted opportunity for vicarious beastliness'. To the critic of the *Sunday Times*, the play represented 'a clear demonstration of what is permissible, what is not, and why' (Elsom 1981: 176).

That *Saved* was interpreted as a social realist account of a certain kind of working-class experience, was partly to do with its setting. However, this is not quite the social environment of the traditional working-class, and is at some remove from the nostalgic northern landscapes of *Coronation Street* and the poeticised back lanes of the film version of *A Taste of Honey*. The play is set amongst the affluent working-class of South London in the sixties, and Bond is careful to establish that the characters are all in work (although what they work at is rarely mentioned). The men who are implicated in the stoning of the baby are clearly young *men*, and not delinquent teenagers. They are, in a sociological sense, more 'typical' than the drifting and peripheral characters that inhabit *A Taste of Honey* and Behan's plays. Unlike many other plays of the New Wave, *Saved* is not a drama of social mobility or escape, and there is no outsider with a privileged view of the events, a Beattie Bryant or Jimmy Porter, with whom the audience may align itself (Len, the central character, has a different role in relation to the character and action than prevails in most social realist plays).

However, both *Saved* and *The Pope's Wedding* have a relationship to dominant forms of realism that is more complex than this kind of sociological account would allow. At one level, the plays push towards a form of 'ultra naturalism', which would appear to be on familiar territory: 'an accurate and minutely detailed picture of life' (Hirst 1985: 49). This was, for many critics, part of the problem with the play; it was not so much that the events of the play were incredible, but that their depiction in such a detailed and 'documentary' manner, unmediated by the playwright's explicit condemnation, was immoral. As one reviewer argued:

> It [modern drama] is becoming more sharply and urgently associated with contemporary life than it has been for centuries, if ever. Things as horrible as this baby-killing, and worse, happen every day; but it is not enough merely to enact them. Without the shaping hand of art, the result is only reporting.
>
> (quoted Elsom 1981: 177)

The reference to the 'shaping hand of art' here was an echo of the opposition between art and documentary that we have encountered

147

elsewhere in the discussion of New Wave realism, and captured both the aesthetic and moral anxieties of reviewers and audiences.

That Bond was assumed to be concerned with depicting a 'way of life' in terms that were recoupable within an available model of realism, obscured the fact that he was, in several important respects, attempting to redefine realist languages and concerns. Unlike Wesker or Osborne, Bond did not so much break out from naturalism, as work at the confluence of different dramatic and theatrical traditions, drawing on both current varieties of natural- ism and Brechtian epic theatre. Indeed, Bond's work at this time is a reminder that Brecht's practice and the realist/naturalist tradi- tion are not as antithetical as we often assume them to be; freed from the precise political context of Brecht's opposition to all forms of illusionist theatre, their common materialism emerges.

There is no doubt that Bond is pursuing a realist project in these plays – to show 'how things really are' – and that this can't be achieved either within domestic naturalism or Brechtian didacti- cism (although Bond's plays have become progressively more didactic). Bond's use of dramatic form places him, at a theoretical level, within the kind of political definition of realism articulated by Brecht and discussed in the previous chapter; 'Reality changes', Brecht argued, 'in order to represent it, modes of representation must also change' (Brecht 1977: 82). One problem remains, however, that is of interest here: Brecht argued that one of the defining criteria of realism was 'making possible the concrete, and making possible abstraction from it' (Brecht 1977: 82). 'Abstract- ing' from the 'concrete' events and actions that Bond explores in his plays is not always easy, however. The difficulty is partly that which faces traditional forms of realism, that is, of negotiating and exploiting the metonymic and synecdochal functions of the local situation of the narrative. Bond is clear that his plays should, as he put it, 'open out all the while, so one has the sense of a feeling of the society outside' (Hay and Roberts 1978: 43). It is, however, also a question of explaining motivation; what is it that makes people behave in this way? What is the root cause of their actions? Bond has been equally clear that his plays should 'explain' the actions they depict: 'my plays are not descriptive. They are analytical' (Bond 1979: 111). The causes of all the problems that his characters experience and of the violence that they sometimes visit on each other are, for Bond, rooted in the social. This perception of how human 'reality' is constructed, which is in the tradition of sceptical, secular realism since the nineteenth century, implies a particular role for the plays themselves; they should 'understand all the pressures that went into the making of [the] tragedy' and move an audience to 'take action' (Bond 1972: 13). The problem is that Bond does not provide his audiences with an obvious course of action to take, largely because he does not provide an obvious context in which to assess motivation. This is partly because little of the wider social world intrudes into the action of either *The Pope's Wedding* or *Saved*, and there are no representatives of the dominant classes in either play. It is also that he has denied himself the obvious devices of the two traditions he so consistently reworks; there is no Weskerian hero (or heroine) to articulate the play's preferred point of view, or, at the very least, to point to a level of metaphor which might deepen the resonance of the action; nor does Bond wish to follow Brecht towards a dramatic form that utilises a range of theatrical means (songs, captions, etc.) – what Raymond Williams has termed 'complex seeing'. The problem was exacerbated in the context in which the plays were originally produced, being performed to a largely middle-class audience in the West End, where it became easy to blame, and thus dismiss, the characters themselves, and this explains much of the initial critical response that greeted them.

However, an answer to questions of motivation and point of view – although it may be only a partial one – lies in the way that Bond refashions the naturalist and Brechtian traditions. The connection with the realist/naturalist tradition is not limited to certain similarities of method. Both *The Pope's Wedding* and *Saved* are classically naturalist in their emphasis on environmental determinism. There is a strong sense in the plays that characters are produced by their environment, that they are not responsible for the situations in which they find themselves, nor do they understand those situations; they are victims, with little possibility of escape from the society that determines their actions, and even less of transforming it. The parallel with early naturalism goes further. Zola, influenced by Darwin, frequently drew attention to the animal nature of human beings, sometimes, as in *Thérèse Raquin*, portraying characters at the mercy of animalistic desires. This is also an element in *Saved*, one which contributed to the unease felt by some contemporary reviewers: 'it amounts to a systematic degradation of the human animal' (Roberts 1985: 16). The play itself draws attention to this level of determinism. The young men persuade themselves that the baby has no feelings, 'like animals', as one puts it. Bond develops this by suggesting, through a stage direction at the end of the stoning ('They go off up left, making a curious buzzing'), a direct parallel with animal behaviour. 'Instead of being an identifiable gang', Bond later said, 'their behaviour is so horrendous that it blurs over into something that can only be described in terms of the animal kingdom, and that's the buzzing of a swarm of bees' (Hay and Roberts 1978: 50).

It is largely through language that this process of determinism is made concrete. The language of both plays is deliberately anti-rhetorical, consisting largely of an impoverished, limited 'everyday' vocabulary, often explicitly sexual and deliberately clichéd. Bond also writes the dialogue phonetically in an approximation of the dialect of the play's setting. Speeches are rarely more than a few sentences long, or, indeed, are complete sentences at all, and questions are usually blocked. This kind of staccato, apparently inexpressive dialogue appears at first sight very much like Pinter's, but the effect over the play as a whole is not so much to concretise the experience of 'non-communication' as to provide a tangible sense of the limitations on the characters' control over their environment.

In a very real sense, society 'speaks through' the characters, and language becomes both an index of ideological repression and one of its chief means; people are deprived of power in society, and cannot use language either to describe their situation or to gain mastery over it. Pam in *Saved*, for example, can only express her despair through progressively more incoherent and broken speech. 'I can't go on . . . No 'ome. No friends. Baby dead. Gone. Fred gone' (Bond 1971: 113). Clichés are a clear example of the way that an inherited mode of speaking and thinking shapes consciousness; 'Cloutin's good for 'em, I read it', says Pete in the course of the progressive dehumanisation and murder of the baby, and Fred, from his prison cell, claims without irony, 'There's bloody gangs like that roamin' everywhere. The bloody police don't do their job' (Bond 1971: 75). Language is a battleground, as it is in Wesker's plays, but the contrast between the ways that Bond and Wesker view language – and, beyond language, culture in general – is marked. In *Roots*, through the way that the play's central protagonist is delineated, Wesker provides the audience with a model of how individuals may take control of their lives through taking control of language; in Bond's plays, no such empowerment is possible. In

The Pope's Wedding, the central character, Scopey, murders and then assumes the identity of, a hermit, Allen, unable to express any clear idea of why he is doing so; and Len, the protagonist of *Saved*, is complicit in the stoning of the baby, and his only act of transformation is not expressed verbally but through the mending of a chair in the last scene.

Bond's relationship to Brecht was an equally complex one. Whilst admitting in 1972 that he admired Brecht, Bond nonetheless found the plays 'naive melodramas' (Bond 1972: 13). Yet his own practice has increasingly paralleled that of Brecht, and he has termed much of his more recent work epic theatre. The influence of Brecht was registered partly through the writer's group at the Court, which, as Holland has argued, was one of the first conduits through which Brecht's ideas were assimilated into British theatre practice (Holland 1978). The early plays were all directed by William Gaskell, who was closely associated with Brechtian directoral practice (see Holland 1978 and Gaskell 1988). Holland has suggested that Bond's reading of Brecht was mediated through Gaskell's concern with Brechtian gestus.

The relationship with Brecht – and the connection between Bond's reading of Brecht and an opening up of the possibilities of traditional realism/naturalism – is most apparent in the approach to design and *mise-en-scène*. Gaskell described the style of *Saved* as 'a kind of pared down naturalism' referring not only to the design but to the way that actors should inhabit the set: 'the actual placing of everyone on the stage is very important, and the actors have to have a kind of awareness of the economy of themselves' (quoted Hay and Roberts 1978: 58). The set of the original production was extremely simple:

> eight of the play's thirteen scenes were played on a set enclosed by a triangle of flats. The three park scenes took place on a bare stage, the café scene had chairs and tables without the flats, and the cell scene was set with a simple door-flat.
>
> (Hay and Roberts 1978: 57)

This approach was similar to that adopted by Brecht, who wrote about the need for a 'selective realism' in the design of the set and the choice of props. This was not the 'poetic realism' that was in evidence elsewhere at the Court (see Chapter 4), and its appeal was not primarily an aesthetic one: indeed, when read as a context for the action, the set was deliberately unaesthetic in any accepted sense, an element in the conscious de-dramatisation of the play. It was in the way that the setting and props were actively used that the departure from naturalism, with its implied personal and psychological orientation, was most evident:

> Instead of scenery I use objects as elements in a society. Somebody has had to pay for every object on my stage, somebody has had to work for it. And so it is the relationship to what is invested in those objects by society, the relation of the characters to those objects that, for me, becomes very telling.
>
> (Bond 1979: 112)

This way of viewing the use of scenic elements has been analysed by Holland, who has drawn attention to the way that objects help to define personal relationships in economic and social terms: Fred's fishing rod or cigarettes in Scene Six of *Saved*, for example, become the means by which his social, economic and sexual dominance over Len is made concrete (see Holland 1978: 28–9).

This emphasis on the social significance of props and their use occurs in a context where some traditional Brechtian concepts were being rejected. Brecht, famously, sought to create a critical distance between spectator and theatrical event, to emphasise theatrical communication as an essentially rational process. Despite the fact that Bond calls his theatre a 'rational' theatre, his plays are often built around powerful, sometimes violent dramatic images, the effect of which is anything but rational; the stoning scene in *Saved*, or the last scene of *The Pope's Wedding*, which opens with Scopey sitting in Allen's coat in the hermit's shack, its owner dead on the floor surrounded by 500 tins of meat. Bond has termed these 'aggro-effects', arguing that, 'In contrast to Brecht, I think it's necessary to disturb an audience emotionally, to involve them emotionally in my plays . . . or as a way of forcing an audience to search for reasons [explanations] in the rest of the play' (Bond 1979: 113).

Aggro-effects are not, however, conceived outside the dramatic traditions within which Bond is working; their effect(s) are variable and achieved by the careful manipulation of theatrical form and audience expectation. In Scene Four of *Saved*, the baby is left to cry for the entire scene off-stage, and at the end of Scene Six, Pam simply wheels the pram away, unaware that the baby is dead: in both scenes, the audience are denied the expected response. This is accomplished by a consistent de-dramatising of the situation, which is achieved by pushing the elements of realism in the scenes in two directions. On the one hand, the crying baby is disturbing because it is ignored, or discussed as an object; a decision that might be justified naturalistically, as a 'plausible' element in a situation, nevertheless produces an effect that resonates as both significant and shocking. On the other hand, Scene Six shifts from a familiar kind of naturalism (established through dialogue) to a more heightened realism and metaphor, achieved out of the collision between a realism of performance style and an abstraction in the props and setting. The baby has been given aspirin, and does not cry when it is stoned, nor were real stones used in the first production. Gaskell has written of the intended effect:

> The killing of a child in a pram when it doesn't care – it can make no statement about the pain it feels – has already a kind of abstract, symbolic quality about it, although one tries to do it as naturalistically as possible. . . . You are watching a kind of ritualised action. What you are watching really is the boys.
> (Hay and Roberts 1978: 50)

The audience is denied a cathartic release, and Bond wrote that he made Pam exit with the pram at the end because he 'didn't want the scene to escape into classical cries of horror' (Hay and Roberts ibid.).

It may be, however, that the central mechanisms of both plays are only tangential related to the naturalist/Brechtian axis. One context that Bond does provide is that of Freud and the Oedipus complex. This has sometimes been overlooked by critics reading the intentions of the plays through the prism of Bond's critical writing, which tends to pursue the themes of the plays by other means, rather than provide a commentary on them. Bond has drawn attention to the Oedipal structure of *Saved*, and, if that play is optimistic, it is because Len refuses to fulfil the Oedipal expectation and kill his symbolic father (Harry). Within this framework, the murder of the baby 'shows the Oedipus, atavistic fury fully unleashed' (Bond 1977: 310). However, this is not simply a means of returning motivation from the social to the psychological, for the implication is that such psychoanalytical drives are socially located. As Jenny Spencer has persuasively argued, this may be one of the central achievements of these plays (Spencer 1993). Bond, himself, however, seemed from the seventies onwards to have opted for a more 'rational' and recognisably Brechtian trajectory, although unlike some of his fifties contemporaries, his relationship to Brecht was always a political one.

BRECHT, HISTORY AND REALISM

One sign of the breaking up of the moment of Working-Class Realism was the reappearance of history plays. By the mid-sixties, plays that were set wholly in the past constituted a significant proportion of new work on the London stage. Some of these plays were written/produced by writers/companies that were associated with the New Wave; Osborne's *Luther* (1961), Arden's *Serjeant Musgrave's Dance* (1959) and *Armstrong's Last Goodnight* (1964), Theatre Workshop's *Oh What a Lovely War* (1963), and Robert Bolt's *A Man for All Seasons* (1960) – these are the most relevant examples. Set in a defined period of history – and therefore not 'contemporary' in the sense in which it was normally used – these plays, and their productions, were connected to the opening out of the realist stage, with an extensive, episodic narrative, a movement beyond the 'domestic' situations of the earlier plays, and with conventions of performance that were anti-naturalistic, frequently drawing on popular genres.

This renewed interest in history may be seen as a rejection – or at least a superseding – of the early concerns of the New Wave. There was a sense, for example, that to write history plays was to have 'grown up', and to have connected with legitimate drama. Writing on *Luther*, Michael Foot commended Osborne for having written a play that stepped 'with such assurance from his crowded bed-sitting rooms and sleazy music halls on to the stage of world history' (Page 1988: 31). This kind of judgement not only erects a hierarchy, in which the local concerns of contemporary realism are seen to be less important – because less ambitious or far-reaching – than the 'universal' themes of history, but also blurs the degree to which plays about history are connected to the present, if only implicitly. In fact, the relationship between past and present in the history plays of this period is often complex and varied; indeed, in some senses, many of them are not 'history' plays at all.

One recurrent point of reference in the discussion of history plays was Brecht, who provided one of the main European models of a serious and committed historical drama. Brecht and the

Berliner Ensemble visited Britain in August of 1956. The company brought three productions, *Mother Courage*, *The Caucasian Chalk Circle* and *Trumpets and Drums*, which were generally met by a contradictory response from the West End audience, attracting 'much attention but not much critical acclaim' (Elsom 1976: 113). However, the visit did have an impact on British theatre practitioners and critics, erecting a set of criteria against which political/ historical drama could be judged. Both Milne (in *Encore*) and Tynan (in the *Observer*) compared Bolt's *A Man for All Seasons* unfavourably to Brecht's plays in general, and *Galileo* in particular. Tynan also used *Galileo* as a point of reference for his review of *Luther*, a play which was also seen more generally in relation to a Brechtian dramaturgy.

The influence of Brecht (and his company) was, and continues to be, complex and to stretch beyond the practice of playwrighting. With its emphasis on a permanent working group, on collective effort, and the value of the ensemble as a means of organising a company, the Berliner was a clear alternative to the ethic of the star system and the half-hearted amateurism that was one of the most persistent criticisms of British theatre. Devine visited the Berliner in East Berlin in 1955 and was clearly impressed by both the professionalism and the 'artistic dedication' in what he saw there. 'The group appears to function in a natural and unneurotic manner', he noted, linking the fact that it was an ensemble to a 'strong artistic conception' (Devine 1970: 16). What Devine saw in the Berliner was the fulfilment of his ambitions for the English Stage Company; a theatre heavily supported by the State, with a permanent company, a strong professionalism, a clear artistic policy (although Devine did not share this) and a popular audience.

What was missing from British Brechtianism in the late fifties was a clear engagement with Brecht's politics.[4] The idea of Brecht as a committed artist was an attractive one. The editors of *The Encore*

---

4 That this was not an inevitable process, but rather one that was specific to British theatrical and intellectual formations in the period, is apparent when the British response is compared with that of a group of French intellectuals who were encountering Brecht at about the same time. Roland Barthes, for example, responded to very different themes in Brecht's work. In an article written in 1956, Barthes considered the implications of Brecht's thinking in the fields of sociology, ideology, semiology and morality, arguing that 'A knowledge of Brecht, consideration of Brecht – in short, Brechtian criticism – is by definition to cover the basic issues of our time' (Barthes 1979: 25).

Reader argued that 'there was no question about the pervasive all-infecting influence of Bertolt Brecht', and that 'To be Brechtian was to be politically concerned, theatrically bold and artistically disciplined' (Marowitz *et al.* 1970: 135); there is little doubt that it was really the latter two qualities that were most influential – and, to illustrate the paradoxical nature of the appropriation of Brecht, they were not the exclusive properties of a 'Brechtian' theatre.

The marginalisation of Brecht's politics was a result of both the difficulty of finding a coherent politics within the New Wave itself, and of the persistence of a Cold War rhetoric that automatically coloured perceptions of Brecht's relationship with the East German government (a relationship that was not without its paradoxes). Mathers has argued that *Encore's* interest in Brecht was 'almost exclusively centred on certain aesthetic criteria, on the "technical elements of alienation"' (Mathers 1975: 81). And although *Encore* did not have a particular 'line' on Brecht, or anyone else, it is certainly the case that Brecht was appreciated mainly as a 'professional' and to the degree to which he could be used to contribute to, and shape, debates that had already been established. On the one hand, this led to an emphasis on Brecht as a poet (Ernest Bornemann lionised him as a 'lyric poet' whose gifts 'transformed everything he touched'; Bornemann 1970: 141). On the other, Brecht's name became a shorthand for a general anti-naturalism, particularly in performance. Lindsay Anderson, for example, commended Avis Bunnage's performance in *A Taste of Honey* as 'real Brechtian playing' (Anderson 1970b: 80).

The influence of Brecht on most British history plays did not proceed, therefore, from a similar politics but tended to focus on particular narrative techniques. Like Brecht's plays, *A Man for All Seasons* and *Luther* use a particular period of history, and are written in an episodic manner, with a narrative of self-contained actions that appears to fracture the strict temporal unity and cause and effect logic of the three-act drama. Both use a form of narration; *A Man* has a recurrent character, the Common Man, who gives a view of the events of the play, whilst in *Luther* each scene is announced by the figure of a knight. However, these connections are at best superficial and at worst misleading, not least because 'history' is largely absent from both of these plays.

The comparison with Brecht threw up the degree to which the precise contours of another historical period and society were the subject of the plays, even when the ultimate lessons to be learnt were about contemporary Britain. Brecht's history plays, notably *Galileo* and *Mother Courage*, set the main narratives within a carefully drawn historical context, one which is defined in terms of the social and political processes that govern the relationships between his characters. For Tynan, this was precisely what was missing from *A Man*.

> Mr Bolt is primarily absorbed in the state of More's conscience, not in the state of More's England or More's Europe.
> . . . Brecht, on the other hand, though he gives us an intimate study of Galileo's conscience, takes pains to relate it at every turn to Galileo's world and to the universe at large.
>
> (Tynan 1984: 287–8)

Gascoine, in a generally favourable review, observed a similar lack in *Luther*: 'The play offers no analysis of the causes of the Reformation, no explanation of Luther's magnetism, nor even the picture of an age' (Page 1988: 29).

Both *Luther* and *A Man*, in fact, show quite marked and unexpected connections to the earlier, more intensive naturalism – and in Osborne's case, to the intensive form of his own earlier plays. Both centre on a dominating central protagonist, who is constructed as a psychologically rounded individual, pitted against a 'society' that is outside him. This was emphasised in production with the casting in the central roles of charismatic actors, Paul Scofield (More) and Albert Finney (Luther), and was perfectly compatible with an episodic scene structure and a design that eschewed naturalism. As Martin Priestman has argued, 'the disturbance of the unities by back-projections and over-familiar narrators was actually quite helpful in allowing classical stars . . . to wrestle tragically with their consciences in full costume' (Priestman 1992: 119). This view of psychology is also at odds with Brecht's concept of the individual as the site of social contradictions, the point where social and historical forces meet and are played out. One result of this is that the conflicts that are then explored – More's crises of conscience, for example – appear 'timeless', very much like our own. Raymond Williams argued that *A Man* exemplified a kind of history play that is really 'a kind of ante-dated naturalism: the characters talk and feel in the twentieth century, but for action and interest are based in the sixteenth' (Williams 1978: 505). The effect is not of one historical period finding a resonance in another, but of history itself being obliterated, dissolved into a pool of universal human concerns.

Luther is also remarkably like Osborne's other protagonists at this time; Tynan remarked that he was remarkably like Osborne himself. 'Why . . . should John Osborne have wanted to write a play about the founder of Protestantism?' he asked. 'Is there not something here that might speak to the author of *Look Back in Anger*, embarrassed to find himself dubbed an apostle of social revolution when in fact, like Luther, he preached nothing but revolutionary individualism?' (Tynan 1984: 314). Like both Jimmy Porter and Archie Rice, Luther is almost outside history altogether, the essential conflicts that trouble him arising not out of his time but out of a kind of original sin of self-doubt and a compulsion towards the truth as he sees it. He is a character who is not produced by history, but rather acts upon it, his inner conflicts played out on a world stage.

A different attitude towards history – and a different relationship to Brecht – is revealed in Arden's writing. Arden's plays are unlike any others in the New Wave, drawing on a range of popular and literary forms to engage not only with the processes of history, but also to explore, along a different path from his contemporaries, the possibilities of a contemporary political theatre. Although both *Serjeant Musgrave's Dance* and *Armstrong's Last Goodnight* were set in the past, the impetus for both of them was contemporary political events – as it was for all of Arden's plays. Arden wrote *Musgrave*, a play about the impact of a group of deserters from a British colonial war on a northern mining town in the mid to late nineteenth century, after reading a newspaper account of an incident involving British troops in Cyprus. And *Armstrong*, set in late medieval Scotland, was written after reading Conor Cruise O'Brien's *To Katanga and Back*, an account of events in the Belgian Congo. In neither play are these original sources openly acknowledged, and the connections are partly at the level of the issues explored. Thus *Musgrave* is a play about the nature of pacifism and the correct response to acts of violence, colonial or otherwise, and *Armstrong* discusses questions of political morality. However, the choice of period was not arbitrary, nor was it based on an attraction to particular individuals from the past, but arose out of similarities between the two historical situations. Therefore, *Musgrave*, a play written in response to contemporary colonialism, was set in the period of colonial expansion; and *Armstrong* was set in a period of European history that had clear parallels to the Africa of the mid-1950s.

Theatre Workshop: De-mythologising History

After 1956, Theatre Workshop was best known for its productions of new plays with contemporary low-life settings. Its reputation before that time, however, rested on its productions of classical plays, particularly Shakespeare and other writers in the European literary and popular tradition, as we have seen. The connection between the 'classics' and contemporary plays in the repertoire was not as clear-cut as this convenient chronological separation would suggest, however. The approach to classical drama was always rooted in contemporary concerns; as Tom Milne put it, 'Theatre Workshop produces Shakespeare or Marlowe as though the play had only just been written, and the playwright were commenting on life as we know it today' (Milne 1970: 81). Conversely, both *The Hostage* and *Oh What a Lovely War* are, amongst other things, about the processes of history, even though the former is set in a time contemporary to its first performance. However, the relationship between history and the contemporary in these plays is different in some ways from that found in the texts discussed so far. One of the central intentions of both texts is the desire to de-mythologise history, to contest some of the main assumptions and beliefs that attach to particular historical events. In the case of *The Hostage*, it is Irish history, especially the 'Troubles' and the Civil War, that is subject to scrutiny; in *Oh What a Lovely War*, it is the First World War.

Oh What a Lovely War (1963) was one of the most innovative productions in the period, and also one of the most influential (see Goorney 1981 and Bradby and Williams 1988). The impetus for the play was a radio programme by Charles Hilton on the popular songs of the First World War. Goorney has noted that the play was originally designed as a way of setting these songs (Goorney 1981: 125), which, in the words of one of the actors in the original production, Brian Murphy, 'trace a period of history which can be presented without the realistic background that you would need in a film' (Goorney 1981: 125). The songs, therefore, were both a form of social history and a springboard into the main conventions of the performance.

The narrative model was radically different from the intensive forms of the naturalist theatre, dramatising the war not by focusing on one particular moment (the strategy adopted by R.C. Sheriff's *Journey's End*, a naturalist play that examined the war through the relationships between a small group of soldiers), but by finding a form that attempted to represent the entire duration of the conflict. The play did this by using a variety of modes of address and theatrical genres: documentary slides projected onto a large screen at the back of the stage; a 'ticker tape' newspanel reminiscent of advertisements which relayed statistics about the war, especially its casualties; realistic scenes of life in the trenches; scenes reminiscent of pre-war agit-prop, such as the one that represented the machinations of the arms manufacturers who wished to keep the war going for their own profit; sequences of pure music-hall, such as the recruiting song in Act One; and, of course, the songs themselves, threaded throughout the action, and presented in a variety of ways.

At the centre of the production was a unifying theatrical device, that of presenting the action in terms of the routines of the Merry Roosters (who actually existed), an end-of-the-pier Pierrot show of the kind that were popular in seaside resorts around 1914. As part of his sceptical account of the viability of popular forms for a contemporary audience, David Edgar has noted that the Pierrot show was a genre that was 'peripheral to the urban British working-class' (McGrath 1981: 33), but it is not so much the specific resonances of the type of entertainment offered by the Merry Roosters that was important in the play as the way that they functioned theatrically in relation to other performance elements. The costumes of the troupe, which consisted of the traditional baggy white trousers with black collar and prominent black buttons, were worn throughout by a cast that played multiple roles. This meant that, whether in a trench or the drawing-room of an upper-class British house, such costumes were a distancing device, in Brechtian terms, a constant reminder of the theatricality of the piece. Such visual dissonances were part of a system of ironic contradiction that structured the performance as a whole. The pious and self-interested hopes of General Haig that one last push would lead to break-through was contradicted by statistics of the actual dead and scenes of actual soldiers from the front; the newspanel announcement of losses of 85,000 men at Verdun was juxtaposed with the singing of 'Goodbye-ee', an ironic song about a soldier leaving to go off to war.

And whole scenes were positioned against each other, Haig and his Generals ineptly planning the campaign and pursuing their own private vendettas, followed later by scenes which demonstrated the human consequences of their actions.

Oh What a Lovely War was undoubtedly a political play. There are, however, two versions of how its politics worked. Commenting on the way that the play rejected conventional 'realism', Clive Barker, who was in the original production, argued that the play was 'a celebration of human resourcefulness in the face of the most appalling catastrophic conditions . . . [and] courage, humour, comradeship, the triumph of life over death and the international solidarity between soldiers' (Goorney 1981: 126). It was also, clearly, a reinterpretation of the events of the war from a perspective that saw the conflagration as at root an Imperial one, resulting from the organised greed of international capitalism, and the ineptitude of the European ruling-classes.

It was, in addition, possible that its abundant theatricality could be read, not as ironic or 'estranging', but rather as sentimental. The criticism here is partly one that comes from the ease with which the songs could be seen as merely nostalgic, and several critics have pointed out the way that the play's impact was muted on its transfer to the West End. The ending, in particular, was changed. The original ending had the MC coming onto the stage and making a short speech, which according to Frances Cukor 'went something like "The war game is being played all over the world, by all ages, there's a pack for all the family. It's been going on for a long time and it's still going on. Goodnight".' However, after the transfer the show ended with a reprise of the songs, which was generally felt to have weakened the impact of the performance and to have been 'calculated to send the audience home happy' (Goorney 1981: 127). The political problem here has both aesthetic and institutional aspects, which relate not just to *Oh What a Lovely War* but to the project of the company as a whole.

Littlewood and Theatre Workshop recognised, as Brecht had done, that questions of organisation, form and audience are, at some level, political questions. Commenting on the effects that moving to a London base had on the values and objectives of the company, Ewan MacColl argued thus:

Before this, the level of discussion had been 'What are we doing wrong when we take a play about mining to the Welsh coal villages and the miners don't care?' This is a perfectly valid question, and by answering it we could formulate a way of dealing with the situation. But new questions were going to be 'How are we going to get Harold Hobson? What is he going to think of us?' I don't think anybody at that particular time realised what was involved in trying to make the critics happy.

(Goorney 1981: 88)

6

THE TWO NEW WAVES
Realism in theatre and film

That there was a close relationship between theatre and cinema in the late 1950s and early 1960s has often been remarked, even if comparative analyses of plays and films are rare. It has been a characteristic of post-war culture that writers as well as actors, directors and other theatre practitioners have worked not only in theatre but in film and television as well; however, at this cultural moment, the relationship between theatre and film was more than just a particular example of a more general drift towards the new possibilities of the electronic media. Not only did some of the central figures in the debates around New Wave theatre also work in the cinema, but the two media had several key objectives in common, not the least of which was the ambition to work outside (at least, partially) the dominant institutions of each medium. And it is in the cinema that the moment of Working-Class Realism finds its most coherent expression.

The term New Wave in the cinema is usually applied to a series of films that were made between 1959 and 1965 by film-makers generally new to the industry, and which were based on successful novels and plays. These included: *Look Back in Anger* (1959), *The Entertainer* (1960), *A Taste of Honey* (1961), *Room at the Top* (1959), *Saturday Night and Sunday Morning* (1960), *A Kind of Loving* (1962), *The Loneliness of the Long Distance Runner* (1962), *This Sporting Life* (1963) and *Billy Liar* (1963). In addition, two other plays associated with the new theatre were made into films, although they play a lesser part in the critical debates; *The Kitchen* (1961) and *The Quare Fellow* (1962). It was not just the texts that theatre and film had in common, it was also key personnel. Lindsay Anderson and Tony Richardson, two of the directors most closely associated with the Royal Court, directed in both media; Woodfall Films, which produced *Look Back in Anger, The Entertainer, Saturday Night and Sunday Morning* and *A Taste of Honey,* was formed by Richardson and John Osborne as the only satisfactory means of filming Osborne's plays. The films also used new acting talent drawn from the theatre – Albert Finney, Tom Courtney, Rita Tushingham and Rachel Roberts, for example, appeared in central roles, assuring them almost star status as the success of the films grew. The Royal Court provided a virtual repertory company of actors in many of the smaller parts.

Even more than the new theatre, New Wave cinema was discussed in terms of its realism. As John Hill has put it, 'What, above all, seemed to distinguish this new cinema was its commitment to "realism", a determination to tackle "real" social issues and experiences in a manner which matched, a style which was honest and "realistic" as well.' (Hill 1986: 127) However, as we have seen in relation to New Wave theatre, realism has no absolute character-istics, but is seen in terms of – as a rejection of – the 'realism' of what preceded it. Realism in this sense relies for its effect on being different from anything else around it. Its innovations are towards a greater 'truthfulness' in its depiction of social reality and its representations are 'how things really are'. The realism of both New Waves was of this kind. 'How things really are' frequently meant dealing with subjects that were taboo in most mainstream cinema (as they had been in theatre); this was especially true of the depiction of sex. However, the rejection had different aspects, and was not simply confined to 'content' in the films any more than in the theatre.

Realist cinema adopted a similar position in relation to the existing British film industry as its counterpart in the theatre occupied in relation to the established theatre structures. Just as the new drama was the product of minority theatres attempting to operate in distinctive ways, the new cinema was associated with independent companies and producers; and both appeared at a time when the mainstream was in crisis. In the cinema, the most dramatic manifestation of this crisis was the rapid decline in attendance that characterised the decade as a whole. Audiences fell from 1396 million in 1950 to 1082 million in 1955, and then to 581 million in 1959 (the period of most rapid decline). By 1963 this figure had fallen still further, to 357 million. The most obvious reason for this, in the opinion of contemporary commentators, was the rise of television. We have already seen how the increase in the

164

number of television sets from 1953 onwards became symbolic of affluence itself, and by the end of the 1950s, television had become the dominant mass entertainment. As in the theatre, one result of this was the concentration of economic power in the hands of a small number of powerful companies – notably Rank and ABC – whose main influence was felt in cinema ownership and distribution, over which they dominated. The independent companies associated with the New Wave were not, however, able to operate outside this system any more than the English Stage Company or Theatre Workshop could operate outside the economic constraints that governed the theatre industry, and their freedom for manoeuvre was severely circumscribed. The films were commercially financed, and distributed as any other British film might be – often, as in the case of *The Entertainer*, in the face of considerable hostility and distrust. That Osborne and Richardson (who had no track record as a film director, having joined the English Stage Company from television) were able to make films at all was a result of the success of the stage plays, rather than any judgement about the value of letting 'new' directors into an ossified system. In fact, it was often in the interests of the major distributors – as it was in the interests of the commercial theatre – to allow new, independent productions into the circuit, particularly when they proved to be successful; as Durgnat observed, 'the British cinema renewed itself . . . by orthodox commercial procedures' (Durgnat 1970: 129).

However, it is unlikely that companies such as Woodfall would have been set up at all if there had been no possibility of some degree of creative freedom, of a relative autonomy that would retain power in the hands of the company itself. This meant not a rejection of a commercial system, but rather developing distinctive working patterns. As Richardson put it: 'It is absolutely vital to get into British films the same sort of impact and sense of life that what you can loosely call the Angry Young Man cult has had in the theatre and literary worlds' (Hill 1986: 40). Just as Devine and Littlewood had to create new companies in order to establish new ways of working, New Wave film directors used the relative freedom of the independent company to make films in a different way; shooting on location (usually outside the affluent heartlands of southern England), using largely unknown actors, and occasionally improvising performances all placed the new cinema in opposition to 'the "phoney" conventions of character and place characteristic of British studio procedure' (Hill 1986: 127).

The rejection of the studio system was tied closely to a rejection of a particular view of the world, which both the theatre and the cinema attacked as being 'snobbish, anti-intelligent, emotionally inhibited, wilfully blind to the conditions and problems of the present, dedicated to an out-of-date, exhausted national ideal' (L. Anderson 1957: 157). The initial reviews of the films usually highlighted this sense that what was being represented was both different from existing British film and closer to 'reality'. 'If it did nothing else', wrote the reviewer in the *New Statesman*, 'Jack Clayton's *Room at the Top* . . . would be remarkable in being a British film that shatters the pattern' (Whitebait 1959a: 144). The film version of *Look Back in Anger* was similarly lauded for its 'adult' content and the ways in which it differed from other British films. The *Monthly Film Bulletin* noted that Richardson had given the play a 'tough vital style which represents something new in British cinema' (Hill 1986: 195), whilst a review in the *New Statesman* observed that the film had 'the urgencies and contacts the British film has been drearily drifting away from ever since the War' (Whitebait 1959b: 758).

Many of the concerns – and some of the personnel – that dominate the new realist cinema came out of the Free Cinema movement of the middle years of the decade. Free Cinema consisted of six programmes of films shown at the National Film Theatre between 1956 and 1959 that were linked by a series of manifestos cum press-handouts, which sought to connect the programmes to a set of interests shared by the programme organisers and film-makers. The group responsible for the NFT seasons was informally constituted, but Anderson, Richardson and Karel Reisz were prominent. The characteristic Free Cinema product was the short documentary about an aspect of contemporary British life – for example, *We Are the Lambeth Boys* (1959, Reisz), which was about a London youth club and its members, and *Everyday Except Christmas* (1957, Anderson), filmed in and around Covent Garden market. The critical work that accompanied the programmes, and which spilled out into the pages of *Universities and Left Review*, helped to focus the underlying concerns of the movement. These have been summarised by Hillier and Lovell:

> a sympathetic interest in communities, whether they were the traditional industrial ones . . . or the new, improvised one of

the jazz club . . . fascination with the newly emerging youth culture . . . unease about the quality of leisure in an urban society . . . and respect for the traditional working-class.

(Hillier and Lovell 1972: 172)

The new realist films were not simply Free Cinema under another banner; as Raymond Durgnat has pointed out, 'while the partisans of Free Cinema were directing stage plays and T.V. commercials, the New Wave arose from the responses to the work of other media' (Durgnat 1970: 129). However, in some respects, Free Cinema did influence the development of both the films and the critical context that was there to interpret them. On the one hand, there is a certain continuity in visual style from documentary to feature film (despite the obvious differences between the two forms), and, on the other, many of the intentions that surfaced in Free Cinema can also be traced in the commercial films – especially the fascination with traditional working-class culture and the ambition to represent what is contemporary about contemporary Britain. And whilst none of the feature films is a documentary, the concern with 'contemporaryness', with life-as-it-is, reinforced realist and documentary readings of them, just as the critical writing (particularly Anderson's) helped to set the agenda for the discussion of New Wave cinema.

A simple, but essential, point needs to be made at this juncture; New Wave screen adaptations are not merely the 'films of the plays'. The latter were, in significant ways, radically reconstituted on the journey from stage to screen. An indication of this is that frequently writers other than the original dramatists were involved in producing the screenplays. Nigel Kneale wrote the screenplay for *Look Back in Anger* (although Osborne is credited with having provided 'additional dialogue'); Kneale and Osborne also collaborated on *The Entertainer* (although Osborne took over from Kneale, who was originally contracted to produce the script); *A Taste of Honey* was co-written by Delaney and Tony Richardson; the screenplay for *The Kitchen* is credited to Sidney Cole (Wesker is not mentioned); Keith Waterhouse and Willis Hall are exceptions to this trend, writing the screenplay of *Billy Liar* from their own play and novel. In addition, films are, of course, largely authored by their directors; in the reviews it is Tony Richardson's *Look Back in Anger, The Entertainer* and *A Taste of Honey*, not Osborne's or Delaney's. This is both a function of the way that they are made as well as the way that they are distributed and promoted; certainly, one of the impulses behind New Wave cinema was the desire for creative freedom for the director, a freedom to evolve a style and a personal 'vision' (in the case of many of the adaptations we shall be considering here, it was the vision of Tony Richardson).

PLAY-TO-FILM: THE USE OF SPACE IN NEW WAVE FILMS

One of the main limitations of stage realism has always been the physical constraints it places on the action of the play. The cluttered domestic interiors of Working-Class Realism, as much as the bourgeois living-room of high naturalism, actively prevented the drama from representing in a direct manner the reality beyond the walls of the box-set. However, the mobility of the camera has meant that neither film nor television need suffer from these constraints. One of the most obvious and important differences between the films and the plays on which they are based is the way that the former take advantage of the camera to transform the spatial systems of the latter, opening up the action in ways that lead to a radical transformation of the narratives. This usually takes the form of representing directly on screen situations and locations that are only referred to in the plays. The film of *Look Back in Anger* takes us to the jazz club/pub; to the street market where Jimmy and Cliff have their street stall; to the funeral of Mrs Tanner; to the streets of the Midland town in which the action is set. The ending of the film relocates the entire action from the flat to a railway station. *A Taste of Honey* uses two different flats (where the play text specifies only one) as well as representing the streets around them both; we are shown the shop in which Jo works; the film takes us to Blackpool, rather than simply noting that the trip has taken place; we see the canals as well as the ship on which Jimmy, Jo's black sailor lover, is the cook. In *Billy Liar* we see Billy's place of work (the funeral parlour), the dance-hall, the station and the cemetery; we also see extensive shots of the town in which the action is set, as well as of the countryside around it. The play specifies a single set of a house and adjacent street corner. Only *The Kitchen* retains a focus on the same single playing space as the play (although there is one short sequence in which we follow the central character into the street).

One of the results of this opening out of the action is that far more of the society in which the characters move is actually shown rather than being referred to in the dialogue or mediated through the characters, as is usually the case with the plays. It is on this basis that a considerable part of the films' claims to realism is constructed. The showing of British society in this way makes it possible to read the films as 'documentary', connecting them to a realism which captures the surface of a contemporary Britain that is different from the one typically represented on screen. As a reviewer of *The Entertainer* put it, the film 'can't help catching the eye, jabbing at the mind, bringing up another England than the usual one. . . . Jaunts along the front, a bathing-beauty contest, a holiday camp . . . they represent a fearsome documentary of seaside pleasures' (Whitebait 1960: 154).

This kind of realism is reinforced by the way that some of the main theatrical conventions that govern the plays are removed in the screen adaptations. Both *The Entertainer* and *A Taste of Honey* have, as we have seen, self-reflexive elements. *The Entertainer* contains a framing device, in which the stage action is set within the larger context of a music-hall performance; and *A Taste of Honey* contains direct address to the audience and a jazz band that comments on the action and is visible throughout the play. That a cinematic equivalent of this kind of theatricality would not be used in the screen adaptation is not the result of any innate difference between the two media, but is bound up with the desire of the film-makers to be more unproblematically 'realistic'. Walker has noted that Kneale 'felt that [*The Entertainer*] should have been completely recast for the screen, even if it meant forfeiting Olivier, since this was the only means he envisaged of getting carte blanche for a completely naturalistic approach' (Walker 1974: 76). It was, however, the cause of much adverse critical comment. John Russell Taylor, for example, called the film 'totally misconceived' on the basis that it 'tries to transplant all the least realistic sections unchanged into a setting of documentary realism' (Walker 1974: 76). That this was, by definition, a failure is open to argument.

British society is present in the films in different ways, but largely as a rhetoric of place, as a set of familiar, repeated and therefore expected locations; the pub, the back street, the dance-hall, the interior of the working-class terraced house. These locations are typically framed not only to further the narrative but also to create a focus of attention (often assisted by music) on the social milieu itself. As Hill has argued:

> In many of the 'New Wave' films. . . it is common to delay the fixing of a place as a locale for action, either by introducing places initially devoid of action (or characters) or by extending the number of establishing shots involved in the introduction of a scene.
>
> (Hill 1986: 129)

In *Look Back in Anger*, for example, we see the morning ritual of the street market being set up for some time before the camera settles on Jimmy and Cliff with their barrow. And in *A Taste of Honey*, the sequence in which Jo and Geoffrey meet at a street parade contains, as Hill has pointed out, about twenty-seven seconds of establishing shots before Jo is picked out in the crowd and the scene enters the narrative proper (Hill 1986: 130). This use of space, which is not immediately narrativised into setting but remains present in its own right, is one of the principal ways in which New Wave films appear different from mainstream cinema; it becomes one means of 'inscribing a distance between these films and the overtly contrived "fictions" of Hollywood, with their tightly structured narratives and avoidance of "residual" elements' (Hill 1986: 131).

NEW WAVE CINEMA AND POETIC REALISM

This treatment of place, of the real locations of a mainly northern Britain, is not only 'documentary' in its appeal. If we look more carefully at the way that the 'real' social geography of industrial landscapes are integrated into the narrative, then a number of different impulses – and therefore different readings – emerge. One of these impulses is an aesthetic one, which at first sight sits in uneasy alliance with notions of documentary realism. We have already noted how both Free Cinema and the New Wave privileged the role of the director-as-author, in a bid to create a space for personal 'vision'. This emphasis on the autonomy of the director is a paradoxical legacy of Free Cinema; paradoxical, because the claim of documentary is that it represents the objective 'truth', reality as it 'really' is, unmediated by aesthetics or authorial intervention (this is also the claim of certain forms of realism). Free Cinema documentarists explicitly denied this version of the status of the form. Anderson asserted that 'we all believe that "objectivity" is no part of the documentary method, that on the contrary, the documentarist must formulate his attitude, express his values as firmly as any artist' (L. Anderson 1958: 51). This is an attempt to reconstitute the basis for documentary in a way that overcomes some of the traditional distinctions between it and 'fiction' – fact/interpretation, capturing reality/constructing reality, the primacy of actuality/the primacy of creative vision. Reisz argued that documentarists should learn from writers and film-makers working in fictional forms; 'the terrible joylessness of British documentary is directly the result of this sort of mistrust of the artist's insights' (Reisz 1958: 25). Anderson stated the position succinctly:

> the only vital difference between making a documentary and making a feature film is that in documentary you are using 'actual' material, not invented situation and actors playing parts. But this actual material still has to be worked on creatively, or we are left with nothing but publicity.
>
> (L. Anderson 1958: 52)

Working on reality creatively and poetically was an essential part of the project of realist cinema; Walter Lassally, the cinematographer on both *The Loneliness of the Long Distance Runner* and *A Taste of Honey* said that what was 'remarkable' about such films was not they 'treat working-class people, working-class problems, but that they have a very poetic view of them' (Higson 1984: 2), and contemporary reviews frequently acknowledged the poetic standpoint and contribution of the director (and cameraman) even as they were praising the truth of the depiction of social reality. Reviewing *A Taste of Honey* for the *Daily Herald* Paul Dehn wrote that 'The film's real heroes are Mr Richardson and his masterly cameraman Walter Lassally, who between them have caught Manchester's canal threaded hinterland to a misty, moisty, smokey nicety' (Higson 1984: 9).

The term 'poetic' in this context implied exactly what it did in the theatre, an 'aestheticisation' of a fictional world (in this case a meticulously 'captured' social environment) that was at the same time being lauded as 'realist'. In other words, that which was subject to documentary readings – the social geography of a Britain that could only be implied in the plays – could also be read in terms that drew attention to the language in which that geography was represented. 'Poetic realism', therefore, registered a tension between a

171

style of film-making that simply aimed to 'record' social reality and one which aimed to draw attention to its own activity.

To take one recurrent example: most of the films contain a sequence (at least one) in which the characters escape to the countryside. At some point, they look back towards the town in a panoramic shot that is self-consciously beautiful; one critic, recognising that such sequences had become almost a cliché in the rhetoric of realist cinema, referred to it as 'That Long Shot of Our Town from That Hill' (Higson 1984: 2). The appeal of these sequences is partly aesthetic – we take in and admire the scenery as spectacle – and partly sociological; the town/city is laid bare, its shape and outline caught often within a single frame. In *A Taste of Honey* (which has the obligatory scene on a hill) there is a similar use of urban landscapes. To take one example; in the play, the moment when Jo informs Geoff that she is pregnant takes place in the flat. In the film, it is introduced in a sequence in which Jo is initially framed in long shot under (presumably) a railway arch. The immediate appeal of this image is aesthetic; the curve of the arch is striking, its visual impact heightened by its being darkened into silhouette, and its clear lines contrasted with Jo, hunched against one of its pillars. The voices, when they come, are distorted by an echo. This image can also be read as a metaphor for entrapment, of course, the arch containing and constraining Jo as her pregnancy is about to do; the point is that it is so in a way that asks the spectator to admire its aesthetic composition, its suitability as metaphor. It is also an image that holds Jo at a distance, that removes us initially from her situation.

This objectivity is a particular instance of a more general characteristic of the films – that the foregrounding of the way that reality is represented opens up a distance between the spectator and character/action. We are 'removed' from the characters, who become, literally, figures in a landscape. This is not, however, a Brechtian distance, for its aim is not to create a spectator who is critically active, but rather the reverse – it assumes a spectator who is comfortable with his/her sense of separation. The observing gaze, which might in other contexts become voyeuristic, is permitted by the 'moral realism' of the commitment to the political project of social extension; it does, though, construct aesthetic distance as social difference. This distance/difference has been allied to the critical stance of the directors themselves, who were similarly 'outside' the subject matter they represented. It is not

172

simply that the directors did not necessarily come from working-class backgrounds themselves, but that the distance created by the aestheticisation of industrial squalor, particularly in *A Taste of Honey* and *Saturday Night and Sunday Morning*, can be constituted as a class difference. As Higson has observed, 'it is only from a class position outside the city that the city can appear beautiful' (Higson 1984: 18). This is clearly related to the critical context surrounding working-class realist theatre, which, as we have seen, constructed readings that emphasised an almost anthropological detachment from, and superiority towards, the social world being represented. In both media, situations are observed, and characters become objects of our concern rather than figures for our identification.

THE CHANGING CONTEXT OF SOCIAL REALISM

It is worth reminding ourselves that the films under discussion appeared some years after the plays on which they were based. Three years separated the two versions of *Look Back in Anger*, *The Entertainer*, *A Taste of Honey* and *Billy Liar*, whilst there were two years between the appearance of *The Kitchen* on stage and on screen. In many ways, the historical moment had changed. This was registered in different ways in different films, and valued differently by contemporary critics. *Look Back in Anger* and *The Entertainer* received mixed reviews, with some critics applauding the relative realism of the films, whilst others responded to both films and plays in terms which echoed a more widespread re-evaluation of the project of anger itself from the vantage point of having 'moved on'. It may be hard to pin-point the exact moment at which 'Anger' becomes 'Working-Class Realism', but there is a clear sense that change had indeed occurred. 'How long does it take a sensational, shocking and timely play to become digestible and mildly dated?' asked the *Daily Express*. 'Answer: the time it takes to transfer it from the stage to the screen' (Hill 1986: 196). Both the Osborne plays also suffered by comparison with later New Wave films, being viewed as 'apprentice work', suggesting a potential (especially in relation to an idea of poetic realism) that was only realised later. Thus, in the course of a review of *A Taste of Honey*, the *Daily Herald* observed that 'Tony Richardson's direction fulfils the poetic prom-ise and avoids the technical pitfalls of *Look Back in Anger* and *The Entertainer*' (Higson 1984: 9). That 'poetic realism' seems less fully achieved in the earlier films may be more a question of subject matter than of mastery of technique; for in many ways the realism of the films was being judged in relation to a new set of ideas, often present in the plays, but given a different emphasis in this changed context.

One way of viewing this is to argue that these films are not simply concerned with the cultural and social experience of the northern working-classes, but also with the problem of 'culture' itself – and especially the encroachment of mass culture on the lives and opportunities of the communities represented. This concern with the debilitating effects of mass culture is a current that runs deep in the period, as we have seen, crossing artistic forms and surfacing in a range of discourses, and centring on a fear for the political and cultural homogeneity of the working-class. In this way, the concern with traditional working-class communities is of a piece with the hostility towards mass culture, and is reflected in the way that New Wave realist films are overwhelmingly set in domestic and leisure spaces (the pub, the club, the dance-hall, the fairground) – and hardly ever in the workplace.

In some New Wave films (though not those based on plays), the main target is television (see especially *Saturday Night and Sunday Morning* and *Loneliness of a Long Distance Runner*), but of the texts under consideration here, the trip to Blackpool in *A Taste of Honey* is one of the clearest, and most often cited, examples of the way that mass leisure is represented (even though Blackpool offers a more traditional form of working-class entertainment than is normally associated with fifties consumerism). In the play, the trip is simply reported and happens off-stage. In the film, we follow Jo, Helen and Peter to Blackpool in the company of two new characters (friends of Peter's). The sequence is clearly constructed to invite our disapproval both of the adult characters (Jo is consistently shown as an 'outsider', ill at ease and unwanted) and of the entertainment itself, which is shot in an almost expressionistic way, emphasising the grotesque (the characters are at one point seen as literally 'distorted' in a hall of mirrors) and the shallow (the words of a pop song – 'I'm gonna grab it. I'm gonna have it. Why not? Why not?').

The vacuity of modern leisure is even more central to *The Entertainer*, where it functions as part of a complex structuring device linking the major themes of the narratives of both play and film. In the play, music-hall is part of the theatrical structure of the performance, as we saw earlier, as well as a metaphor for the state of the nation itself. At the heart of both texts, however, is the juxtaposition between the traditional music-hall and its insipid post-war manifestation, which functions as the nexus of a complex series of oppositions – between past and present, authentic and in-authentic, rewarding and enervating, a 'rich' human and cultural experience and a shallow one. This is represented indexically by Billy Rice, Archie's father, who is one of the last surviving artists from that time. Archie's current review, in contrast, is not only sleazy and exploitative (once again, rock 'n' roll is used as a sign for contemporary kitsch), it is also unsuccessful. The terms of the opposition are demonstrated in the film in a cut between a sequence in which Billy is asked to sing, spontaneously, in a pub (which is not in the play) and one of Archie's routines (which is substantially one of Archie's front-cloth routines from the stage version). Billy's song is warmly received by an audience that fills the frame, whilst Archie plays to a half empty house, the only response being the salacious laughter of the family of his young mistress, with whom he is about to go into business.

The film that uses the most obviously contemporary symbols of mass culture is probably *Billy Liar*, where the by now conventional signs for affluence are not so much referred to as on display; supermarkets, the radio, and television are amongst the main targets. The play has no direct equivalent to this kind of criticism, keeping the action within a single set and a limited range of characters. Only a reference to a letter from Billy's mother to a radio programme can be found in both film and play. Conceived like the novel and the play in essentially comic terms, the film adopts a more satirical stance towards the culture it represents than many of the other films of the New Wave. This is manifest partly through the characterisation of Billy's family and fiancées, but mainly through a number of set-piece routines. At one point, the comic Danny Boon, with whom Billy is attempting to find work as a scriptwriter, opens a supermarket. A shot sweeps across an array of identical tills (the uniformity and impersonality of mass culture), and the opening is conducted to the wonderfully incongruous strains of a pipe band (the appalling bad taste of mass culture). The figure of Danny Boon himself is presented in terms that emphasise his duplicity (his relationship to his employees contrasted with his public persona, replete with catchphrase and catch-all smile) and the shallowness of the 'entertainment' he offers. An important corollary to this is the way that the audience for Boon and the kind of popular culture he represents are represented in the film. The dialogue he is given at the opening of the supermarket is reminiscent of that given to Archie Rice as he compères a beauty contest in *The Entertainer*; that is, it draws attention to itself as being meretricious and cheap. The fact that it also draws a positive response from the screen audience of shoppers (*Billy Liar*) and trippers (*The Entertainer*) constructs an essentially manipulative relationship between entertainer and entertained, which – when it is confirmed as a system across the films as a whole – constructs a view of the broader, un-named public as a duped 'mass'. The audience for the film itself, then, is placed in a superior position to the characters within it, particularly the crowds (again, partly a function of its comic conventions), able to see and criticise what is hidden from the characters themselves.

This relationship between mass entertainment and its audience, and between that audience and the implied one for the film itself, is best illustrated in the opening sequence, which is very different from that of the play. The opening image is of a clock on the wall of a radio studio, where an early morning programme is being broadcast. The presenter (Godfrey Wynn) announces 'Good morning housewives' and begins to read from listeners' letters. The camera then pans across a series of identical houses and flats in a rapid and broad sweep that both catches a cross-section of society (the sequence includes both houses and flats, suggesting different classes as well as the 'old', pre-war terraces and the 'new', modern semis) and provides a humorous suggestion of an essential similarity (conformity) between those that live behind their doors. The camera eventually settles on one house, and then one interior – that of the Fisher household; at this point the film picks up the story at the same point as the play. This opening also functions to situate the Fisher household as 'representative' of a society that lies beyond it, and in this case it is the lower-middle rather than working-class that is being typified. This is something that the play does not have to establish in the same way, for it is a characteristic of the basic form of the play (which, although comic, shares many of the features of the realism that characterises other plays of the period) that both characters and situation are automatically representative of a wider society, and will be read as such.

In fact the genres of popular art and culture (as distinct from the trappings of an affluent society) are present in the film at a number of levels, in particular through the way that Waterhouse and Hall (and the director, John Schlesinger) have chosen to dramatise Billy's fantasies. In the play, these day-dreams and fantasies of wish-fulfilment are kept within the naturalism of its dominant form, never disturbing the illusion of an observed reality. What we see as a theatre audience is a character fantasising rather than the fantasies themselves. The effect of this is always to keep Billy's imaginings within the context that gives rise to them; indeed, they appear either as responses to the situations in which his habitual lying lands him, or as a means of defending himself against the demands of his family (his father especially) and of the social values they represent. In dramatising and elaborating on the fantasies, the film explodes with the kind of playfulness that, although it is never entirely absent from the play particularly in performance, is kept in check by its realism. The film uses its comic form both to disturb an illusionism that would otherwise prevail and to play with forms of representation; for the retreats into day-dream are presented mainly in terms of recognisable fictional genres. For example: the kingdom of Ambrosia to which Billy repeatedly escapes (and to which the play only refers as it nears its conclusion) is seen largely in terms of varieties of war films; the Fisher family are at one point transposed into the world of a Noel Coward play; Billy begins to write a novel, which is a romanticised pastiche of northern realist fiction about grinding poverty; and Billy's relationship with his boss is reversed in a sequence in which Billy imagines himself as a political leader, solving the nation's problems in terms of an heroic drama of stiff-upper-lip integrity. In each case, the sequence is shot and scripted in a way that both evokes the genre that is being utilised and draws attention to its clichés; Billy as a conscious-stricken Rommel figure striding stiff-legged across a battlefield, or receiving the salute at a march past; Billy in prison, framed by the bars of his cell.

One effect of this is to satirise the conventionality of the largely popular genres that are co-opted, although the appeal is not disruptive of an audience's expectations but rather relies on a sense of recognition of the kinds of texts that are being referred to; we are nudged into a conspiratorial laughter rather than being made aware of the ideological implications of the conventions employed. At another level, however, Billy's fantasies draw attention to the way that other characters live by fantasies that are no less damaging or evasive. Barbara, for example, his 'respectable' fiancée, fantasises about a cottage in Devon and the (improbable) life she will lead with Billy when they are married. And Billy's mother uses the radio as a form of escape from the routine of her life; 'we are only normal people', she writes to Godfrey Wynn in a letter that Billy refuses to send for her. In this way, the generic references to popular culture and art stand both as comments in themselves and are integrated into the main themes of the film, which revolve around the seductiveness of fantasies of escape and magical resolutions – and their ultimate destructiveness.

The most popular, and widely debated, New Wave films were those that had protagonists who could be read as new social archetypes, as their prototypes had been in the novels and plays in which they originated. This was most obvious when such characters were also upwardly mobile (Vic in *A Kind of Loving*, for example). What is distinctive about the film versions, though, is the way that this can be seen as a response to the changing nature of the cinema audience itself, which, whilst being in general decline, contained a high proportion of young adults. As Laing has observed, '44 per cent of those between 16 and 24 still attended cinemas at least once a week [in 1960] and a further 24 per cent at least once a month' (Laing 1986: 110). In a period where the main studios seemed unable to stop the haemorrhage of spectators to television, part of the attraction of the products of the new independent companies was their ability to capture this younger (though still adult) audience.

The desire to appeal to a young audience may be one reason behind some of the most important changes made to the narratives on their journey from stage to screen. *Look Back in Anger*, for example, begins not in the bed-sit but in a pub/club, where Jimmy is playing the jazz trumpet. Jimmy's trumpet playing is important in the play, of course, but is often more a reminder of Jimmy's presence in the flat when he is not on-stage rather than having a value in its own right. What is noticeable about the environment of the club is that it is peopled by the young (male and female, black and white). This located one element of the social world of the play in a precise way – as precise as the seediness of the Midlands garret that was such an important signifier for the original audiences for the play. The music itself is important here, for jazz is by no means an arbitrary or innocent choice. In context, jazz carried a range of connotations that go far beyond the film (or the play). On the one hand, it is part of a systematic 'internationalising' of the film, which, as Walker argues, 'divorces [Porter] from his specifically English background . . . and sets him against three themes that meant most in international cinema in the 1950s – the generation gap, race prejudice and jazz music' (Walker 1974: 61). On the other, jazz was the 'respectable' face of popular culture, an essential part of the cultural style of the new, young, left-inclined intelligentsia. Like music-hall, it was 'authentic' and complex, and could be lined up against pop and rock, 'an infinitely richer kind of music both aesthetically and emotionally' (Hall and Whannell 1964: 72). This quotation comes from *The Popular Arts* by Stuart Hall and Paddy Whannell, which was an important attempt by two writers closely connected with the New Left to open up a discussion of popular culture and reclaim it for serious attention. In particular, Hall and Whannell attempted to recast the opposition between 'high' and 'low' culture, between the traditional art forms and the mass media in terms that were echoed elsewhere on the left; 'what is good and worth while and what is shoddy and debased is not a struggle *against* the modern forms of communication, but a conflict *within* these media' (Hall and Whannell 1964: 15). Jazz was valued because it had 'much of the expressive intensity of folk art' yet was a 'sophisticated urban form' (72) which had a direct relationship to its increasingly wide audience. Jazz was allowed in the cultural festivals organised by Centre 42, whereas rock 'n' roll was not.

Look Back in Anger furnishes us with another example of the way that characters are redefined under the pressure to respond to new social archetypes. The first is Cliff; in the play, he is defined as 'short, dark, big-boned, wearing pullover and. . . very creased trousers. He is easy and relaxed, almost to lethargy. . . . He is a soothing, natural counterpoint to Jimmy' (Osborne 1957a: 10). As Micheline Wandor has observed, 'although Cliff is statedly hetero-sexual, his stage presence is sexually neuter' (Wandor 1987: 41). In the film, however, he is more recognisably a late-fifties figure, his presence signifying not only in relation to Jimmy, but also as a young, single and sexually available refugee from the provinces. Although the film maintains his Welsh (i.e. non-metropolitan) origins, Gary Raymond, who plays Cliff, is a more obviously sexually attractive (and sexually active) character than Cliff appears to be in the play. He is first seen in the club in the company of a young woman; there are semi-nude pictures on the walls of his room; and the dialogue is occasionally explicit about his sexual conquests. However, it is in the character of Jimmy himself that the most significant changes are made.

Much of the power and dramatic intensity of the stage play lies in the way that Jimmy (Richard Burton in the film) is constructed as a character who is 'blocked', unable to find a course of action that will change his situation. His manifest energy is displaced from the social world that offers him no creative outlet, and is directed instead at those around him. The emotional claustrophobia that results, which is at once both personal and symptomatic of a wider social neurosis as we have seen, is therefore dissipated in the film, where the opening out of the narrative action allows Jimmy not only a range of different relationships (including ones that are hinted at in the play, such as that with Ma Tanner) but also different kinds of action, relocating him as a protagonist in the process. He and Helena go to the cinema, which leads to his becoming involved in an altercation with a fellow member of the audience as he attacks the (contrived and out-dated) representations the film (a war film) contains. He and Cliff also go to the theatre and disrupt the play that Helena is rehearsing (it is a bourgeois drawing-room drama called *The Forgotten Heart*, the kind of play that *Look Back in Anger* was said to have replaced). These sequences not only make Jimmy more 'active', they also, paradoxically, reconstitute him in terms of a later, more developed version of the Angry Young Man stereotype, particularly in its radical, instinctively anarchic form; Jimmy Porter on screen is, perhaps, more like the mid-century dissident that Tynan characterised in his review than is the stage incarnation to which that review referred.

The relocation of Jimmy Porter as a distinctively leftish figure is also connected to the way that the film attempts to respond to the new context in which it appears. One of the clearest examples of this is the inclusion of a sub-plot that has no counterpart in the play; the racism inflicted upon an Indian street trader, Kapur, in the market where Jimmy and Cliff run their sweet stall. Victimised first by the market inspector, Hurst, defended by Jimmy and Cliff, and then forced to leave the market because of the actions of the other traders, the Indian stall-holder is the centre of a narrative line that can be read as a response to the emergence of race and racial discrimination in the late fifties. In 1958 Britain saw its first post-war 'race riots' in Nottingham and Notting Hill, which represented an attack on the consensus from the political right. In fact, these were not race riots in the sense the term is normally used, for they consisted mainly of attacks on black people and their property – attacks that were, by the mid-fifties, by no means infrequent. The main effect was to highlight the issue of 'race' (usually by defining it as 'a problem with the blacks') whilst marginalising the role of racist organisations, and leading to calls for stricter immigration controls. It is, then, possible to see the inclusion of this theme as an attempt by Richardson (whose idea the market scenes were) to update the film's social concerns. It is also possible to read it in terms of the conscious 'internationalising' of the film, to which we have already referred – in particular, the attempt to cast it in a mould that would appeal to an American audience. The film was financed by Warner Brothers, largely because of contractual reasons to do with Richard Burton (who was nobody's first choice for the role). Harry Saltzman, an entrepreneur who worked closely with Osborne and Richardson at Woodfall, later referred to the casting of Burton as 'a monumental miscalculation' arguing that he was 'too old' and that his presence made 'nonsense of the text' (Walker 1974: 58). However, as Walker has argued, Burton/Jimmy, 'looks forward in anger to social intolerance, thus linking him, however tenuously, with a viewpoint already familiar to American liberals and film-goers' (Walker 1974: 62).

However, the actual exploration of the race theme in the film is more complex and contradictory than this version of Jimmy as an active, liberal protagonist suggests. Jimmy is simultaneously 'active' and 'blocked' in relation to the racism he encounters. He is able to stand up to the inspector, thwarting his early attempts to intimidate Kapur. He also confronts Hurst on learning that the Indian has been forced off the market. He cannot, however, defeat the more pervasive – the more 'institutionalised' – racism of the other stall-holders, acting out of both instinctive fear and self-interest. No course of action is possible for either Jimmy or Kapur, and the film's final emphasis is the same as the play's; whilst Jimmy may feel genuine sympathy for Kapur and outrage at what has happened to him, there is no possibility of real change in the social situation in which either of them finds himself. This is made clear in a short scene that Jimmy and Kapur have alone (the last in which we see the latter). Shot largely from Jimmy's point of view, the sequence draws an implicit parallel between the two figures, as Kapur confides that he is an 'untouchable' in his own country, an outcast whose situation echoes Jimmy's own.

The later films of the New Wave negotiate not only the transition between the moment of Anger and that of Working-Class Realism, but also look forward to a new context, that of the mid to late 1960s.

It is particularly interesting to look at *Billy Liar* with this in mind, especially those elements that do not come from the play. Much of the film occurs outside the domestic interior of the Fisher home, as we have seen; however, the images of the city contained in the film are in many ways very different from those found in other New Wave films. The city in which the narrative is set (Bradford) is clearly in the process of change and redevelopment. There are numerous shots of buildings being demolished or renovated, of open land waiting to be filled with new housing, and the sound of reconstruction often dominates the soundtrack. The opening sequence (see above) concludes when the camera comes to rest on an image of a house in the process of being knocked down, disrupting both the rhythm and the content of the scene. And a crucial sequence (in narrative terms), in which the camera follows the figure of Liz (Julie Christie) through the streets of the city constantly picks up images of urban renewal, occasionally dwelling on them and allowing her to move out of frame. The effect is of a city that is in transition, shedding much of its dominant icono-graphy along with its architecture; what it is in transition to, however, is not contained in the cityscape itself (which contains images of destruction, of the sweeping away of the old, rather than the contours of the new) but in the description of affluent consumerism, to which we have already referred.

This image of a city, which is both fully active and in the process of considerable change, is in contrast to the townscapes of many of the other New Wave films. *A Taste of Honey*, for example, typically inhabits the empty back lanes and derelict industrial wastelands of a largely deserted town, that is clearly reliant on older, heavy industry. And most of the action of *Saturday Night and Sunday Morning* occurs within a community that is defined largely in terms of traditional working-class terraced housing.

It is not that *Billy Liar* contains radically different elements within its rhetorical pattern, but rather that it redefines many of them. It contains the by now almost obligatory 'shot of our town from that hill', in which characters obtain a sense of distance from their immediate situation, and a perspective that is both actual and metaphorical. However, in *Billy Liar* it is not Billy himself who is afforded this moment of reflection and escape (although he is present in the scene) but Councillor Duxbury, Billy's employer. Duxbury is given a certain status in the film, both within this scene and more generally (he both 'sees through' Billy and offers him a paternal sympathy). More than any other character (with the possible exception of Billy's grandmother) he embodies the past. This is present not only in his person (he clearly belongs, in his dress and mode of speech as well as his age, to another world) but also in his reflections on the harshness and poverty of his youth. These are both comic – they are, generically speaking, satirised through the novel that Billy is fitfully attempting to write – and, in the scene in question, serious. He is one of the only characters who actually registers the general social and economic changes that are so evident in the *mise-en-scène* of the film; 'trams are gone', he notes, 'the city centre, that's all new'. In this way, the film recognises the genre of films to which it belongs by utilising a narrative element that is familiar from a range of texts in a different way, in order to remark on the processes of social change in which the film is clearly interested.

THE REPRESENTATION OF WOMEN AND GENDER RELATIONSHIPS IN NEW WAVE FILMS

Although there are elements in New Wave films that look forward to a new context, there are others that reach back to the 'Angry' texts. It is, perhaps, in the way that the films represent women and deal with questions around gender definitions and relations that these links back to the earlier cultural moment are most apparent.

A large part of the realism of both the New Wave films, and the plays and novels on which they were based, lay in the way that they were seen to break taboos around certain subjects, notably sex. Social extension is connected, as it were, with the willingness of the film-makers to open up areas of social and personal experience that, like the situation of the working-class, had been unrepresented. Commending the 'lively and local accents' of *A Room at the Top*, for example, one reviewer noted in the same sentence that it had 'more than a smack of real sex' (Whitebait 1959a: 59). However, the realism at issue here is essentially to do with an explicitness in the depiction or discussion of sexual activity (as it had been in the plays) rather than the result of a radically new way of thinking about issues of gender or sexuality.

This frankness is related primarily to male sexuality, however, for it is usually the sexual/social identity of the (male) protagonist that the films centre on. This has clear implications for the way that women are represented in the films. Hill has argued that the New

Wave as a whole tends to reproduce a division between women as sexually active and adulterous on the one hand, and women as wives and symbols of entrapment on the other (Hill 1986). The trajectory of the male heroes is frequently from bachelorhood to marriage via an adulterous affair, often with a more mature woman (who may herself be unhappily married); this is the narrative path trodden by both Arthur in *Saturday Night* and Joe Lampton in *Room at the Top*. Marriage is characteristically represented in terms of conformity and/or compromise. These narrative resolutions are, then, largely conservative or defeatist both in the proffered solution to the sexual dilemma of the protagonist and in the way that marriage itself is defined.

The film version of *Look Back* takes over the structure of gender representation from the play. If Jimmy is newly active on the screen, Alison is still largely passive; indeed, her passivity is more apparent in comparison. We first encounter Alison via Jimmy, who attempts to wake her up so that he can make love to her. The scene is a literal representation of a verbal metaphor from the play – Jimmy speaks of wishing to arouse her 'from her beauty sleep'. This becomes an image that explicitly equates her waking into self-knowledge with his sexual desires. It is not that Alison is not allowed by the film to leave the flat as other characters do, but rather that she does so mainly in sequences that are primarily about Jimmy; for example, a scene in a pub, in which Jimmy and she meet Ma Tanner, focuses mainly on Jimmy's reaction to her unease with the older lady. Elsewhere, she is allowed to go to the (male) doctor alone where her pregnancy is confirmed; her tentative suggestion that an abortion may be possible is met by a patrician disdain, which effectively removes from her any possibility of choice in the matter.

Although the film removes many of the set-piece monologues that characterise the play, what remains are chiefly the tirades against Alison. The basic pattern of their relationship is therefore confirmed, as is the disquieting nexus of contradictory emotions that Jimmy feels for her. Both texts locate the relationship between Jimmy and Alison in terms of his problematic sexual needs; the object of his desire is also the source of the greatest danger. Alison's own sexuality, which is described in terms of the consuming passion of a python, is similarly a threat. She is, therefore, in a situation in which she cannot win: if she is passive, she cannot fulfil Jimmy's need for an equal, if she is active (especially sexually) she is a danger to him. The solution is a pathological destruction of her self-respect, symbolised by the child that she loses, and the concluding scene retains the lines from the play that make this explicit.

Not all the New Wave films that are of primary concern here simply replicate the way that women and gender differentiation are constructed in the plays. *The Entertainer, A Taste of Honey* and *Billy Liar* all disturb – or develop – the pattern of gender representation that the plays adopt (although the movement is not unproblematically towards a greater freedom of action or self-definition for the women within them).

In the play version of *The Entertainer* Archie Rice is not only the structural centre of the narrative, but also the dominating presence in performance. In the film, however, much greater importance is attached to his daughter Jean. The characterisation of Jean in the play may have been criticised for being vague and lacking any political centre, but she is a much more substantial presence in the film. The play opens with Billy, whereas the film opens with Jean. From then on, her situation, dilemmas and decisions are one of the main focuses of the narrative; indeed, the first fifteen minutes of the film is concerned largely with Jean. Events and characters that relate to her (and which are only alluded to on the stage) are represented on the screen; Jean's work in a youth club, and her fiancé, Graham, for example. Only Jean and Archie of the central knot of characters have scenes of their own, in which their specific choices and problems are explored. In fact, Jean is in many ways a more consistent focus of identification than Archie in the film. It is not only that she almost displaces him at the centre of the narrative, but that she provides us with a point of view of him (and one which is more sympathetic than the play). The opening sequence is, in fact, a literal indicator of this function, as the opening shot (of Archie's face on the hoarding, filmed from below) is framed from her point of view. This is immediately established by a cut to Jean looking up. The ending is even more telling; in the play, Archie delivers his final speech on the music-hall/theatre stage, then goes to Phoebe, who gives him his hat and coat. After the final line, the stage directions state that they both walk upstage into darkness. The film gives this supportive role to Jean – indeed, it turns the final image from one which is motivated by Archie (he goes to Phoebe) to one that is motivated by Jean. After the last line, which is the same in both play and film, the curtain drops and Jean goes on stage to comfort her father. The final image is of them both staring out into an empty auditorium, Archie's audience (both symbolic and actual) having deserted him.

Jean, then, is given both dilemmas and choices of her own, unlike Alison in *Look Back*, and is seen in situations in which she is allowed to be active in ways that do not always relate to men. But the situation is more contradictory than this, for her basic dilemma – the choice she is asked by both play and film to make – is essentially between a man (Graham) and her family – both conventional choices for a woman to have to make. This is to a degree obviated by the characterisation of Graham, who is portrayed in a far more sympathetic light than he is in the play. On stage, he appears only once and is described unambiguously as the kind of young man that is 'well dressed, assured, well educated, their emotional and imaginative capacity so limited it is practically negligible' (Osborne 1957b: 83). On screen, he is far less of a younger version of brother Bill; indeed, he turns down the opportunity to go to Africa in order to remain with Jean.

A rather different set of contradictions emerge if we look at the way that some of these issues are played out in *A Taste of Honey*. Alone among New Wave plays, it was written by a woman, directed on the stage by a woman, centres on a relationship between a mother and her daughter within a domestic context, and is concerned, as we saw earlier, with issues that are usually thought of as 'female', especially the nature of motherhood – issues that were largely ignored, or defined in other terms, by the predominantly male critics that reviewed it. The film, similarly, foregrounds those elements of the text that can be understood within the context of Working-Class Realism, with the result that some elements in the play are either marginalised or redefined. This is particularly true of the central relationship of the play, that between mother and daughter, to which the film is more ambivalent. The implications of this are most evident in the way that the ending of the film shifts the emphasis from the renewal of Jo's relationship to Helen to the severing of her relationship to Geoff: the final scene in the play is between Jo and Helen alone, whereas the concluding sequence in the film concerns all three and is shot partly from Geoff's point of view; the penultimate shot is of Geoff walking off, unseen.

The reworking of these elements from the play is partly the result, as Lovell has noted (Lovell 1990), of a 'Hoggartian' structure of feeling; that is, it proceeds from a set of concerns that link the film to the New Wave generally – the anxiety about traditional forms of working-class culture, the destabilising effects of newer forms of mass leisure. In the course of an extended and complex analysis of the relationship between the play and the film (in particular the way that questions around gender are posed and the role of the female spectator is addressed), Lovell has argued that this is also the point of view of Hoggart's 'scholarship boy' (sic). This is not so much an 'outsider's' perspective, but rather 'that of someone deeply implicated in and familiar with what is being observed: someone who has left that life behind, yet with a considerable sense of loss in moving through the educational system', bringing to bear 'the knowledge of the insider combined with the distance achieved by the move outside and beyond' (Lovell 1990: 370). This point of view, which Lovell argues is the 'point of enunciation' of the New Wave films as a whole, is connected to the anxiety arising out of the experience of a class fraction on the way from one class to another. It is also predominantly a male perspective, and one which necessarily underplays the mother/daughter relationship, the latter having little real presence in the Hoggartian social landscape.

On top of this, the film develops a perspective on the 'youth' debates (which is arguably there in the original anyway), demonising Helen (and adults generally) as the agents of an 'unsavoury' sexuality. Also, adults, rather than the ubiquitous 'youth', are the repository of anxieties about the effects of mass leisure and affluence. The Blackpool sequence discussed earlier, for example, can be read as a critique of mass leisure, but Blackpool is clearly an adult space in the film, and the satirical horror with which the film depicts the entertainments on offer is partly a criticism of adults, and especially Helen. Indeed, Blackpool is paralleled with a later sequence, in which Jo and Geoff go to a funfair, which is represented in a far more positive light, consciously reflecting the mutually supportive, spontaneous, almost childlike, nature of their developing relationship. These sequences seem to invite two differing readings, which originate in both the concerns of the filmmakers and of Delaney/Littlewood. In this way, the film cannot entirely 'rewrite' the story of the play, and elements of the latter continually emerge, particularly through the dialogue. Lovell refers to this as a 'double-vision', in which the main themes of the New Wave generally cannot be satisfactorily pursued through the characters and relationships of the original, which constantly asserts itself through the gaps in the film's additions.

The terms in which Jo and Helen are defined in *A Taste of Honey* raises wider questions about the way that gender is represented in New Wave films, and in particular the way that character diferentia- tions based on gender are sometimes submerged in those that originate in the debates about post-war youth. It is probable, for example, that Jean's prominence in *The Entertainer* is related to a sense that the film is aimed at a young audience. Jean is a figure from a recognisably contemporary world; she has attended the massive anti-Suez rally in Trafalgar Square, she teaches art in a youth club, and this allies her with that young and educated intelligentsia discussed above. 'Youth' here is not an abstract category but has precise social contours. In *Billy Liar*, similarly, certain characters function as signs of a new social typology that prefigures the debates about social change (and not only the role of youth within these debates) that were characteristic not so much of Working-Class Realism as of the historical moment that followed it. The key figure here is Liz.

In all three versions of *Billy Liar*, Billy has a third woman with whom he is involved, Liz, who occupies a position in the narrative that is denied both the ostensible fiancées, Barbara and Rita. In both play and film, Liz is clearly constructed as 'different' from not only the other young female characters, but from the men as well. She is also simultaneously connected to Billy (she is the only character who understands and shares his fantasies) and separate from him, enjoying a freedom he aspires to but cannot achieve. This sense of difference is, as Laing has noted, constructed differ- ently across the three versions of the story. In the novel, she is referred to as 'Woodbine Lizzy', and her sense of otherness is connoted by the fact that she is 'scruffy'. In the play, this scruffiness is partly the result of other characters' perceptions of her; the skirt she habitually wears is perceived as being 'dirty', reproducing a connection between dirt and the 'other' that is often made. When she appears, however, wearing the skirt, we are told in a stage direction that it is not as soiled as we have been led to believe. By the time she appears on the screen, scruffiness is, as Laing has observed, 'no longer an issue' (Laing 1986: 220), even if the sense of difference still is. This is apparent from the moment she is introduced into the narrative. Her arrival is noted by Billy, yet she is kept at a distance from the spectator, talked about and watched, yet initially having no voice herself. The camera follows her – in a sequence that has no counterpart elsewhere in the film – through the streets of the city almost fetishistically, singling her out from the crowds in which she moves, to the accompaniment of a jazz soundtrack that supplants the 'real' noises of the street.

The casting of Julie Christie as Liz is of significance – although this is partly retrospective, relying on a subsequent knowledge of her role in such seminal films of the mid-sixties as *Darling*. However, even if such associations are discounted, she is clearly a different kind of presence from, say, Rita Tushingham or Joan Plowright, and was not a member of the repertory of actors from the English Stage Company that peopled this and many other New Wave films. John Schlesinger was initially worried about casting her, fearing that she might appear 'too gorgeous'. 'But when I look back on it', he said later, ' her first entrance gives the precise feeling of liberation I was after' (Walker 1974: 166). The sense of otherness that attaches to Julie Christie and Liz has implications that go far beyond the world of the film itself, presenting an image of 'femaleness' that conspicuously rejects the domestic terrain that imprisoned many New Wave women, and simultaneously marked a significant shift in the wider cultural context.

IN CONCLUSION
The 1960s – new definitions of 'What Britain is Like'

In retrospect, the final sequence of *Billy Liar* has acquired an acute symbolic significance. In looking south, the film was consolidating much of the imagery of a society in flux that was such an important part of its narrative, and which registered the terms of a new cultural moment, a new set of explanations of 'What Britain is Like' in the post-war period. The shift from one moment to another – from Working-Class Realism to the 'Swinging Sixties' – was dramatic, generating a new mythology that has since engulfed the decade as a whole, 'with its King's Road boutiques, Mayfair Art galleries and fashionable glitterati; the enamelled butterflies of the summer of love . . . its ambience of marijuana and sitar music; or protesting students battling with police outside the US Embassy in Grosvenor Square' (Moore-Gilbert and Seed 1992: 1). Theatre had a relatively minor presence on this landscape, which is dominated instead by many of the products of the despised mass culture, now hedonistically celebrated.

It is, in this context, ironic that the demise of Centre 42 should have been bound up with the Round House, which became the venue for a number of events that symbolised the contours of the new era. In 1967, it housed both an 'Angry Arts Week' in opposition to the Vietnam War, and 'The Dialectics of Liberation – Towards the Demystification of Violence'. This latter event attracted a range of key figures, such as R.D. Laing and Stokeley Carmichael, who were central to the growing counter-cultural movement that was assuming shape as the decade drew to a close. And in 1970, Kenneth Tynan mounted *Oh Calcutta!* in the venue; billed as an erotic revue, the show was both a commercial success and a symbol of sixties permissiveness.

This was a cultural landscape that derived, as Moore-Gilbert and

Seed have argued, 'from a composite of media-constructed images evoking material prosperity, cultural innovation and youthful rebellion' (Moore-Gilbert and Seed 1992: 1). However, it is worth pointing out that all of these elements – of affluence, of cultural change and advance and of youthful revolt – were also central to the fifties as well; and, in one sense, Julie Christie was simply following a well-trodden path from the provinces to the metropolis – one that had been taken by many of the New Wave of theatre intellectuals in the previous decade. There are, then, important continuities underpinning this apparently dramatic sense of change.

Clearly, in the few years between the collapse of Centre 42 and the Dialectics of Liberation conference, the debates about class and culture had moved on and become politicised – and polarised – in new and unexpected ways; in the theatre, the problems did not go away, however, but remained to be addressed by a new generation of theatre practitioners – on the fringe, in the new socialist touring companies, in feminist theatre – as the sixties gave way to the seventies, and theatre began to move along several different paths.

There is not the space here to do more than register some of the indices of change. Initially, the mid to late sixties sees a thorough rejection of realism, both as a set of practices and an available framework for debating political intentions. This is evident in, for example, Peter Brook's experiments in Artaudian theatre at the Royal Shakespeare Company around 1964, and in Joe Orton's savage, Dionysiac comedies from later in the decade, both concerned not so much with representation as with confrontation. Realism – or rather the political intentions that its critical language encapsulates – returns with a sharper ideological focus in the political theatre of the seventies; in the work of Trevor Griffiths, political commitment was accompanied by the exploration of the familiar forms of the naturalist/realist dramatic tradition. The re-emergence of realism in this later period is an indication that, although no longer the symbolic centre of a specific cultural moment, contemporary theatre working in relation to the realist tradition could still be resolutely anti-consensual, could still develop a cultural and political identity that first emerged in the late fifties and early sixties.

BIBLIOGRAPHY

Abrams, M. (1959) *The Teenage Consumer*, London: Odhams.
—— (1964) *The Newspaper Reading Public of Tomorrow*, London: Odhams.
Addison, P. (1975) *The Road to 1945: British Politics and the Second World War*, London: Cape.
Allen, W. (1973) 'Review of Lucky Jim' in G. Feldman and M. Gartenberg (eds) *Protest*, London: Quartet.
Allsop, K. (1958) *The Angry Decade*, London: Peter Owen.
Alvarez, A. (1959) 'As We Like It: *The Kitchen*', *New Statesman*, Sept. 11 p. 304.
Amis, K. (1961) *Lucky Jim*, London: Penguin.
—— (1973) 'Socialism and the Intellectuals' in G. Feldman and M. Gartenberg (eds) *Protest* London: Quartet.
Anderson, L. (1957) 'Get Out and Push' in T. Maschler (ed.) *Declaration*, London: MacGibbon and Kee.
—— (1958) 'Free Cinema', *Universities and Left Review*, Vol. 1, No. 2, pp. 51–2.
—— (1970a) 'Vital Theatre?' in C. Marowitz, T. Milne and O. Hale (eds) *The Encore Reader*, London: Eyre Methuen.
—— (1970b) 'Review: *A Taste of Honey*' in C. Marowitz, T. Milne and O. Hale (eds) *The Encore Reader*, London: Eyre Methuen.
Anderson, M. (1976) *Anger and Detachment*, London: Pitman.
Arden, J. (1959) 'Letter to Ted Willis', *Encore*, May/June, p. 41–3.
—— (1960) *Serjeant Musgrave's Dance*, London: Methuen.
—— (1969) *John Arden: Three Plays*, London: Penguin.
—— (1970) 'Telling a True Tale' in C. Marowitz, T. Milne and O. Hale (eds) *The Encore Reader*, London: Eyre Methuen.
—— (1971) *The Workhouse Donkey*, London: Methuen.
—— (1977) *Collected Plays: Vol. 1*, London: Methuen.
—— (1979) *To Present the Pretence*, London: Eyre Methuen.
Baldry, H. (1981) *The Case for the Arts*, London: Secker and Warburg.
Banham, M. (1969) *John Osborne*, London: Oliver and Boyd.
Barker, C. (1966) '*Look Back in Anger*: The Turning Point' in *Zeitschrift für Anglistik und Americanistik*, No. 4, pp. 367–71.
Barstow, S. (1962) *A Kind of Loving*, London: Penguin.

Barthes, R. (1979) 'Barthes on Theatre' trans. Peter Mathers, *Theatre Quarterly*, Vol. 9, No. 33, pp. 25–30.

Beckett, S. (1965) *Waiting for Godot*, London: Faber.

Behan, B. (1978) *Collected Plays*, London: Methuen.

Bennedetti, J. (1982) *Stanislavsky: An Introduction*, London: Methuen.

Bentley, E. (1975) *The Theory of the Modern Stage*, London: Penguin.

Billington, M. (1973) *The Modern Actor*, London: Hamish Hamilton.

Birmingham Feminist History Group (1979) 'Feminism as Femininity in the Nineteen-fifties?', *Feminist Review*, No. 3, pp. 48–65.

Blaug, M. (1976) *The Economics of the Performing Arts*, Boulder, Colorado: Westview.

Bogdanor, V. and Skidelsky, R. (eds) (1970) *The Age of Affluence: Britain 1951–1964*, London: Macmillan.

Bond, E. (1971) *Saved*, London: Methuen.

—— (1972) 'Drama and the Dialectics of Violence', *Theatre Quarterly*, Vol. 2, No. 5, Jan./March.

—— (1977) *Plays: One*, London: Methuen.

—— (1979) 'Edward Bond: From Rationalism to Rhapsody', interview in *Canadian Theatre Review*, No. 23, summer.

Bornemann, E. (1970) 'The Real Brecht' in C. Marowitz, T. Milne and O. Hale (eds) *The Encore Reader*, London: Eyre Methuen.

Bowlby, J. (1953) *Child Care and the Growth of Love*, London: Penguin.

Bradbury, M. (1972) *The Social Context of Modern English Literature*, Oxford: Blackwell.

—— (1976) 'Afterword' to *Eating People is Wrong*, London: Arrow.

—— (1987) *Oh No, Not Bloomsbury*, London: André Deutsch.

Bradby, D. and Williams, D. (1988) *Directors' Theatre*, London: Macmillan.

Braine, J. (1959) *Room at the Top*, London: Penguin.

Brecht, B. (1965) *The Messingkauf Dialogues*, London: Methuen.

—— (1977) 'Against George Lukacs' in E. Bloch, G. Lukacs, B. Brecht, W. Benjamin and T. Adorno, *Aesthetics and Politics*, London: New Left Books.

Brien, A. (1959a) '*A Taste of Honey*', *Spectator*, Feb. 20, p. 251.

—— (1959b) '*Roots*', *Spectator*, July 16, p. 28.

Brooks, J. (1960) 'Chunks of Life: Review of *The Lion in Love*', *New Statesman*, Sept. 17, pp. 377–8.

Brown, I. (1956) *Theatre: 1955–56*, London: Reinhardt.

Brown, J.R. (1963) (ed.) *Modern British Dramatists*, New Jersey: Spectrum.

—— (1969) *Effective Theatre*, London: Heinemann.

—— (1972) *Theatre Language*, London: Allen Lane.

Browne, T. (1975) *The Playwright's Theatre: The English Stage Company at the Royal Court*, London: Pitman.

Calder, A. (1969) *The People's War: 1939–45*, London: Cape.

Caughie, J. (1981) 'Progressive Television and Documentary Drama' in T. Bennett (ed.) *Popular Television and Film*, London: BFI and the Open University.

Cohen, M. (1985) 'The Politics of the Earlier Arden', *Modern Drama*, No. 2, June, pp. 198–210.

Cohen, S. (1973) *Folk Devils and Moral Panics*, London: Paladin.

Cooper, D.E. (1970) 'Looking Back on Anger' in V. Bogdanor and

R. Skidelsky (eds) *The Age of Affluence: Britain 1951–1964*, London: Macmillan.

Coppetier, F. (1975) 'Arnold Wesker's Centre Forty-Two: A Cultural Revolution Betrayed', *Theatre Quarterly*, Vol. V, No. 18.

Crick, B. (1980) *George Orwell: A Life*, London: Secker and Warburg.

Crossland, A. (1961) *Can Labour Win?*, Fabian Tract No. 324.

Crossman, R. (ed.) (1950) *The God that Failed: Six Studies in Communism*, London: Hamish Hamilton.

Curran, C. (1956) 'The Passing of the Tribunes', *Encounter*, June, p. 21.

Davison, P. (1982) *Contemporary Drama and the Popular Dramatic Tradition*, London: Macmillan.

Delaney, S. (1959) *A Taste of Honey*, London: Methuen.

—— (1960) *Lion in Love*, London: Methuen.

Devine, G. (1957) 'The Royal Court Theatre' in Harold Hobson (ed.) *International Theatre Annual*, No. 2, London: John Calder.

—— (1959) 'Vital Theatre', *Encore*, March/April, pp. 23–6.

—— (1962) 'The Birth of the English Stage Company', *Prompt*, No. 1.

—— (1970) 'The Berliner Ensemble' in C. Marowitz. T. Milne and O. Hale (eds) *The Encore Reader*, London: Eyre Methuen.

Dollimore, J. (1983) 'The Challenge of Sexuality' in A. Sinfield (ed.) *Society and Literature: 1945–70*, London: Methuen.

Driver, C. (1964) *The Disarmers: A Study in Protest*, London: Hodder and Stoughton.

Durgnat, R. (1970) *A Mirror for England*, London: Faber.

Dyer, R., Geraghty, C., Jordan, M., Lovell, T., Paterson, R. and Stewart, J. (eds) (1981) *Coronation Street*, London: BFI Television Monograph.

Eatwell, R. (1979) *The 1945–51 Labour Governments*, London: Batsford Academic.

Edgar, D. (1981) 'Putting Politics on Stage', *New Socialist*, Nov./Dec.

—— (1988) *The Second Time as Farce*, London: Lawrence and Wishart.

Ellis, J. (1982) *Visible Fictions*, London: Routledge and Kegan Paul.

Elsom, J. (1971) *Theatre outside London*, London: Macmillan.

—— (1976) *Post-War British Theatre*, London: Routledge and Kegan Paul.

—— (1981) *Post-War British Theatre Criticism*, London: Routledge and Kegan Paul.

Encore (editorial) (1957) Jan./Feb., pp. 1–2.

—— (editorial) (1958) Jan./Feb., pp. 1–2.

Esslin, M. (1968) 'Naturalism in Context', *Tulane Drama Review*, Vol. 13, No. 2, pp. 67–76.

Fiedler, L. (1958) 'The Unangry Young Man', *Encounter*, Jan., pp. 5–9.

Findlater, R. (1952) *The Unholy Trade*, London: Gollancz.

—— (1967) *Banned*, London: MacGibbon and Kee.

—— (1981) *At the Court: Twenty-Five Years of the English Stage Company*, London: Amber Lane.

French, S. (1991) 'Diary', *New Statesman and Society*, November 1, p. 8.

Furst, L. and Skrine, P. (1971) *Naturalism*, London: Methuen.

Gamble, A. (1974) *The Conservative Nation*, London: Routledge and Kegan Paul.

Gardner, C. and Wyver, J. (1986) 'The Single Play: From Reithian

Reverance to Cost-Cutting Censorship', Official Programme, Edinburgh International Television Festival.

Gascoine, B (1962) *Twentieth Century Drama*, London: Hutchinson.

Gaskell, W. (1988) *A Sense of Direction*, London: Faber and Faber.

Gilliat, P. (ed.) (1959) 'Vital Theatre: A Symposium', *Encore*, May/June, pp. 21–7.

Goetschuis, G. (1966) 'The Royal Court in its social context' in *10 Years at the Royal Court*, published by the theatre as a souvenir programme.

Goorney, H. (1981) *The Theatre Workshop Story*, London: Eyre Methuen.

Goorney, H. and MacColl, E. (1986) *Agit-Prop to Theatre Workshop: Political Playscripts 1930–50*, Manchester: Manchester University Press.

Gramsci, A. (1971) *Prison Notebooks*, London: Lawrence and Wishart.

Gray, F. (1982) *John Arden*, London: Macmillan.

Hall, S. (1970) 'Beyond Naturalism Pure' in C. Marowitz, T. Milne and O. Hale (eds) *The Encore Reader*, London: Eyre Methuen.

Hall, S., Crichter, C. and Jefferson, T. (eds) (1978) *Policing The Crisis*, London: Macmillan.

Hall, S. and Jefferson, T (eds) (1976) *Resistance Through Rituals*, London: Hutchinson in association with the Centre for Contemporary Cultural Studies.

Hall, S. and Whannell, P. (1964) *The Popular Arts*, London: Hutchinson.

Harris, J.S. (1970) *Government Patronage and the Arts in Britain*, Chicago: University of Chicago Press.

Hartley, A. (1963) *A State of England*, London: Hutchinson.

Hay, M. and Roberts, P. (1978) *Edward Bond: A Companion to the Plays*, London: Eyre Methuen.

Hayman, R. (1973) *The Set-Up*, London: Eyre Methuen.

—— (1979) *British Theatre since 1955: A Re-assessment*, Oxford: Oxford University Press.

Hebdige, D. (1979) *Sub-Cultures: The Meaning of Style*, London: Methuen.

—— (1982) 'Towards a Cartography of Taste' in B. Waites, T. Bennett and G. Martin (eds) *Popular Culture: Past and Present*, London: Croom Helm and the Open University.

Herbert, J. and Courtney, C. (1993) *Jocelyn Herbert: A Theatre Workbook*, London: Arts Book International.

Hewison, R. (1981) *In Anger: Culture in the Cold War 1945–60* London: Weidenfeld and Nicolson.

Higson, A. (1984) 'Space, Place and Spectacle', *Screen*, No. 4/5, pp. 2–21.

Hill, J. (1986) *Sex, Class and Realism: British Cinema 1956–63*, London: British Film Institute.

Hillier, J. and Lovell, A. (1972) *Studies in Documentary*, London: Secker and Warburg.

Hirst, D. (1985) *Edward Bond*, London: Macmillan.

Hobsbawm, E. (1969) *Industry and Empire*, London: Penguin.

Hobson, H. (1953) *The Theatre Now*, London: Longman.

—— (1984) *Theatre in Britain: A Personal View*, London: Phaidon.

Hoggart, R. (1971) *The Uses of Literacy*, London: Penguin. First published 1957.

Holland, P. (1978) 'Brecht, Bond and Gaskill', *Theatre Quarterly*, Vol. VIII, No. 30, summer.

Hopkins, H. (1963) *The New Look: A Social History of the Fifties*, London: Secker and Warburg.

Hunt, A. (1960) 'Another Taste: Review of *The Lion in Love*', *Encore*, Nov./ Dec., pp. 40–1.

—— (1961a) 'Only a Soft-Centred Left', *Encore*, May/June, pp. 5–12.

—— (1961b) 'Around us . . . Things are there', *Encore*, Aug./Sept., pp. 25–9.

—— (1974) *John Arden: A Study of his Plays*, London: Eyre Methuen.

Hutchinson, R. (1982) *The Politics of the Arts Council*, London: Sinclair Brown.

Innes, C. (1992) *Modern British Drama: 1890–1990*, Cambridge: Cambridge University Press.

Itzin, C. (1980) *Stages in the Revolution: Political Theatre in Britain since 1968*, London: Eyre Methuen.

Jacobs, N. and Ohlsen, P. (eds) (1977) *Brecht in Britain*, London: Theatre Quarterly Publications.

James, L. (1981) 'Introduction', in D. Bradby, L. James and B. Sharratt (eds) *Performance and Politics in Popular Drama*, Cambridge: Cambridge University Press.

Jordan, M. (1981) 'Realism and Convention' in R. Dyer, C. Geraghty, M. Jordan, T. Lovell, R. Paterson and J. Stewart (eds) *Coronation Street*, London: BFI Television Monograph.

Kavanagh, D. and Morris, P. (1994) *Consensus Politics: From Attlee to Major*, Oxford: Blackwell.

Kumar, K. (1981) 'The Nationalisation of British Culture' in S. Hoffman and P. Kitromilides (eds) *Culture and Society in Contemporary Europe*, London: Allen and Unwin.

Laing, S. (1973) 'The Idea of a Post-War Britain: A Case Study in the Cultural Analysis of Literature', unpublished Ph.D thesis, University of Birmingham.

—— (1986) *Representations of Working-Class Life*, London: Macmillan.

Leeming, G. (1985) *File on Wesker*, London: Methuen.

Leeming, G. and Trussler, S. (1971) *The Plays of Arnold Wesker: An Assessment*, London: Gollancz.

Lehmann, J. (1956) *The Craft of Letters in England*, London: Cresset.

Lessing, D. (1957) 'The Small Personal Voice', in T. Maschler (ed.) *Declaration*, London: MacGibbon and Kee.

—— (1959) *Each His Own Wilderness*, in *New English Dramatists*, London: Penguin.

Lewis, N. (1960) 'Without Nostalgia? Review of *Sparrers Can't Sing*', *New Statesman*, Sept. 3, p. 303.

Lewis, R. and Maude, A. (1953) *The English Middle-Classes*, London: Penguin.

Losey, J. (1970) 'The Individual Eye' in C. Marowitz, T. Milne and O. Hale (eds) *The Encore Reader*, London: Eyre Methuen.

Lovell, A. and Hillier, J. (1972) *Studies in Documentary*, London: Secker and Warburg.

Lovell, T. (1980) *Pictures of Reality*, London: BFI.

——— (1990) 'Landscape and Stories in 1960's British Realism', *Screen*, Vol. 31, No. 4.

Lukacs, G. (1977) 'Realism in the Balance' in E. Bloch, G. Lukacs, B Brecht, W. Benjamin and T. Adorno, *Aesthetics and Politics*, London: New Left Books.

——— (1978) 'Narrate and Describe' in *Writer and Critic*, London:Merlin.

MacCabe, C. (1974) 'Realism and the Cinema: Notes on Some Brechtian Theses', *Screen*, Vol. 15, No. 2.

——— (1977) 'Television Drama: The Case against Naturalism', *Sight and Sound*, Vol. 46 No. 2.

McGrath, J. (1975) 'Better a Bad Night in Bootle', *Theatre Quarterly*, Vol. 5, No. 19.

——— (1979) 'The Theory and Practice of Political Theatre', *Theatre Quarterly*, Vol. IX, No. 35, autumn.

——— (1981) *A Good Night Out*, London: Eyre Methuen.

——— (1990) *The Bone Won't Break*, London: Methuen.

MacInnes, C. (1959) 'A Taste of Reality' *Encounter*, No. 67, April pp. 70–1.

——— (1966) *England, Half-English*, London: Penguin.

Mander, J. (1961) *The Writer and Commitment*, London: Secker and Warburg.

Marcorelles, L. (1960) 'Where Have You Been, Billy Boy?', *Encore*, Nov./Dec., pp. 30–4.

Marowitz, C. (1961) 'A Cynic's Glossary', *Encore*, May/June, pp. 32–2.

——— (1973) *Confession of a Counterfeit Critic*, London: Methuen.

Marowitz, C., Milne, T, and Hale, O. (eds) (1970) *The Encore Reader*, London: Eyre Methuen.

Marquand, D. (1959) 'Lucky Jim and the Labour Party', *Universities and Left Review*, Vol. 1, No. 1, pp. 57–9.

Marshall, N. (1947) *The Other Theatre*, London: John Lehmann and Purnell and Sons.

Martin, T. Kennedy (1964) 'Nats Go Home', *Encore*, March/April, pp. 5–14.

Marwick, A. (1968) *Britain in the Century of Total War*, London: Pelican.

——— (1982) *British Society Since 1945*, London: Penguin.

Maschler, T. (ed.) (1957) *Declaration*, London: MacGibbon and Kee.

Mathers, P. (1975) 'Brecht in Britain: From Stage to Television', *Screen*, Vol. 16, No. 4.

Mikhail, E.H. (ed.) (1979) *The Art of Brendan Behan*, London: Vision Press.

Miliband, R. (1973) *Parliamentary Socialism*, London: Merlin.

Miller, J. (1961) 'Kitchenette', *New Statesman*, July 21, p. 96.

Milne, T. (1961) 'Touch of the Poet' *New Left Review*, Jan./Feb., pp. 35–48.

——— (1970) 'Art in Angel Lane', in C. Marowitz, T. Milne and O. Hale (eds) *The Encore Reader*, London: Eyre Methuen.

Milne, T. and Goodwin, C. (1960) 'Working with Joan', *Encore*, July/August, pp. 9–20.

Moore-Gilbert, B. and Seed, J. (1992) *Cultural Revolution? The Challenge of the Arts in the 1960s*, London: Routledge.

Morrison, B. (1980) *The Movement: English Poetry and Fiction in the 1950s*, London: OUP.

Mulgan, G. and Worpole, K. (1986) *Saturday Night and Sunday Morning?*, London: Comedia.

Orwell, G. (1980) 'England your England' in *Inside the Whale and Other Essays*, London: Penguin.

Osborne, J. (1957a) *Look Back in Anger*, London: Faber.

—— (1957b) *The Entertainer*, London: Faber.

—— (1957c) 'They Call it Cricket' in T. Maschler (ed.) *Declaration*, London: MacGibbon and Kee.

—— (1959) *The World of Paul Slickey*, London: Faber.

—— (1961) *Luther*, London: Faber.

—— (1973) 'Sex and Failure' in G. Feldman and M. Gartenberg (eds) *Protest*, London: Quartet.

—— (1982) *A Better Class of Person*, London: Penguin.

—— (1991) *Almost a Gentleman*, London: Faber and Faber.

Osborne, J. and Creighton, A. (1960) *An Epitaph for George Dillon* in *New English Dramatists: 2*, London: Penguin.

Owen, A. (1962) *Progress to the Park* in *New English Dramatists: 5*, London: Penguin.

Page, M. (1988) *File on Osborne*, London: Methuen.

Parkin, F. (1968) *Middle-Class Radicalism*, Manchester: Manchester University Press.

Pick, J. (1983) *The West End: Mismanagement and Snobbery*, London: Offord.

Pinter, H. (1976) *Plays: One*, London: Methuen.

Priestley, J.B. (1947) *The Arts under Socialism*, London: Fabian pamphlet, Turnstile Press.

Priestman, M. (1992) 'A Critical Stage: Drama in the 1960s' in B. Moore-Gilbert and J. Seed (eds) *Cultural Revolution? The Challenge of the Arts in the 1960s*, London: Routledge, Chapter 6.

Quigley, I. (1963) 'A Kind of Truth', *Spectator*, August 10, p. 204.

Ratcliffe, M. (1995) 'An Anarchist's Agenda', *Observer*, January 1.

Reckford, B. (1963) Introduction to *Skyvvers*, *New English Dramatists: 9*, London: Penguin.

Reisz, K. (1958) 'A Use for Documentary', *Universities and Left Review*, Vol. 1, No. 3, pp. 23–5.

Ritchie, H. (1988) *Success Stories: Literature and the Media in England 1950–1959*, London: Faber.

Roberts, P. (1973) *Theatre in Britain: A Playgoer's Guide*, London: Pitman.

—— (1985) *Bond on File*, London: Methuen.

Sanderson, M. (1984) *From Irving to Olivier: A Social History of the Acting Profession*, London: Athlone.

Scott, M. (ed.) (1991) *Harold Pinter: 'The Birthday Party', 'The Caretaker' and 'The Homecoming': A Selection of Critical Essays*, London: Macmillan.

Seed, J. (1992) 'Hegemony Postponed' in B. Moore-Gilbert and J. Seed (eds) *Cultural Revolution? The Challenge of the Arts in the 1960s*, London: Routledge.

Segal, L. (1990) *Slow Motion*, London: Virago.

Shils, E. and Young, M. (1963) 'The Meaning of the Coronation', *Sociological Review*, Dec., pp. 63–81.

Sigal, C. (1962) 'Serials', review of *Coronation Street* in *New Statesman*, Jan. 12, p. 63.

Sillitoe, A. (1960) *Saturday Night and Sunday Morning*, London: Pan.

—— (1961) *The Loneliness of the Long-Distance Runner*, London: Pan.

Sinfield, A. (1989) *Literature, Politics and Culture in Post-War Britain*, Oxford: Blackwell.

Sinfield, A. (ed.) (1983) *Society and Literature: 1945–70*, London: Methuen.

Sked, A. and Cook, C. (1983) *Post-War Britain: A Political History*, London: Penguin.

Shiach, M. (1989) *Discourse on Popular Culture*, Oxford: Polity Press/Blackwell.

Smith, A.C.H. (ed.) (1975) *Paper Voices: The Popular Press and Social Change 1935–65*, London: Chatto and Windus.

Spencer, J. (1992) *Dramatic Strategies in the Plays of Edward Bond*, Cambridge: Cambridge University Press.

Stevenson, R. (1987) 'Scottish Theatre 1950–1980' in C. Craig (ed.) *The History of Scottish Literature Vol. 4: 20th Century*, Aberdeen: Aberdeen University Press, Chapter 23.

Storey, D. (1962) *This Sporting Life*, London: Penguin.

Symons, J. (1971) *The Thirties: A Dream Revolved*, Westport, Connecticut: Greenwood Press.

Taylor, J.R. (1962) *Anger and After*, London: Methuen

—— (1968) *'Look Back in Anger': A Casebook*, London: Macmillan.

—— (1978) *The Second Wave*, London: Methuen.

Thompson, E.P. (1964) 'The New Left in Britain' in D. Boulton (ed.) *Voices from the Crowd*, London: Peter Owen.

Trussler, S. (1969) *The Plays of John Osborne: An Assessment*, London: Gollancz.

Tschudin, M. (1972) *A Writer's Theatre*, Frankfurt: Frankfurt University Press.

Tynan, K. (1957) 'Theatre and Living' in T. Maschler (ed.) *Declaration*, London: MacGibbon and Kee.

—— (1984) *A View of the English Stage*, London: Methuen.

Wager, W. (ed.) (1969) *The Playwright's Speak*, London: Longman.

Wain, J. (1960) *Hurry on Down*, London: Penguin.

Waites, B., Bennett, T. and Martin, G. (eds) (1982) *Popular Culture Past and Present*, London: Croom Helm and the Open University.

Wall, R. (1979) '*An Giall* and *The Hostage*' in E. H. Mikhail (ed.) *The Art of Brendan Behan*, London: Vision Press.

Walker, A. (1974) *Hollywood England: The British Film Industry in the Sixties*, London: Michael Joseph.

Wandor, M. (1986) *Carry On, Understudies*, London: Routledge and Kegan Paul.

—— (1987) *Look Back in Gender*, London: Methuen.

Wardle, I. (1984) *The Theatres of George Devine*, London: Eyre Methuen.

—— (1991) *Theatre Criticism*, London: Routledge.

Warren, T. (1969) *I was Ena Sharples' Father*, London: Duckworth.

Waterhouse, K. and Hall, W. (1966) *Billy Liar* in *Plays of the Sixties*, London: Pan.

BIBLIOGRAPHY

Wesker, A. (1960a) *The Kitchen* in *New English Dramatists: 2*, London: Penguin.
—— (1960b) *The Modern Playwright or 'Oh Mother is it Worth it?',* Oxford: Gemini.
—— (1962a) 'An Interview with Arnold Wesker on Centre 42', *Encore,* May/June, pp. 39–44.
—— (1962b) 'Where Civilisation Begins', *Anarchy,* No. 19, pp. 267–70.
—— (1970) 'Let Battle Commence' in C. Marowitz, T. Milne and O. Hale (eds) *The Encore Reader,* London: Eyre Methuen.
—— (1973) *The Trilogy,* London: Penguin.
—— (1985) *Distinctions,* London: Cape.
—— (1990) *Chips with Everything,* London: Penguin.
Westergaard, J.H. (1971) 'The Myth of Classlessness' in R. Blackburn (ed.) *Ideology and Social Science,* London: Fontana.
Whitebait, W. (1959a) 'Having a Bash', *New Statesman,* Jan. 31, p. 144.
—— (1959b) '*Look Back in Anger*', *New Statesman,* May 30, p. 758.
—— (1960) '*The Entertainer*', *New Statesman,* July 30, p. 154.
Whiting, J. (1970) 'At Ease in a Bright Red Tie' in C. Marowitz, T. Milne and O. Hale (eds) *The Encore Reader,* London: Eyre Methuen.
Willett, J. (ed.) (1982) *Brecht on Theatre,* London: Eyre Methuen.
Williams, R. (1958a) 'Culture is Ordinary' in N. Mackenzie (ed.) *Conviction* London: MacGibbon and Kee.
—— (1958b) *Culture and Society,* London: Penguin.
—— (1959) 'Drama and the Left', *Encore,* March–April, pp. 6–12.
—— (1965) *The Long Revolution,* London: Penguin
—— (1967) *Culture and Society,* London: Penguin.
—— (1975) 'Base and Superstructure in Marxist Culture Theory', *New Left Review,* Summer.
—— (1976) *Keywords,* London: Fontana.
—— (1977) 'Lecture on Realism', *Screen* Vol. 18, No. 1, spring.
—— (1979) *Politics and Letters,* London: New Left Books.
—— (1978) 'Recent English Drama' in B. Ford (ed.) *the Pelican Guide to English Literature No. 7: The Modern Age,* London: Pelican.
—— (1980) *Problems in Materialism and Culture,* London: Verso.
—— (1981) *Culture,* London: Fontana.
—— (1983) *Drama from Ibsen to Brecht,* London: Penguin.
Williams, R. and Axton, M. (1977) *English Drama, Forms and Development,* Cambridge: Cambridge University Press.
Willis, T. (1947) 'Mobilise the Theatres' in *New Theatre,* December.
—— (1959) Contribution to symposium on vital theatre, *Encore,* March/ April, pp. 21–9.
Wilson, C. (1959) 'The Writer and Publicity' *Encounter,* No. 74, Nov.
—— (1976) *The Outsider,* London: Picador.
Wilson, E. (1980) *Half-Way to Paradise: Women in Post-War Britain,* London: Tavistock.
Woodcock, G. (1979) 'Anarchism Today' in T. Perlin (ed.) *Contemporary Anarchism,* New Jersey: New Brunswick.
Worsley, T.C. (1959) 'The Sweet Smell' in *New Statesman,* Feb. 21, p. 252.

Worswick, G. and Ady, P. (1962) *The British Economy in the 1950s*, Oxford: Oxford University Press.
Worth, K.J. (1972) *Revolutions in Modern British Drama*, London: Bell.
Young, M. (1959) *The Rise of the Meritocracy*, London: Pelican.

INDEX

affluence: ideology of 10–11, 81;
  statistics of 10; and women
  92–3; and youth 26–7
Allen, Walter 24, 30
Amis, Kingsley 17, 23–4, 25, 32, 34
An Giall 137–8
anarchism 127
Anderson, Lindsay 3, 33, 37, 38,
  54, 111, 112, 163, 166, 170–1
anger 7, 8, 27, 32, 34, 68, 78, 173,
  181, 183; critical context of 17,
  24–5; and *Look Back in Anger* 17;
  as moral panic 27–8
angry young men 1, 17, 30, 165,
  180; and gender 30–1, 183; and
  youth 25–8
Arden, John (see also individual
  plays) 7, 37, 48, 59–60, 100,
  141; and Brecht 158–9; and
  libertarianism 128, 130–5; and
  the popular 124, 128–30 and
  social realism 103, 110, 130–1
Armchair Theatre 71, 116
Armstrong's Last Goodnight 158–9
Arts Council of Great Britain
  42–3, 59
audiences: cinema 164–5, 178,
  188; theatre 48, 51, 53, 54–7,
  59–60, 84, 90, 124–5, 134, 135

Bakhtin, Mikhail 129–30
Barthes, Roland 11, 155n
Beckett, Samuel 2, 141
Behan, Brendan 49, 50, 51, 109, 139

Big Flame, The 122–3
Billy Liar; film 93, 163, 167, 168,
  173, 175–8, 182, 185, 188–9, 190;
  play 69, 79, 80, 84, 167–8, 175–7
Birthday Party, The 140–2, 144, 145
Blond, Neville 44
Bolt, Robert (see also individual
  plays) 37, 154, 157
Bond, Edward (see also individual
  plays) 7, 48; and Brecht 151–4;
  and naturalism 149–50; and
  realism 146–9; and Royal Court
  Theatre 48, 145–6
Bowlby, John 91
Brecht, Bertolt 39, 48, 50, 53, 63,
  148, 160–1, 172; British
  Brechtianism 155–7; and
  history plays 154–7; and the
  popular 124, 126; and realism
  7, 100, 102–3; the visit to Britain
  of the Berliner Ensemble 154–5
Bunnage, Avis 137, 156
Butskellism 12

Campaign for Nuclear
  Disarmament (CND) 36–7, 127;
  and theatre 37; and the
  Committee of 100 37, 127
Caretaker, The 140, 141, 144
Cathy Come Home 10, 116, 121
censorship 33
Centre 42 6, 60–2, 89–90, 179, 190
Chekhov, Anton 63, 65, 101
Chicken Soup with Barley (see also

202